Metadata Applications and Management

Edited by

G. E. Gorman

School of Information Management,
Victoria University of Wellington

Associate Editor

Daniel G. Dorner

School of Information Management,
Victoria University of Wellington

facet publishing

© This compilation: G. E. Gorman 2004
The articles: The contributors 2004

Published by
Facet Publishing
7 Ridgmount Street
London WC1E 7AE

Facet Publishing is wholly owned by CILIP: the Chartered Institute of Library and Information Professionals.

First published 2004

British Library Cataloguing in Publication Data

A catalogue record for this book is available from the British Library.

ISBN 1-85604-474-2

Typeset from editor's disks by Facet Publishing Production in 10.5/14.5pt New Baskerville and Franklin Gothic Condensed.
Printed and made in Great Britain by MPG Books Ltd, Bodmin, Cornwall.

Dedicated to our many friends in the Greater Mekong Sub-region for whom metadata applications are a dream awaiting realization

Contents

Editorial Advisory Board 2003/2004

Australasia

- **Dr Peter Clayton**, University of Canberra, Canberra 2614, Australia. E-mail: prc@comedu.canberra.edu.au
- **Dr Rowena Cullen**, School of Information Management, Victoria University of Wellington, Wellington, New Zealand. E-mail: rowena.cullen@vuw.ac.nz

East Asia

- **Dr Schubert Foo**, Division of Information Studies, School of Communication and Information, Nanyang Technological University, Nanyang Link, Singapore. E-mail: assfoo@ntu.edu.sg
- **Dr Jianzhong Wu**, The Shanghai Library, 1555 Huai Hai Zhong Lu, Shanghai 200031, China. E-mail: jzwu@libnet.sh.cn

South Asia

- **Dr M. P. Satija**, Department of Library and Information Science, Guru Nanak Dev University, Amritsar 143005, India. E-mail: satija_mp@yahoo.com

Southern Africa

- **Mr Stephen M. Mutula**, Department of Library and Information Studies, University of Botswana, Private Bag 0022, Gaborone, Botswana.
  E-mail: mutulasm@mopipi.ub.bw

North America

- **Dr D. Grant Campbell**, Faculty of Information and Media Studies, University of Western Ontario, London, Ontario N6A 5B7, Canada.
  E-mail: gcampbel@uwo.ca
- **Ms Peggy Johnson**, University Libraries, 499 Wilson Library, University of Minnesota, 309 19th Avenue South, Minneapolis, MN 55455, USA.
  E-mail: m-john@maroon.tc.umn.edu

United Kingdom

- **Dr Gobinda G. Chowdhury**, Graduate School of Informatics, Department of Computer and Information Sciences, University of Strathclyde, 26 Richmond Street, Glasgow G1 1XH, Scotland.
  E-mail: gobinda@dis.strath.ac.uk
- **Dr Mike Thelwall**, School of Computing and IT, Wolverhampton University, 35-49 Lichfield Street, Wolverhampton WV1 1EQ, England.
  E-mail: m.thelwall@wlv.ac.uk

Western Europe

- **Mr Paul S. Ulrich**, Information Services, Zentral- und Landesbibliothek Berlin, Haus Amerika Gedenkbibliothek, Bluecherplatz, 10961 Berlin, Germany.
  E-mail: pulrich@zlb.de
- **Dr Kristina Voigt**, GSF - National Research Center for Environment and Health, Institute of Biomathematics and Biometry, Ingolstaedter Landstrasse 1, 85764 Neuherberg, Germany. E-mail: kvoigt@gsf.de

About the contributors

Dr D. Grant Campbell is Assistant Professor in the Faculty of Information and Media Studies at University of Western Ontario, Canada. Dr Campbell's research currently focuses on information resource description, with a special emphasis on the description, classification and access of electronic resources using traditional and non-traditional methods. One of his current grant-funded research projects is on the role of semantic markup in the creation of electronic versions of primary texts in the humanities.

Priscilla Caplan is Assistant Director for Digital Library Services at the Florida Center for Library Automation, USA. She was previously Assistant Director for Library Systems at the University of Chicago, and before that at the Harvard University Library. She is the author of *Metadata Fundamentals for All Librarians* (ALA Editions, 2003) and of numerous articles on metadata, reference linking, and standards for digital libraries.

Louise Craven is the Archival Cataloguing Programme Manager at the National Archives of the UK, where she is responsible for Access to Archives (A2A) and PROCAT (the online catalogue of the National Archives of the UK).

Michael Day has worked for UKOLN, the UK Office for Library Networking, since 1996, taking part in a number of metadata-related research projects. As Research Officer, his main interests include metadata content rules for subject gateways, subject access and crosswalks between metadata formats. Between 1998 and 2002 he participated in the Cedars Project, where he contributed to the development of the Project's outline preservation metadata specification. More recently, he has produced a feasibility study into web archiving on behalf of the Joint Information Systems Committee (JISC) and the Wellcome Trust. He also co-operates with the National Library of Australia on the production of a quarterly current awareness bulletin on digital preservation topics. From 2000-2002, he was a member of the international Working Group on Preservation Metadata supported by the Research Libraries Group and OCLC.

Dr Daniel G. Dorner is Senior Lecturer and Director of LIM Programmes in the School of Information Management at Victoria University of Wellington, New Zealand. He is also a contributor to two volumes of the *International Yearbook of Library and Information Management* and has been involved in various metadata-related research projects for the National Library of New Zealand.

Dr Anne Gilliland-Swetland is Associate Professor and Director of the Center for Information as Evidence in the Department of Information Studies at the University of California, Los Angeles, USA. Her research and teaching interests are in the areas of electronic records management, metadata management, and the design and evaluation of evidence-based information systems.

Dr G. E. Gorman is Professor of Library and Information Management and Head of the School of Information Management at Victoria University of Wellington, New Zealand. He is the founding general editor of the *International Yearbook of Library and Information Management* and the author or co-author of more than a dozen books and more than 100 refereed journal articles. He is also editor of *Online Information Review* (Emerald), Associate Editor of *Library Collections, Acquisitions and Technical Services* (Elsevier), a member of the editorial boards of several other journals, and currently Chair of the Regional Standing Committee of IFLA for Asia and Oceania.

Dr Ingrid Hsieh-Yee is Associate Professor in the School of Library and

Information Science at the Catholic University of America in Washington, DC. Her areas of research interest are: organization of information, metadata, information architecture, users' interaction with online information systems, digital collections and research methods.

Shirley Hyatt is currently Communications and Business Transitions Director of the Office of Research, OCLC (Online Computer Library Center), Inc., USA. Her responsibilities include recognizing the potential of technologies and innovations, and incorporating them into OCLC's development and marketing environments. Prior to joining OCLC's Office of Research, she served as Director of Distributed Systems, and Manager of OCLC's Access Services product line. She has over 20 years' experience in library access services.

Wei Liu is Director of the Digital Library Research Institute at the Shanghai Library, Vice-President of the Digital Library Research Institute of Shanghai, and Visiting Professor at East China Normal University. He took part in research and development of key technologies for the digital libary in China, and since 1996 has been involved in most key national projects on digital library and metadata implementation. He is a member of IFLA's Standing Committee on Information Technology, of the Advisory Board of the Dublin Core Metadata Initiative (DCMI), and of the Chinese Library Association's Special Committee on Digital Libraries. Since 2000, he has been a columnist on the application of new technologies for *Library Journal* (China). He is a doctoral candidate of the Computer Science Department of Fudan University, Shanghai.

Patrick McGlamery is Map Librarian at the Map and Geographic Information Center (MAGIC) in the Homer Babbidge Library at the University of Connecticut, USA. He is also co-Director of the University of Connecticut Center for Geographic Information and Analysis. He has been involved with computer mapping in a library environment since 1987 and is active in the American Library Association Map and Geography Roundtable and in the IFLA Geography and Map Section. His professional activities include promoting access to GIS resources for students, developing integrated statistical and geographic systems, promoting best practice for GIS services, and incorporating innovations in technology – for example handheld technology for remote users to access digital collections of spatial information.

Jon Mason is Director of Strategic Initiatives at education.au limited, and Assistant Director of IMS Australia. He has an advocacy role in developing interoperability standards relevant to internet-enabled education and training in Australia. His other roles include: Co-chair of the Dublin Core Metadata Education Working Group; member of the IEEE-LTSC; Australian delegate to ISO/IEC JTC1 SC36, IT in Learning, Education and Training; Chair of Standards Australia IT-19-1; member of the Standards Australia Knowledge Management reference group; member of the Standards Sub-committee of the Australian ICT in Education Committee; and co-lead of IMS Global Learning Consortium, Digital Repositories Interoperability Working Group.

Dr Paul Miller is Interoperability Focus at UKOLN, the UK Office for Library and Information Networking, based at the University of Bath. His job deals with a wide range of issues related to enabling and maintaining the exchange of electronic information in an interoperable fashion between communities such as museums, libraries and archives so that potential users of such resources may interact with them as seamlessly as possible. He has been closely involved with the Dublin Core process for some years, and has been a member of the Dublin Core Executive Committee.

Dr Simon Pockley is the Collections Manager for Australia's newest cultural institution, The Australian Centre for the Moving Image (ACMI). He has been an active participant in the development of the Dublin Core Metadata Standard since its conception in 1995 and has recently led the submission of linked DC.Type (moving image/still image) proposals to the Dublin Core Usage Board. He is an advisor to the National Library of Australia on digital preservation and a member of the Committee of Experts for the Government of Victoria.

Eileen Quam is Information Architect in the Minnesota Department of Natural Resources, Minnesota Office of Technology, USA. She has been a cataloguer, indexer and metadata specialist. She worked full-time as a MINITEX contract cataloguer before taking her current position. Her lead work on the Foundations Project culminated in Best Practice Guidelines for Web Metadata for the State of Minnesota. Eileen continues to be involved in metadata and records management standards, as well as occasional indexing and contract cataloguing. She teaches indexing and abstracting at the College of St Catherine's Graduate School of Library and Information Science.

Bill Stockting, an expert in archival metadata, is currently Access to Archives (A2A) Senior Editor at the UK's Public Record Office at the National Archives in Kew. He has contributed to the development of the online catalogue of the National Archives of the UK (PROCAT), is a member of the international working group that maintains Encoded Archival Description (EAD) and also sits on the Research Libraries Group's EAD Advisory Panel.

Dr Stuart A. Sutton is Associate Professor in the Information School of the University of Washington, USA. He has served on the faculties of Syracuse University and San José State University and in a visiting position at the University of California at Berkeley. Dr Sutton's research areas include metadata and networked information discovery and retrieval; technology-mediated teaching and learning; cognition and the information-seeking behaviour of discourse communities; mental models in information system design; and the law and policy of intellectual property.

Dr Sherry L. Vellucci is Director of the Division of Library and Information Science at St John's University, Jamaica, New York. She has served on the Board of the Music Library Association (US) as Treasurer and Member-at-Large, and is currently editor of the MLA Technical Reports Series. She is also active in the International Association of Music Libraries, Archives, and Documentation Centres (IAML), currently serving as President of the IAML-US Branch and Vice Chair of the IAML Cataloging Commission. In 1998 Dr Vellucci received the Music

Library Association's Special Achievement Award in recognition of her path-breaking research in the area of bibliographic relationships in music catalogues and their implications for system design in future catalogues. Dr. Vellucci serves on the editorial board of *Cataloging & Classification Quarterly* and is the author of numerous publications on bibliographic relationships and metadata.

Introduction

Regular readers of the *International Yearbook of Library and Information Management* will know that each year we nominate a specific theme to be treated by a group of international experts. The 2003–2004 volume is no different, the theme being metadata applications and management. Metadata emerged as a driving force behind a number of chapters in the 2002–2003 volume, *The Digital Factor in Library and Information Services*. One chapter in particular suggested that metadata warranted a volume of its own in the series – this was 'Making Sense of Metadata: Reading the Words on a Spinning Top' by my colleague Dr Daniel G. Dorner, who in fact has been invited to serve as Associate Editor of this year's compilation. In this chapter Dorner showed that in just a decade metadata as a concept and a professional tool came from nowhere to be about as hot a topic as one can have in the information professions.

As Dorner indicated, the prevalence of metadata in the professional literature is easily demonstrated through a search of *Library and Information Science Abstracts*, using 'metadata' or 'meta' and 'data' as search terms. According to results of his LISA search, the term first appeared in print in 1978, and was then more or less moribund until 1994, when it appeared 12 times. Since then, the citations have grown exponentially: 32 times in 1996, 80 times in 1997, 104 in 1998, 196 in 1999 and 209 in 2000 – a dramatic increase indeed.

This growth has probably been due in part to the gradual acceptance of a broader definition of metadata. In common with most experts and commentators, we have adopted that proposed by the Association for

Library Collections and Technical Services Task Force on Metadata (2000): 'metadata are structured, encoded data that describe characteristics of information-bearing entities to aid in the identification, discovery, assessment, and management of the described entities'.

With this definition in mind we set out in this year's volume of the *International Yearbook of Library and Information Management* to offer a broad overview of the current state of play with regard to metadata developments and applications both generally and in selected disciplines. Inevitably the constraints imposed by a single volume mean that we have been selective in terms of topics, but overall we trust you will agree that the chosen authors represent the best international thinking on metadata and its present impact on the information professions.

The 15 chapters are divided into six parts, covering what we believe are key issues related to the emergence of metadata.

Part 1   Perspectives on Metadata

Part 1 addresses Perspectives on Metadata, with two overview chapters by acknowledged metadata experts. Dr Paul Miller of UKOLN addresses 'Metadata – What It Means for Memory Institutions'. This chapter confirms that metadata is becoming increasingly prevalent among archives, libraries and museums. Accordingly, the need for an understanding of the term and its implications continues to grow as exchange of data and information between practitioners blossoms, and provision of access to a broader set of potential users becomes increasingly important for learning, for inclusion, and also for continued social relevance. Miller's chapter introduces the basics of metadata clearly and simply, and it then goes on to explore some examples of metadata in use.

In Chapter 2 ('Metadata – Where Are We Going?') Dr Anne Gilliland-Swetland of UCLA continues Miller's theme of the importance and complexity of metadata in a wide range of institutions. She argues that key areas of current growth can be identified in terms of dimensionality (i.e. the application and use of metadata to bridge temporal, activity, community and domain boundaries) and plurality (i.e. the development, extension and revision of ever-increasing numbers, types and versions of metadata schema for a range of purposes within and across a growing number of domains). Her chapter also argues that key considerations we face in moving forward relate to how to manage this plurality, and how to support the efficient creation of appropriately rich metadata by the development of tools for the automated capture and creation of metadata and by distributing responsibilities for metadata creation and management more widely.

The remaining five parts of the *Yearbook* focus on metadata applications in selected fields (humanities, government, education) or specific metadata applications (bibliographic organization, spatial data, preservation, etc.). Some will notice the lack of chapters on metadata applications in the sciences, which we recognize as a shortcoming in this volume. But it was not for want of trying – there are actually very few experts working in this area, and those who were available did not meet our criteria. This lacuna aside, we believe that the volume covers fields where important and innovative work is being done, and which can be applied to other disciplines or areas of professional practice with slight modification.

Part 2 Metadata in the Humanities

The broad field of the humanities is represented by two chapters, one on music and the other on the arts generally. In 'Music Metadata' Dr Sherry L. Vellucci of St John's University in New York looks at both conceptual and practical issues associated with music metadata. The former are important, for

> conceptual issues must be grasped because they underpin the fundamental principles of organising music resources and account for many of the practical problems. Understanding the various ways in which music resources are used will allow the metadata creator to resolve the practical problems when determining the type of metadata information required to meet the search and retrieval needs of musicians.

In Vellucci's perception the current issues and problems we face when organizing music resources fall into two categories: creating music metadata and using music metadata. She discusses both in considerable detail through her analysis that ranges from current music metadata solutions (AACR2, MARC, etc.) to new directions such as Dublin Core initiatives and EAD, and including examples of major music library metadata projects. She concludes that the complexities of music information organization and retrieval are compounded by the many metadata options available today. 'It is possible', she maintains, 'that a music-specific metadata scheme will be developed in the future, but it is just as possible that the music community will continue to use a variety of existing metadata schemes and adapt them to their music needs.'

Chapter 4, 'Metadata and the Arts – The Art of Metadata' by Dr Simon Pockley (Australian Centre for the Moving Image), begins from the premise that access to structured metadata in the arts is a radical idea. It can, he says, be compared to the challenge of building a nation out of a group of warring states, where assembly is characterized by friction and tension. When those who create it do not share the values residing in its use and distribution, metadata becomes unreliable. In a federated repository, it becomes useless. Understanding the importance of such cultural values may be as important a step in building a sustainable back-of-house infrastructure for generating quality metadata, as building the front-of-house services that can understand it. Against this background, Pockley's general discussion of metadata in the arts is illustrated from research into collaborative metadata production conducted at the Australian Centre for the Moving Image (ACMI). The research demonstrates how the values of the various practitioners can have a significant impact on the quality of metadata and hence an organization's ability to participate in an arts cluster or a cultural network. These values reach into the fabric of how ideas and thoughts are expressed in an electronic environment. They also play an important role in the durability of artistic expression. Ultimately, they point towards the development of a poetic for the art of metadata.

Part 3 Metadata in Government

In Part 3 we turn to government information, a major area for research and development of metadata initiatives, and one that is likely to be increasingly metadata-dependent as e-government continues to spread rapidly. In Chapter 5, 'Metadata and Taxonomy Integration in Government Portals', Eileen Quam (Minnesota Office of Technology) focuses on government websites and portals, most of which rely on content management systems to manage the data. This being the case, why is it, Quam asks, that developers give so little thought to metadata, metadata standards and controlled vocabularies in product creation? The same may be said of the purchaser, who more often than not gives little consideration to the importance of metadata. Quam's chapter looks at metadata as a management tool from the dual perspective of content manager and user/searcher – a most useful approach. She discusses integration issues of metadata, controlled vocabularies and taxonomies in content management solutions, as well as search engine integration and tuning. In her chapter the State of Minnesota and other government web portals provide real-life examples of successful implementation and lessons learned.

Moving from the US to Britain, in Chapter 6 Bill Stockting and Louise Craven discuss 'Metadata and the UK Archives Network'. Because British archivists have been particularly active in resolving issues relating to key metadata about their holdings with the aim of providing easy and comprehensive online access to users, this national case study offers significant insights that may be applicable in other countries beginning to grapple with some of the same issues. Stockting and Craven discuss the series of agreed international and national standards for content and data exchange, and they show how these have allowed the development of frameworks for dealing with issues such as how to present legacy data and the appropriate depth for new cataloguing and indexing. This in turn has led to the development of a number of complementary online services offering access to information about archives. All of this is given shape by reference to access metadata examples from the UK National Archives, which many regard as setting the standard for the archives community internationally.

Part 4 Metadata in Education

Part 4 moves from the government sector to education, with two chapters, one from the USA and one from Australia. Dr Stuart A. Sutton of the University of Washington opens with 'Metadata and the Education Sector'. This begins by defining a set of core terms, followed by a general discussion of the categories of metadata (or categories of attributes) necessary for various functions in resource discovery, and, to a certain degree, to the use of those resources as teaching and learning instruments. Sutton then focuses on those metadata issues that he regards as unique to education and training and, having framed a set of issues regarding the attributes of educational resources, he then describes the technical architecture necessary to effective metadata generation, deployment and use. Given the vastness of the topic, Sutton concentrates only on metadata as it relates to the process of educational resource discovery. 'The base premise of the discussion is that while educational resources share common attributes with all other digitally available entities, they also possess attributes that are either unique to, or are in need of unique treatment in, the domain of education and training.'

Jon Mason follows in Chapter 8 with discussion of 'Educational Metadata in Transition: An Australian Case Study'. This paper is presented in two parts, as two aspects of an evolving context. First, it discusses the development and application of metadata standards as a feature of the evolving requirements of the Australian education and training sector as it harnesses the capacities of the internet. Second, the notion of value creation in the development of metadata standards and knowledge-based economies is explored. The latter discussion is informed by the experience associated with the first, given that knowledge-driven work practices depend upon a technical infrastructure. This range of topics is brought together with a view to discussing the wide and complex context in which metadata standards are developed and utilised for learning, education, and training. Pragmatics demands that current and next generation metadata standards require simultaneous application and development, with outputs from each informing the other. Within both these scenarios attention is given to the notion of value – a key organizing principle in managing information and knowledge. In the digital domain value is developed in numerous ways, characterized by a meshing of recursive relationships between data, information and knowledge.

Part 5 Metadata and Bibliographic Organization

Traditionally metadata has been associated with bibliographic organization, and it is perhaps for this reason that this section seems to tie together many of the ideas raised in the preceding discipline-specific chapters. Dr D. Grant Campbell of the University of Western Ontario opens this key section with a provocative discussion of 'The Metadata–Bibliographic Organization Nexus'. Chapter 9 explores the relationship between metadata systems and bibliographic organization systems. On the one hand these two traditions of development exhibit striking similarities, which suggest that libraries have much to give and to receive in collaborating with and participating in digital information projects of many kinds. On the other hand the persistent differences in language, technological infrastructure and approach between these two traditions continue to make collaboration problematic. In this chapter Campbell maintains that these problems can be highlighted by examining two fundamental tensions that are common to both traditions: the tension between information storage and information transfer, and the tension between human-understandable and machine-understandable data.

In Chapter 10 Dr Ingrid Hsieh-Yee (Catholic University of America) discusses 'Cataloguing and Metadata Education'. The growth of interest in metadata, in her view, is a reflection of the widespread need to organize information in many sectors, from educational institutions to government agencies to the corporate sector. Accordingly, expertise in organizing information is needed in many places, and LIS education programmes have a unique opportunity to meet that need and shape the future of information organization. A particularly telling question, however, is whether there room for metadata education in LIS programmes. Further, if metadata education is being provided, what is the current state of the offerings? These are important issues for educators as well as practitioners, and Hsieh-Yee addresses them directly in her chapter. Data from recent research shows that metadata education in LIS programmes is a work in progress. While metadata topics have been integrated into many courses, the coverage seems to remain at the introductory level. There are several reasons that metadata education remains a work in progress. First, new metadata schemes continue to emerge, and no scheme has been considered 'the' standard for organizing resources in all disciplines, Second, development and implementation of metadata schemes have taken place mainly in the field, and few educators are able to keep up with all the new developments. Third, the library and information science field is still struggling to find its niche in the digital environment, where many more new players have arrived and the competition has become keener than before.

Chapter 11 ('Developments in Cataloguing and Metadata') by OCLC's Shirley Hyatt examines some of the transformations occurring in the metadata environment that are affecting libraries, collection managers and online information providers. Following a brief synopsis of some legacy issues Hyatt discusses some of the trends that are near-future givens. These include growth in the shared networked space and proliferation and movement of communities using that space, an emphasis on simplification, a renewed interest in and ability for collocation, and an increase in modularity and recombination of metadata. She closes with a high level overview of research that OCLC is presently exploring related to these trends.

Part 6 Metadata and Other Applications

In the final part we have a set of four chapters covering preservation metadata, spatial data, international metadata initiatives, and the development of metadata initiatives in China – further evidence that metadata has an application in every field and every country.

Chapter 12, 'Preservation Metadata', is by Michael Day, Research Officer for UKOLN at the University of Bath, and a recognized expert on metadata and preservation. This is an absolutely key chapter in the overall perspective that the volume seeks to convey, for ensuring the long-term preservation of information in digital form counts as the greatest challenge for the information professions this century. Day introduces some proposed digital preservation strategies, noting how metadata comprises a key component of them all. This is followed by brief introductions to the influential Open Archival Information System (OAIS) reference model and a number of other selected initiatives, based on projects originating from national and research libraries, digitization projects and the archives community. The final sections highlight some major issues and needs for the future, including interoperability, costs, more detailed practical experience, increased co-operation and more relevant metadata research.

Chapter 13, 'Metadata and Spatial Data', is by Patrick McGlamery of the University of Connecticut. This chapter explores the history and nature of digital geo-spatial data, Geographic Information Systems (GIS) and metadata. McGlamery focuses on current best practices and points toward the emerging use of metadata in the field., starting from a discussion of maps and GIS and then moving to issues of institutional sharing of spatial data and directed spatial information policy. The main thrust of the chapter is a discussion of metadata standards for geo-spatial data and in-depth discussion of the types of metadata information appropriate for this field. McGlamery concludes with discussion of some emerging trends likely to have some impact on the future direction of metadata applications to digital geo-spatial data.

Priscilla Caplan of the University of Florida has contributed Chapter 14, 'International Initiatives in the Implementation of Metadata Standards'. Suggesting that the usefulness of metadata schemes to supplement traditional library cataloging seems to be well accepted within the library community, Caplan gives an update on activities within selected metadata initiatives in the last few years, and finds some common trends. These include efforts to develop content standards and application profiles, a clear preference for XML as a transport syntax, a trend towards developing non-descriptive metadata schemes (particularly preservation metadata, structural metadata, and content packaging), and a renewed focus on presentation issues. A future trend is likely to be an increasing focus on tools for facilitating metadata creation, use and exchange.

Finally, Chapter 15. cements the international spread of the volume with discussion of 'Metadata Applications in Developing Countries: The Example of China'. In it Wei Liu of the Shanghai Library reviews and highlights the main Chinese efforts on the research and implementation of metadata standards, specifications and applications, by the institutions of national science and technology, education, and culture, and as well as the private sector.

The production team

I continue to owe much to my Editorial Advisory Board – for suggesting topics, cajoling reluctant authors and reviewing completed chapters. This year their task has been especially arduous, with a number of chapters having to be rejected. I also wish to thank, as usual, the team at Facet Publishing, especially Rebecca and Helen, Lin, Alison and Garry for their expertise and good humour in seeing this fourth volume into print. As always, Jackie Bell in Wellington has been a stalwart assistant, always picking up the pieces just in time – IYLIM would never happen without her calming influence. And finally, I express my gratitude to this year's Associate Editor and my good friend, Dr Dan Dorner, for his knowledge of individuals most suited to write about metadata, and of course to the various authors who managed to meet our standards and deadlines without too much complaint – you have all helped to create a commendable survey of metadata activities in 2003.

G. E. Gorman
Victoria University of Wellington

Part 1

PERSPECTIVES ON METADATA

1

Metadata – what it means for memory institutions

Paul Miller

Introduction: Here comes the real 'Renaissance Man'?

Discussion of 'metadata' is becoming increasingly prevalent amongst our 'memory institutions' – archives, libraries and museums. The need for an understanding of the term and its implications continues to grow as exchange of data and information between practitioners blossoms, and provision of access to a broader set of potential users becomes increasingly important for learning, for inclusion, and also for continued social relevance. This paper aims to introduce the basics of metadata clearly and simply. It then goes on to explore some examples of metadata in use.

Long-established boundaries both within and without the cultural sector are beginning to blur as researchers become increasingly interested in the data, knowledge and techniques of disciplines other than their own. This quest for new knowledge is proving far from easy, and invariably requires the tackling of seemingly arcane terminologies, and procedures devised by an apparently alien mindset; yet the rewards are hopefully both evident and manifold.

As becomes rapidly evident to those entering new fields of endeavour, fundamentally similar issues may be addressed in dramatically different fashion from location to location and subject to subject. Despite this, it is becoming more important to enable such inter-disciplinarity in order to forge new insights into extant data. For these efforts at traversing or demolishing boundaries to succeed, the hazy semantic and procedural fortresses within which disciplines sequester themselves, girded about with the strong walls of obfuscation and specialist language, must be undermined with as much vigour as the clearer boundaries of academic subject and faculty.

An endeavour of relevance, both for the opportunity it brings to this work and as a sterling example of what may be achieved when experts from a wide range of disciplines and nationalities actually manage to work successfully together, is the current drive towards the creation of cross-disciplinary standards for metadata.

Introducing metadata

Metadata. The word is becoming increasingly prevalent in the humanities and elsewhere, especially in relation to the online discovery and exchange of electronic information. Metadata, however, is not restricted solely to an electronic existence, and the term applies as readily to the humble card catalogue as to the high-profile electronic indices of initiatives such as the UK's Resource Discovery Network (www.rdn.ac.uk/) and Arts & Humanities Data Service (ahds.ac.uk/) with which it might more commonly be associated.

What, then, is metadata, and what is its role in facilitating collaboration across these artificial barriers erected between disciplinary domains? At the most basic, metadata can be considered as *data about data*. In essence, metadata is the extra baggage associated with any resource that enables a real or potential user to find that resource; to decide whether or not it is of value to them; to discover where, when and by whom it was created, as well as for what purpose; to know what tools will be needed to manipulate the resource; to determine whether or not they will actually be allowed access to the resource itself and how much this will cost them. Metadata is, in short, a means by which largely meaningless data may be transformed into information, interpretable and reusable by those other than the creator of the data resource.

Returning, for a moment, to an analogue paradigm with which readers may be more comfortable, a traditional book, printed on old-fashioned paper, has metadata which clearly includes the book's title (*Foucault's Pendulum*), its author (Umberto Eco), year of publication (1990), publisher (Picador) and International Standard Book Number (ISBN 0-330-31497-1). The price may also be included (£8.99), although this is obviously more subject to change than some of the other elements. In this example, another vital element of metadata is the name of the translator (William Weaver). The fact that the book is written in English, that it was translated from Italian, and that it is a paperback may also be considered worthy of recording, as might the names and dates of those publishing each imprint prior to the one currently sitting by my side (Gruppo Editoriale Fabbri Bompiani, 1988; Picador, 1988; Secker & Warburg, 1989).

Metadata pertaining to access restriction is more normally found with digital data or printed maps than with books, but this book's jacket quite clearly states 'Not for sale in Canada'. Of little relevance to the casual browser in your local bookshop, perhaps, this piece of information gains importance as soon as you consider the possibility of books being sold anywhere in the world from the shop's site on the world wide web.

As suggested above, the concepts of metadata are most commonly applied to resources that are electronic in nature, rather than to the humble book. With resources of this form, further issues gain relevance, such as the format of a resource (HTML web page, Access database file, JPEG image file, etc.), the manner in which it is accessed and the requirements for manipulating it once retrieved. In reality, of course, these issues are addressed in non-electronic resources too, but many of the requirements are either assumed to be fulfilled through the normal completion of primary and/or secondary education – a prospective user of the resource may be assumed to have learned to read, in a way that a prospective user may *not* be assumed to have learned how to handle a .gzip compressed data file – or are considered 'obvious': if you only read English and Portuguese, there is no point attempting to extract detailed information from a textbook written in German or Mandarin, while many users of information technology have an endearingly naïve belief that their computer will 'understand' any file that they manage to get on to it, regardless of format.

Importantly, even if a resource of interest is provided only in

Mandarin, or in some obscure computer format, the *metadata* describing the resource may very well be provided in several languages or electronic formats, such that you are able to read metadata in English about a Mandarin resource and decide whether or not it will be necessary to invest the resources in having it translated so that you might use it. Without intelligible metadata, you would not know what might be hidden behind the language barrier and might therefore either waste effort translating a useless resource or fail to translate something extremely relevant to your needs. Similarly, a well-structured metadata description potentially enables the expert historian to assess the value of a complicated archaeological resource without the need for him or her to also be an expert archaeologist. Should the metadata imply that such an archaeological resource is of value, the historian has the option to either invest time in interpreting detailed archaeological jargon or else request help from an archaeologist in translating the resource in order to make it intelligible. Metadata may therefore be seen as facilitating re-use.

Towards revolution? Metadata for the masses

Use of metadata is widespread, although few resource describers consider that which they are doing to be creation of metadata per se. Instead, they believe their work to be the more academically acceptable *cataloguing* or *indexing*, while 'metadata' is an alien – and, perhaps, slightly frightening – concept discussed by people who spend far too much time in front of computers and too little working with 'real' sources.

Don't panic! Metadata is not (necessarily) arcane, and it's not after your job. Rather, it is a label given to that which you and many others do every day all around the world, either formally as a librarian accessioning new books or informally as you decide whether to categorize your personal compact disc collection by year of release, by artist or on aesthetic grounds so that the colours of all the CD cases form a pretty pattern on your shelf. The simple act of providing an intuitive name for a computer file – I called this paper 'What it Means for Memory Institutions. Paper for IYLIM 2003.doc' while writing it – might also be considered as creating metadata. The intuitive name, after all, makes it significantly easier for me to locate and retrieve the file I want amidst the morass of other documents littering my computer's disk.

As the brief examples above have shown, it is extremely easy to identify attributes of an object that may usefully be identified and noted in order to describe the object in such a way that it may be discovered or recognized at a later date. These attributes may also be usefully considered as a form of abstract, such that the key features of any given object or resource may be imparted to others without you or them actually needing to have access to the physical object itself. Metadata may therefore be seen as a surrogate for the resource (Lagoze, 1997).

Consider, for a moment, an object that you can see from where you sit. What key attributes would you extract from this object in order to describe it? If it is a book, presumably author, title and year of publication are high on your list, but what other attributes do you consider to be important? Choose another – very different – object and carry out the same exercise. How many of the attributes you selected for the first object (a book, say) are of relevance to the second (a desk lamp, perhaps)?

Well done! You have just defined a series of metadata elements (your key attributes) and given each of them values in order to describe a specific resource. Welcome to the world of metadata!

Look again at each object, and at the elements defined to describe them. Think carefully about which of the elements would actually be required in order to enable you – or someone else – to find the resource again, or to decide whether or not it would be worth using for a particular task.

Here, we are introducing the concept of 'resource discovery metadata', or a particular form of metadata intended specifically to enable other users to find a given resource and assess its fitness for their purpose, whatever that might be. In many cases, a great deal of detail may be recorded about a resource, much of which will be essential for particular uses of the resource, or for maintaining it in some fashion. It is normally the case, however, that only a small number of elements are actually required to capture the essence of a resource, thereby facilitating the discovery process. The bulk of this paper deals exclusively with resource discovery metadata, as opposed to other forms of metadata such as those related to the preservation, management or use of a resource.

Requirements for sharing metadata

Leaving aside for a moment the added complexities of interdisciplinary communication, consider the issues involved in sharing any descriptive scheme that is developed to create metadata for a given resource. It is all very well to define a set of elements to describe an object or resource and to give each of these elements a value that seems to adequately capture a particular facet of the object being described, but matters become more complicated with the need to share either the element definition (Title, Author, Date, etc.) or the object description (*Foucault's Pendulum*, Umberto Eco, 1990, etc.) with others.

In order to enable some form of comparability between resources (all books in a library, all libraries in a country or all transcribed texts in an electronic corpus, for example) it is necessary to formulate a framework within which description may take place. At the most basic, this framework will define the essential elements (Title, Author, etc.) that must be recorded about a resource, and more involved frameworks will also be extremely prescriptive about how each of several hundred elements may be completed ('Eco, U.' or 'Eco, Umberto, 1932–', but not 'Umberto Eco' or 'Eco, Umberto', for example). More detailed models may also address the underlying semantics within which elements are defined, tackling the often complex issues of clarifying exactly *what* 'Title', for example, means within the paradigm of expression. In many cases, a term such as Title may be selected by diverse recorders, despite the fact that each may be interpreting the – apparently identical – term in different ways.

In most cases, such frameworks are localized and exist merely to ensure that all records in a single PhD student's database, or all exam results from a single university department for a single year, are recorded in a consistent fashion. Some, however, are more widespread and become adopted as de facto or de jure disciplinary, national or international standards, such as the International Standards Organization's ISO 2709 for describing library holdings, and national implementations such as UKMARC for the UK and MARC21 for Canada and the USA.

Complex structures equivalent to MARC have evolved within many disciplines, each tailored specifically to the requirements and semantics associated with a particular problem area and associated world view. Well known examples of these large schemes include the American Federal Geographic Data Committee's *Content Standard for Digital Geospatial Metadata* (FGDC, 1998), which underpins the major US archiving effort of the National Spatial Data Infrastructure clearinghouse network, and the work behind the Text Encoding Initiative (www.tei-c.org/), used by organizations such as the Oxford Text Archive (ota.ahds.ac.uk/) to describe, or mark up, digitally stored texts from the works of Shakespeare to the speeches of the 1992 US presidential campaign.

Making use of metadata

Accepting, then, that metadata may usefully be recorded about a resource in order to both add value to the resource itself and encourage its re-use by others within the creating organization and beyond, how might the concepts of metadata be applied to the diversity of data to be found outside the theoretical discussions of a paper such as this?

An example from the Archaeology Data Service

As with other service providers of the UK's Arts & Humanities Data Service, the Archaeology Data Service (http://ads.ahds.ac.uk/) is concerned with the development of mechanisms capable of facilitating a degree of integrated search capability between disparate data sources, both within and between subject domains. As well as a strongly held belief that issues of interoperability are important, ADS specifically requires a means by which users may interrogate the distributed holdings of, among others:

- local authority Sites and Monuments Records (SMRs)
  - quasi-statutory record of 'the heritage' for each county and unitary authority in the UK
  - 'living' database – regular addition of new records, as well as amendments to existing ones

— mainframe/PC platforms
— multiple DBMS (database management systems) products
— links to other holdings such as geophysical and aerial photographic data, often by means of reference to hard copies in a filing cabinet or box file, but occasionally as a pointer to other digital holdings
— differential integration with spatial management systems such as GIS
— little integration of glossaries, element definitions, etc. between implementations, although this is improving
- National Monuments Records for England, Scotland, Wales and Northern Ireland
  — nationally relevant subset of the SMRs
  — 'living' database
  — beginning to see some degree of guidance/control exerted upon local Sites and Monuments Records from the organizations responsible for each National Monuments Record, but little integration between the national records themselves
- excavation and fieldwork archives
  — produced by commercial archaeological contractors, university departments, etc.
  — computerized archives of completed archaeological work
  — 'dead' database – no modifications likely, other than extension through reinterpretation
  — likely to be integration between textual databases, maps, drawings, photographs, etc.
  — binary data (geophysical survey, satellite image, etc.) may well be the primary component of one of these archives
- corpora
  — single, definable, act of research to produce a body of knowledge
  — for example, a corpus of all Roman Samian pottery from Cambridgeshire or the catalogue of the Hunter collection of coinage at Glasgow's Hunterian Museum
  — 'dead' database

In many cases, these data sets will not be physically held by ADS, but rather by the data owner or some other relevant agency with whom ADS negotiates access arrangements.

For some of these holdings outside ADS, the data will be accessible via SuperJANET or a similar computer network, but all too many of the data sets will for the foreseeable future be held either behind a firewall or in a non-networked environment. For this body of knowledge, ADS will only be able to provide metadata on the resource and contact details for the host organization, rather than any interactive access to the resources themselves. The main requirement of ADS may therefore be seen as a cataloguing system that allows the construction of a 'meta-database' suitable for recording disparate and distributed data holdings.

Taking a purely fictional example, such a catalogue would enable the user to enter a single search ('Tell me about 12–13th-century coinage from Scotland'), the returned results of which will include metadata about the large Hunter coin collection (the catalogue for which is perhaps on an unnetworked PC database located within Glasgow's Hunterian Museum), the coin holdings of the National Museums of Scotland (possibly in a networked UNIX multiple media database in Edinburgh, accessible over the world wide web via SuperJANET, and including pictures of the coins) and the detailed corpus of a large coin hoard from Elgin in the Scottish Highlands (maybe physically held by ADS in York as a single downloadable dBase file).

The above example illustrates a perfectly feasible query within the structure being constructed by ADS, and it is possible to quickly envisage some of the problems that might be associated with putting such a system into production. Even at a local level, many of the same problems apply for those attempting to facilitate querying between different databases held on the same site.

Such a cataloguing system is *not* envisaged as a means by which users necessarily gain the ability to submit detailed queries on the contents of several databases simultaneously. Rather, the system is intended to enable users to search the *metadata* pertaining to each resource. For those resources felt to fulfil the search criteria, the user may then interact directly with the resource online, download parts of it, or make arrangements to physically visit the resource's location, depending upon each resource's access arrangements and degree of technological sophistication.

However the resources themselves are finally accessed by the user, the metadata repository through which information pertaining to each resource is distributed is required to make difficult decisions as to the manner by which metadata is collected from resource creators, how it is most effectively made available to users, and how it is kept up to date with both alterations to existing resources and the addition of new material.

Models for metadata

There is not necessarily a single correct way in which to deploy a metadata-based solution to all given problems. However, in each case there will tend to be three key components of the resource discovery process, namely the *user* in search of a useful resource, the *resource* itself and some form of *metadata* with which the user may interact in order to discover information about the resource. The three components need not be physically close together and, indeed, may potentially be located *anywhere*.

There are many ways in which a user might interact with metadata to discover a resource, just as there are many ways in which the metadata may be related to the resource itself in order to prevent the two from becoming inconsistent with each other. Three broad approaches might be considered, illustrating the key considerations.

The metadata record

This is the simplest of approaches, where metadata is created manually for a resource in the same way as a librarian might produce a card catalogue entry for a new book. Such an approach is relatively straightforward to implement and is perhaps the most effective means of dealing with distant resources to which the catalogue system has no direct access, such as the example of an offline database at the Hunterian Museum introduced above. Records such as these are expensive to create and maintain, as cataloguers are required to gather and enter data on the resource by hand, and then make efforts to monitor the resource to ensure that its catalogue record entry remains relevant and up to date. Subject hubs in the UK's Resource Discovery Network record electronic resources in this fashion, where the effort expended in record creation and maintenance is felt to be justified by the 'value-added' quality assessments brought to the resource by their expert cataloguers.

The metadata layer

Here, the wherewithal is introduced to generate the metadata from the resource by more automated means than those employed for the metadata record, above. In this case, the concept of a mapping or 'crosswalk' is defined between the structure used to store data within the resource and that used to allow querying of the metadata.

Such a mapping may well be relatively simple, and comprise little more than a set of rules which defines relationships such as that a field called author in the resource is synonymous with creator in the metadata structure. As the metadata layer exists solely to facilitate resource discovery, it is only necessary to map those 'core' elements from the resource that are most likely to prove useful during the resource discovery process. Once the mapping has been satisfactorily defined, simple software scripts may be used to automatically extract information from the resource and parse it correctly for the selected metadata format.

Assuming that straightforward one-to-one or one-to-many relationships may be established between the metadata structure and that for the resource, such a metadata layer approach has the potential to be both successful and cost-effective as duplication of effort is minimized and there is little, if any, re-keying of data.

Two major problems arise with this approach, one of which is merely procedural, but the second of which has the potential to cause great difficulty for some resource cataloguers. The former is the same as that raised for metadata records, above, namely update frequency. As with more basic metadata records, it remains necessary to ensure frequent and systematic regeneration of the metadata layer in order to ensure its congruence to the underlying resource. The second problem is that of many-to-one relationships, where the contents of a single element or field in the resource are required to map on to more than one element in the metadata structure. While it is straightforward to map multiple elements in the resource on to a single metadata element, the converse is far more difficult to accomplish, and may even prove impossible.

The whole metadata layer approach has gained currency recently, largely owing to the great success of the Open Archives Initiative (www.openarchives.org/).

The metadata filter

This is by far the most ambitious of the three approaches to metadata provision, that of a metadata *filter* on the resource. The concept of a metadata filter removes all need for manual or automatic generation of metadata, and in this case the metadata need never exist prior to query submission.

For such a model to function, both user and resource must be connected together by means of a computer network of some form, and technically complex protocols such as ISO 23950/Z39.50 are likely to be required in order to handle the negotiation of requests between computers.

The metadata filter utilizes the same mapping or crosswalk procedure introduced for the metadata layer, above. Under this model, however, the mapping is used to translate a user query for direct submission to the resource, rather than storing the translated metadata permanently for querying as done under the metadata layer model. In practice, the user would appear to be submitting a query directly to one or more resources, but the query would in reality be translated through a filter capable both of translating the user's request into a syntax (or syntaxes) appropriate for each resource and of translating the responses back into a single syntax for interpretation. The system would normally only hold information for translating those elements of the resource defined as useful for resource discovery, and the user would still be required to interact directly with the resource itself in order to gain access to more obscure elements of information.

Moving between domains

Significant effort is already expended on the creation of metadata within particular domains, where great benefits may be seen to accrue in the form of increased dissemination of results and access to information. The potential benefits of working in a cross-domain manner, where scholars make use of resources from subjects other than their own, are undeniably great, although fraught with difficulty. In an environment such as this, metadata potentially takes on a role of greater significance as descriptions created in order to allow the discovery of a resource also serve to describe that resource in a standardized and hopefully intelligible form, thus rendering the resource accessible to those not necessarily equipped with a detailed knowledge of the subject matter or its traditional modes of expression.

Access to information and practices from domains other than that in which a researcher is trained serves to broaden the outlooks of both knowledge donor and recipient. Opportunities are created for accessing related resources (an archaeologist studying the Sutton Hoo ship burial (www.nationaltrust.org.uk/places/suttonhoo/) who gathers background information from, among other sources, a translation of *Beowulf* (http://etext.virginia.edu/etcbin/ot2www-ebooks?specfile=/texts/english/ebooks/ebooks.o2w&act=text&offset=6239122&textreg=2&query=beowulf&id=AnoBeow)) and even for applying apparently unrelated techniques and theories from elsewhere.

Many of the subject domains in which we work today are the result of centuries of scholarly practice, and may – nowadays – be perceived more as a justification of the existing faculty structure within higher education than as an effective compartmentalization of the resources and practices with which modern scholars approach their craft. Archaeology, for example, remains a difficult subject to compartmentalize, drawing upon *anthropological* observation, *geological* notions of deposition and stratigraphy, and *historical* supporting evidence, and deploying a battery of *scientific* techniques every day. Is it, then, *really* an 'Art', a 'Humanity', or a 'Science' and, if so, how effective are these labels?

Rather than seeking to compartmentalize themselves and others within these flawed and outdated disciplinary groupings, modern scholars should be seizing the opportunities offered by globalization and the breaking down of other, more tangible, barriers in order to maximize their use of theory, practice and data from across the spectrum of academic endeavour.

Conclusion

This paper began by defining metadata. There then followed requirements for sharing metadata, and how to make use of it. Several models for metadata were described: records, layers, and filters. Finally, cross-disciplinary use was discussed.

If these data are to be made more widely available, work is required on means by which the specifics of disciplinary language, practice and interpretation may be presented in an accessible fashion, enabling access from outside the community and, hopefully, increasing access and awareness within any given community at the same time.

References

Federal Geographic Data Committee, Metadata Ad Hoc Working Group (1998) *Content Standard for Digital Geospatial Metadata*, version 2, www.fgdc.gov/metadata/contstan.html.

Lagoze, C. (1997) From Static to Dynamic Surrogates: resource discovery in the digital age, *D-Lib Magazine*, (June), www.dlib.org/dlib/june97/06lagoze.html.

2

Metadata – where are we going?

Anne Gilliland-Swetland

Introduction

Given the current ubiquity of research and development in metadata creation, management and use, it is easy to lose sight of the fact that 20 years ago, metadata was still a fledgling and seemingly straightforward construct ('data about data') that was being applied primarily in the management of scientific data. Today it is recognized as a critically important, and yet increasingly problematic and complex concept with relevance for information objects of all types as they move through time and space. Metadata helps users to negotiate a hybrid print and digital world by being able to describe and manage non-digital, born-digital and digitized information objects, as well as document the various relationships between them. Metadata is also what makes it possible to present and preserve multiple views of those objects, to provide and document their various functionalities and behaviours, to support use-driven information tools and services, and to place and sustain information objects within their cultural, historical, procedural, technological and other contexts. Moreover, many kinds of metadata have characteristics that increasingly lead them to be treated as information objects in their own right through processes such as metadata mining and technologies such as evidence-based information systems.

The nature and potential of metadata are continuously evolving as technologies change and new applications are identified. Traditionally, a major role of metadata has been to facilitate resource discovery (e.g. MARC cataloguing by libraries and Dublin Core tagging for web resources). Increasingly, however, metadata is being used to support the management and preservation of dynamic digital resources (e.g. schema and element sets such as XrML, RKMS and the OCLC/RLG Preservation Metadata Framework, www.oclc.org/research/pmwg/pm_framework. pdf). One emerging area is the study of metadata itself as evidence of social and organizational processes and collective memory.

What is particularly striking is how metadata is achieving a prominence that permeates almost all information-related activities, thus making its creation and management no longer the exclusive purview of information professionals. Metadata, albeit often embedded in invisible procedural, policy or technology infrastructures, plays key roles across our digital and information lives. Life-time management of information resources for activities such as digital asset management, recordkeeping, digital rights management, and e-learning, for example, is metadata intensive and requires that all actors in information-related processes, be they the creator, the information manager, the information provider, or the end-user, are not only to able to exploit metadata, but often also to create and manage it.

Such embeddedness and complexity indicate the maturation of metadata as an area not only of development, but also of intellectual debate. The questions this chapter addresses, therefore, are definitional and speculative – what can we say about the nature and roles of metadata today and where do today's developments seem to be leading us? In speaking to these questions, the chapter argues that key areas of current growth can be identified in terms of *dimensionality* (i.e. the application and use of metadata to bridge temporal, activity, community and domain boundaries) and *plurality* (i.e. the development, extension, and revision of ever-increasing numbers, types and versions of metadata schema for a range of purposes within and across a growing number of domains). The chapter also argues that key considerations we face in moving forward relate to how to manage this plurality, and how to support the efficient creation of appropriately rich metadata by the development of tools for the automated capture and creation of metadata and by distributing responsibilities for metadata creation and management more widely. There are also sociological and political aspects to metadata that need continuing attention, including how to ensure that metadata standards and schema can support *pluralism* in terms of diversity of purpose, behaviour, and culture. The chapter illustrates these arguments with brief discussions of some of the domains that provide indicators of where the conceptualization and roles of metadata are evolving.

The evolving concept of metadata

What kinds of relationships exist between metadata and the information objects with which it is associated? When might metadata be treated as an information object in its own right? Which kinds of metadata are neither part of the information object, nor about the information object, but are required to preserve or reconstruct the technological or other contexts of the objects?

What contexts can be identified for information objects and to what extent should these be captured or represented as metadata?

What are the implications for metadata creation and management when the information object(s) with which it is associated need to cross temporal, activity, community or domain boundaries?

These questions illustrate some of the problems that we face in defining the parameters of metadata, both as a tangible entity needing to be created and managed as part of an information system, and as a concept to be explained in a more theoretical manner. However, there are certain assumptions that are likely to continue to hold true, regardless of metadata development that occurs:

- Individual definitions of metadata will, of necessity, vary depending upon one's objective and perspective.
- Metadata and information objects are non-exclusive constructs, bound together by many different potential relationships. These relationships need to be identified and managed as part of information resource

management, but they can also represent tacit understandings and implicit information that can be exploited for knowledge development purposes.

• Metadata is instrumental in establishing the context of information systems, objects and services (however, the notion of *context* is expanding to include not only documentary, creative, historical, associative and social contexts but also policy, technological, juridical-administrative and procedural contexts, among others).

• Over its lifetime, an information system or information object will accrue many different types of metadata, created in different ways by different agents and processes. Some of this metadata will continue to be of value to preserve or reconstruct the system or object and its contexts, and some will not and will need to be purged.

Elsewhere I have argued that information objects, and digital information objects in particular, have a life cycle that begins and ends with creation and multi-versioning, and moves through organization, searching and retrieval, utilization, and preservation and disposition phases (Gilliland-Swetland, 2000). We can view this life cycle as a temporal model relating to the activities in which the information object participates over time. We can place an overlay on this model, however, that indicates the different domains or agents (e.g. authors, publishers, cataloguers, bibliographers, researchers) responsible for relevant metadata. In each case, however, the vocabularies, perspectives and needs of the agents creating or interacting with the metadata change.

Metadata thus created will predominantly take one of three approaches – *object-based metadata* (e.g. MARC) for physical object control, *process-based metadata* (e.g. RKMS) describing or captured by the processes, functions and activities in which that object is instrumental, or by which it is generated or manipulated (McKemmish et al., 1999), and *event-based metadata* (e.g. Harmony, ABC) that show sequences of events in which an object is involved over time and associations between variant manifestations of the object and the agents of those manifestations (Hunter and James, 2000). These approaches at different points have to interact, and managing the increasing dynamism of information objects and environments is an important emerging role for metadata.

Issues of granularity and plurality

There are widely differing opinions about how much metadata is enough, and, by implication, how rich metadata schema and frameworks should be. There is a tension between making the elements sufficiently simple for them to be widely used, and complex enough to describe a wide array of different resources and relationships (Dempsey and Heery, 1998). Simplicity of metadata can assist in helping information creators such as developers of web resources to become metadata creators even if they are not trained information professionals, thus enhancing widespread access to otherwise uncatalogued resources (one objective of Dublin Core) and can help a system to function in a more efficient and elegant manner. Smaller, more generic metadata sets may be easier to manage and perhaps to apply than complex, highly specific ones, but there is a need for much more evaluation of the extent to which they are actually effective.

In counterpoint to the simple and generic metadata approaches, individual domains are increasingly investing considerable resources in developing rich metadata schema that are designed for very specific purposes (such as the capture of context or the preservation of information objects) and user communities. Such developments raise two big questions: how do we create metadata economically and effectively that is still of sufficient granularity to support the use and preservation of information objects? And how do we manage plurality of metadata resulting from the development of multiple metadata schema? In the future, we are likely to see an emphasis on smarter ways to satisfy both sets of concerns that will avoid laborious manual creation of metadata and crosswalks between metadata schema. Several strategies seem to be ascendant. They include enhancing semantic interoperability between schema, exploiting hierarchical relationships to support inheritance of metadata, developing tools that can automatically create or capture metadata, spreading the responsibility for metadata creation and management, and supporting the long-term management and version control of metadata schema and the integrity of mapping between metadata elements in different schema through the development of metadata registries.

Crosswalks, that is formal mappings between corresponding elements in different metadata sets, have become increasingly prevalent as a means to integrate or search across resources described using different metadata sets. For example, mappings exist that would allow one to interoperate between all of the following, either simultaneously or sequentially: MARC, Encoded Archival Description (EAD), Categories for the Description of Works of Art (CDWA, www.getty.edu/research/institute/standards/cdwa/), the Visual Resources Association (VRA) Core Categories (www.vraweb.org/vracore3.htm), Dublin Core (DC, http://dublincore.org/documents/dces) and the Recordkeeping Metadata Schema (RKMS). However, the potential for semantic drift in so doing are manifold and well known. Many types of relationships may exist between elements in different metadata sets, including equivalencies where there is a one-to-one relationship but terminological differences such as synonyms and spelling and language variations, hierarchical relationships such as broader to narrower and part to whole, and associative or peripheral relationships. Moreover, metadata schema are constantly evolving. As a result, manual compilation and updating of robust crosswalks is labour intensive. One important area of development, therefore, lies in finding ways to define the semantics, i.e. the actual meaning of a metadata element within the domain within which it was developed, more closely, and then to automate the process of mapping between corresponding elements and levels across schema. The CORES project (www.cores-eu.net) is an example of an initiative whose objective is to support the sharing of metadata semantics through the development of a data model that will declare the definitions for terms used in metadata schema, including local usage and adaptations, in a way that can be automatically understood by interacting systems.

If rich metadata creation is key to the management of information objects as assets, packaging them according to user need, and demonstrating their continued reliability and authenticity, then future developments need to identify more automatic ways in which metadata can be created and managed by the various responsible agents. Inheritance of metadata created at different levels of aggregation exploits existing structural relationships within individual or collective information objects and provides an efficient method of metadata creation that also potentially enhances access (Baron, 1999; Gilliland-Swetland, 2002). This approach is being used effectively in many new metadata schema that are taking advantage of the hierarchical nature of XML. Other emerging approaches include the creation of metadata automatically based upon the occurrence of specific technological or procedural events, and inferring or deriving metadata as a result of computational analysis of the structures, behaviours, and content of information objects (e.g. the Persistent Archives technology being developed by the San Diego Computer Center in association with the National Archives and Records Administration (Moore et al., 2000)). Development of tools to help end-users to exploit rich metadata and search for and retrieve information packaged according to their needs is another important direction for metadata development.

With the development of metadata, however, also comes a requirement for its ongoing management, both at the levels of the information object and system for purposes such as rights and preservation management, and at the level of maintenance of the actual metadata schema or element sets. Organizations are realizing the asset value of metadata and the amount of resources they have put into its creation, and are managing it as an investment. In the preservation of information objects, they are also encountering issues of metadata version control. For example, how can the links between preserved information objects such as records and associated metadata retain their referential integrity over time in the face of systems obsolescence, data migration and the evolution of metadata schema? Temporal modelling is required to identify the version of metadata in place when objects were created or captured and then embed pointers to locations where that version of the metadata can be invoked. The development of metadata registries in response to some of these issues will likely play a key role in building the metadata management infrastructure that is rapidly becoming necessary. This topic was the subject of the 1997 Berkeley Joint Workshop on Metadata Registries (Joint Workshop on Metadata Registries, 1997), and is being pursued through research and development projects such as DESIRE (http://desire.ukoln.ac.uk/registry/) and InterPARES 2 (www.interpares.org), which have been investigating the necessary functionalities of metadata registries of different types.

The politics of metadata

Every technology and taxonomy has its socio-cultural and political dimensions, and along with the frenzy of all these new metadata initiatives there must be some space to consider the implications of what we are trying to achieve thereby. Common wisdom is that standards are good – that they facilitate data exchange and collaboration across technological, domain and national boundaries and they also provide a more predictable framework within which to undertake the preservation of information objects. Is there, however, a balance that we should be trying to achieve between standardization and customization? Between globalization and support of local practices? As new communities become involved in metadata concerns, they bring with them their own conceptualizations, semantics, behaviours and cultural outlook. Indeed, much of a culture or community of practice is embodied in its metadata structures, and these structures, whether they be recordkeeping procedures, literary genres or taxonomic classifications are more and more the focus of sociological and cultural study. We need to examine the kinds of consensus building we undertake in our processes of developing metadata schema and frameworks to ensure that we are avoiding imposing a metadata imperialism in terms of how we categorize and label things and a technological determinism in terms of how we implement metadata in our systems upon communities that have other ways of doing things but that are less empowered in those development processes. We need to debate whether we should even promote over-arching metadata schema in certain areas, or whether we should be taking a different approach. For example, it may be possible to agree upon metadata requirements, but leave it up to individual communities to decide how they meet those requirements according to their own cultural and domain perspectives and behaviours, and the extent to which they will work toward interoperability with other metadata schema.

On a more pragmatic note, there are several areas that need to be addressed more directly. These include how we ensure that the parties who we need to be creating and managing metadata actually do so (e.g. creators of web resources, records creators), what economic models we should be putting in place to support the creation and management of metadata over time, how we make informed choices between multiple potentially applicable schema, and how we cope with the implications for preservation and use of resources dependent upon proprietary metadata.

Domains doing new things with metadata

This section outlines developments in three areas that have been instrumental in furthering our conceptualization of metadata and the roles it can play. These developments are indicative of many of the themes discussed above and are areas where we can expect to see considerable activity over the next few years.

Recordkeeping

Records are particularly complex information objects because, as both the object and the documentation of business processes, they must move between business, legal, social, historical and cultural contexts: 'records are heterogeneous distributed objects comprising selected data elements that are pulled together by activity-related metadata such as audit trails, reports, and views through a process prescribed by the business function for a purpose that is juridically required. ... Records are temporally contingent – they take on different values and are subject to different values at different points in time' (Gilliland-Swetland and Eppard, 2000). Business and recordkeeping communities are increasingly concerned with the difficulties of ensuring the stability and fixity of records for accountability and historical purposes in environments that also wish those information objects to be highly dynamic and mutable for enterprise activities such as digital asset management. The process of ensuring fixity comes not at the end of the active life of the record, but at the beginning, even before the record is created, by purposefully embedding it in its procedural and documentary context. All this is achieved through metadata.

The area of quality recordkeeping exemplifies several of the directions in which metadata conceptualization is evolving – 'a quality system requires three different types of documentation: records of business processes; business rules that control the business processes; and systems documentation' (Duff and McKemmish, 2000). In recordkeeping, rich metadata is required to document all the dimensions involved in the processes and technologies of recordkeeping, and not just the record or records as information objects. Metadata facilitates the management, continued use and re-use of the records as they move forward through time; and the responsibility for creating that metadata, through both automatic and manual means, is distributed across many different agents and domains of use.

The Australian Metadata Recordkeeping Project identified eight goals or purposes that metadata may serve: unique identification; authentication of records; persistence of records content, structure and context so that they can be re-presented with their meaning preserved for subsequent use; administration of terms and conditions of access and disposal; tracking and documenting use history, including recordkeeping and archiving processes; enabling discovery, retrieval and delivery for authorized users; restricting unauthorized use; and assuring interoperability in networked environments (Duff and McKemmish, 2000). These goals are embodied in the Recordkeeping Metadata Schema (RKMS), which employs a taxonomy of relationships between entity types – business, agent, records, and business recordkeeping processes (McKemmish et al., 1999). Identifying metadata mechanisms for capturing and documenting processes is also a goal being pursued by manufacturing organizations through initiatives such as the Process Specification Language (PSL, http://ats.nist.gov/psl/rationale.html). Manufacturers need to be able to track processes such as production scheduling, process planning, workflow, business process reengineering, simulation and project management, and to exchange information about them with other companies with which they do business.

Calanag, Sugimoto and Tabata (2001) argue that 'while waiting for some "tried and tested" preservation solutions, extensive metadata for the meantime is our best way of minimizing the risks of a digital object becoming inaccessible'. On the archival side of recordkeeping, the Preservation of the Integrity of Electronic Records Project at the University of British Columbia (the UBC Project (Duranti, Eastwood and MacNeil, n.d.)) and the International Research on Permanent Authentic Electronic Records (InterPARES, www.interpares.org) project have been examining the ways by which reliable records can be created and authentic records preserved. One of the impetuses for the strong emphasis on reliability and authenticity is that the rules of evidence for admitting records into legal proceedings have shifted from producing the original to demonstrating the integrity of the system. The notion of an original has also been challenged in the digital environment. Merrill has noted the increased emphasis when determining the legal admissibility of documents distributed on the web on 'authentication of identity of originators of information' and 'authentication of record integrity' (Baron, 1999; Merrill, 1999). The findings of InterPARES indicate that integrity assurance and continuing accessibility are the key outputs of the archival recordkeeping function and that these are primarily assured through procedural and descriptive metadata. Some of the means by which metadata in active recordkeeping systems must document and ensure the records' reliability include maintaining expressions of records' attributes, documenting implementation of creator-defined access privileges, documenting protective procedures to prevent loss or corruption of records and to prevent media and technology deterioration, enforcing any documentary forms for records that are legally or organizationally required, and helping to identify an authoritative record when multiple copies or versions exist. Archival metadata must support the continued authenticity of records by describing the records as they were received from the records' creators and thoroughly documenting the entire process of preservation (Duranti and MacNeil, 1996; Baron, 1999; Gilliland-Swetland, 2003).

Digital rights management

With the rise of networked access to digital resources and the capacity to create multiple derivative versions with comparative ease have also come changes in legislation relating to intellectual property and the desire to use metadata to inform users about, and automatically enforce rights requirements. As a result, metadata for rights management is an area that is developing rapidly, but with varying objectives, within several communities. This is demonstrated by the multiplicity of current initiatives, including eXtensible rights Markup Language (XrML), the Open

Digital Rights Language (ODRL) Initiative, the Digital Rights Expression Languages (DREL) Workgroup, and Online Information Exchange (ONIX). XrML (www.xrml.org) is a language for specifying, managing and enforcing rights and conditions associated with all kinds of resources including digital content as well as services. XrML makes use of hierarchy to assign rights and conditions at different levels of granularity both for individual and groups of users, and can also authenticate those users. ODRL (http://odrl.net/) is seeking to develop a specification of an open standard for an extensible language and vocabulary to express terms and conditions over any content including permissions, constraints, obligations, conditions, and offers and agreements with rights holders. DREL (IEEE Learning Standards Committee, 2003) is an IEEE initiative that is backed by industry groups related to consumer electronics and information technology development and is concerned with identifying requirements to ensure that standardized digital rights expression languages support the learning and training needs of educational communities. ONIX (EDItEUR, n.d.) is a data exchange standard developed by the publishing industry in the USA to exchange information with wholesale, retail, and e-tail booksellers about publications, including extensive or brief descriptions, reviews, abstracts, tables of contents, and author credentials for publications.

Such multiplicity, where metadata is being used for authentication and enforcement as well as notification and description purposes, illustrates well the range of roles that metadata can play as well as the very different perspectives that different communities can bring through their own schema to a common topic such as digital rights management.

Metadata for e-learning

A third area of development that is the site of increasing activity and that moves metadata for end-use beyond traditional description and resource discovery relates to the design and use of digital resources in education ('e-learning'). Educational users often have specific needs in terms of how and why they locate information resources, as well as how they want to use them, and these needs are largely mediated through metadata. They may, for example, need an indication of which resources would be most appropriate for specific curricular uses in terms of coverage and level of difficulty. Key concepts may need to be highlighted and clustered in particular ways, and terms of art used in metadata may need to be searchable also in lay language (Gilliland-Swetland, Kafai and Landis, 1999). Sometimes, a student may be required to demonstrate domain-specific reasoning in how they search for and interpret information. Novice users may need scaffolding that is unnecessary for more advanced learners. Instructors and students may wish to create their own metadata in the form of annotations of content or to record links to other relevant materials for an assignment (Bos, Krajcik and Soloway, 1997).

The Gateway to Educational Materials (GEM, www.geminfo.org/networker.html) is one project that has developed a metadata set that extends Dublin Core by eight metadata elements to assist teachers in the use of uncatalogued materials available on the internet. These include elements such as grade or age of the student, the pedagogy being employed, the quality of the resource for instruction, and the curricular standards to which the resource can be mapped (Sutton, 1998; 1999). One of the most extensive and complex applications of metadata is the IEEE Learning Object Metadata (LOM, http://ltsc.ieee.org/wg12/index.html). IEEE-LOM shares some of the same goals as GEM in terms of supporting the educational activities of instructors and learners, but it also has a strong technology focus in terms of supporting how learning objects are created, shared, exchanged and composed into lessons, as well as facilitating how organizations engaged in educational activities can express educational content and performance standards in standardized ways.

To date, most of these sets have been created for specific communities but much work has still to be done in evaluating the effectiveness of their use by educators and students and assessing their ability to meet the educational needs of wider communities (Greenberg, 2000). One initiative that is undertaking this is the Metadata for Education Group (MEG, www.ukoln.ac.uk/metadata/education), a forum that has been formed to review the diverse developments in educational metadata with a goal of identifying and disseminating best practices based upon existing standards and specifications for all educational levels across the UK

(Miller, 2002). As metadata sets proliferate, we can expect to see similar forums emerge in other areas with common interests seeking to discern, evaluate and promote emergent best practices, rationalize the points of overlap, and identify where any gaps may be and bring them to the attention of the parties best positioned to address them.

Conclusion

The next few years will be busy ones in terms of metadata development. There will be more of an emphasis on managing the dynamics of information objects from creation through preservation, disposition, or re-versioning, and in particular, on how object-, process- and event-based metadata might interact to assist with that management. We can expect to see continued proliferation of new metadata schema and the continuing refinement of existing schema, resulting in more effort being put into metadata management through the development of metadata registries and other mechanisms such as crosswalks for identifying correspondences between metadata elements in different metadata schema. There will be an increasing focus, for those crosswalks, on rules and automated methods for capturing and mapping semantics notions in much more rigorous ways. The demand for rich metadata is likely to encourage more investigation into automatic ways of creating metadata as well as tools designed to help end-users customize information that they have located by exploiting metadata.

Finally, there are two aspects that require a higher level view of metadata development than is currently supported by the fragmented communities who are involved. The first of these is addressing the political and policy implications of metadata developments. The second relates to developing mechanisms to support more holistic approaches to metadata development in specific areas of application such as multi-domain forums.

References

Baron, J. R. (1999) Recordkeeping in the 21st Century, *The Information Management Journal*, (July), 8–16.

Bos, N., Krajcik, J. and Soloway, E. (1997) Student Publishing in a WWW Digital Library – goals and instructional support. In Bell, P. (chair), *Artifact-Building in Computer Learning Environments: supporting students' scientific inquiry*, AERA 1997, http://mydl.soe.umich.edu/papers/.

Calanag, M. L., Sugimoto, S. and Tabata, K. (2001) A Metadata Approach to Digital Preservation. In Oyama, K. and Gotoda, H. (eds), *Proceedings of the International Conference on Dublin Core and Metadata Applications 2001*, Tokyo, National Institute of Informatics, 143–50, www.nii.ac.jp/dc2001/proceedings/product/paper-24.pdf.

Categories for the Description of Works of Art (CDWA), www.getty.edu/research/institute/standards/cdwa/.

Dempsey, L. and Heery, R. (1998). Metadata: a current view of practice and issues, *The Journal of Documentation*, **54** (4), 145–72.

DESIRE Metadata Registry, http://desire.ukoln.ac.uk/registry/.

Dublin Core Metadata Initiative, http://dublincore.org/documents/dces/.

Duff, W. and McKemmish, S. (2000) Metadata and ISO 9000 Compliance, *Information Management Journal*, **34** (1), http://rcrg.dstc.edu.au/publications/smckduff.html.

Duranti, L., Eastwood, T. and MacNeil, H. (n.d.) The Preservation of the Integrity of Electronic Records, www.interpares.org/UBCProject.

Duranti, L. and MacNeil, H. (1996) The Protection of the Integrity of Electronic Records: an overview of the UBC-MAS Research Project, *Archivaria*, **42** (Fall), 46–67.

EDItEUR (n.d.) ONIX for Books, www.editeur.org/onix.html.

Gateway to Educational Metadata (GEM), www.geminfo.org/networker.html.

Gilliland-Swetland, A. J. (2000) Setting the Stage: defining metadata. In Baca, M. (ed.) *Introduction to Metadata: pathways to digital information*, 2nd edn, Los Angeles, Getty Information Institute, www.getty.edu/research/institute/standards/intrometadata/index.html.

Gilliland-Swetland, A. J. (2001) Popularizing the Finding Aid: exploiting EAD to enhance online browsing and retrieval in archival information systems by diverse user groups, *Journal of Internet Cataloging*, **4** (3/4), 199–225.

Gilliland-Swetland, A. J. (2002) Testing our Truths: delineating the parameters of the authentic archival electronic record, *American Archivist*, (Fall/Winter), 196–215.

Gilliland-Swetland, A. J. (2003) Advanced Electronic Records: design implementation and evaluation; presentation given at Southern Illinois University, Carbondale, IL, 20–1 March 2003.

Gilliland-Swetland, A. J. and Eppard, P. (2000) Preserving the Authenticity of Contingent Digital Objects: the InterPARES Project, *Dlib Magazine*, **6** (July/August), www.dlib.org/dlib/july00/eppard/07eppard.html.

Gilliland-Swetland, A. J., Kafai, Y. and Landis, W. E. (1999) Metadata Applications in the Creation and Description of Digital Primary Sources for Elementary School Classrooms, *Journal of the American Society for Information Science*, **50** (14), 193–201.

Greenberg, J. (ed.) (2000) *Metadata and Organizating Educational Resources on the Internet*, New York, Haworth Information Press.

Hunter, J. and James, D. (2000) The Application of an Event-Aware Metadata Model to an Online Oral History Project. In proceedings of Research and Advanced Technology for Digital Libraries Conference, ECDL 2000, Lisbon, Portugal, September 2000, *Lecture Notes in Computer Science*, 1923, 291–304, http://archive.dstc.edu.au/RDU/staff/jane-hunter/OralHistory/paper.html.

IEEE Learning Technology Standards Committee (2003) Digital Rights Expression Language (DREL) Working Group, http://ltsc.ieee.org/wg4/.

IEEE Learning Technology Standards Committee (LTSC) *IEEE P1484.12 Learning Object Metadata Working Group*, http://ltsc.ieee.org/wg12/index.html.

Joint Workshop on Metadata Registries (1997) *Workshop Report*, http://pueblo.lbl.gov/~olken/EPA/Workshop/report.html.

McKemmish, S. et al. (1999) Describing Records in Context in the Continuum: the Australian Recordkeeping Metadata Schema, *Archivaria* **48** (Fall), 4-43.

Merrill, C R. (1999) Legislative Initiatives on the Shift from Paper to Electronic Paradigm: understanding the difference between closed and open systems. In *Public Key Infrastructure (PKI): the right combination for electronic commerce, Internet Security Summit, Washington DC, 8-9 February 1999,* www.pkilaw.com/9902issp-Book/.

Metadata for Education Group, www.ukoln.ac.uk/metadata/education/.

Miller, P. (2002) Taking a Common View of Educational Metadata, *D-Lib Magazine*, (April), www.dlib.org/dlib/april01/04inbrief.html#MILLER.

Moore, R., Baru, C. Rajasekar, A. et al. (2000) Collection-Based Persistent Digital Archives – Parts 1 & 2, *D-Lib Magazine* (March/April), www.dlib.org/dlib/march00/moore/03moore-pt1.html, www.dlib.org/dlib/april00/moore/04moore-pt2.html.

OCLC/RLG Working Group on Preservation Metadata (2002) *Preservation Metadata and the OAIS Information Model: a metadata framework to support the preservation of digital objects*, www.oclc.org/research/pmwg/pm_framework.pdf.

Process Specification Language, National Institute of Standards and Technology, http://ats.nist.gov/psl/rationale.html.

Sutton, S. A. (1998) Gateway to Educational Materials (GEM): metadata for networked information discovery and retrieval, *Computer Networks and ISDN Systems*, **30**, 691–3.

Sutton, S. A. (1999) Conceptual Design and Deployment of a Metadata Framework for Educational Resources on the Internet, *Journal of the American Society for Information Science*, **50** (1–7), 1182–92.

Visual Resources Association (VRA) *Core Categories*, www.vraweb.org/vracore3.htm.

Part 2

METADATA IN THE HUMANITIES

3

Music metadata

Sherry L. Vellucci

Introduction

This paper begins by providing a background to music metadata, outlining the different types of music information, conceptual issues and practical problems. Then the current forms of music metadata are discussed, i.e. AACR2R and MARC. Next we look at new directions and specific examples including Dublin Core, EAD, expanded functions, and multimedia. Following that, some major music library metadata projects are described. Finally, new ideas on access and retrieval are covered.

Types of music information

Music is complex and multifaceted in nature, presenting several challenges to information organizers. A musical work contains a particular musical idea. This musical idea can be expressed through music notation as a printed score; it can be coupled with textual material that becomes an inherent part of the musical work, such as a song or opera; it can be expressed in sound by performance; and a performance can be captured visually. Music information, therefore, can be represented as notation based, text based, audio based or visually based. Each representational form can be considered a type of music information. It is not uncommon for a digital music resource to contain all of these forms of music information with additional interactive capabilities. Neither is it uncommon for users to search for a musical work in any or all of these forms.

Just as the representation of music can be complex, each form of music representation can be presented in a variety of ways. Music notation can appear as printed scores (full scores, vocal scores, instrumental parts, etc.), scanned images of music scores, or computer-encoded music such as MIDI (Musical Instrument Digital Interface) or NIFF (Notation Interchange File Format) files. Text can be underlain beneath the music notation as part of the score, printed independently of the notation or marked up for use on the internet. Audio representations can be analogue or digital and can come in a variety of 'containers' such as LPs, cassettes, CDs or MP3 files. Because of such complexities, music presents both theoretical and practical problems for identification, description and retrieval of music resources.

In most library systems, retrieval of a musical work through a library catalogue is only possible by accessing a metadata record that describes the resource in terms of the physical item and the musical content. Since the metadata is textual, it is not derived from the musical *content* itself; it is transcribed from the bibliographic information associated with the musical work and its specific manifestation. This textual surrogate for the musical resource includes information *about* the musical content, such as title, composer, conductor, key, duration, publisher, etc. A text-based metadata system for music requires a two-step process to retrieve the desired music: first, a text search of the catalogue to find the surrogate record. This requires the searcher to have some factual information about the musical work. Once the metadata record is retrieved, a second search must be performed to physically locate and access the resource. Today's web-based catalogues can provide direct linkage from the metadata record to the musical resource if the resource is available online in digital form.

Conceptual issues

The creators of music metadata must deal with the conceptual issues associated with the complex nature of music, as well as the practical descriptive problems related to the usage of music resources. The conceptual issues must be grasped because they underpin the fundamental principles of organizing music resources and account for many of the practical problems. Understanding the various ways in which music resources are used will allow the metadata creator to resolve the practical problems when determining the type of metadata information required to meet the search and retrieval needs of musicians.

The conceptual issues involve the various manifestations in which a musical work may appear, the universality of music, the continued popularity of some musical works over long periods of time and the pervasiveness of bibliographic relationships. All of these issues are closely interrelated and create challenges for music metadata creation, retrieval and display.

The *work* as an artistic entity separate from its physical container is a fundamental concept for creating music metadata. In the cataloguing world this dichotomy is commonly referred to as 'content vs carrier'. Since notation, text, sound and visual media can represent music information, and in turn each of these representations may have several different presentation formats, it is not unusual for one musical work to appear in many different manifestations. The addition of words to the music further complicates the issue, since poems and libretti set to music are often written by someone other than the composer and may appear as separate but related text documents. Because music resources have different uses, it may be important for the searcher to retrieve all instances of a musical work represented in a catalogue in order to find the appropriate resource that meets the specific need.

Another factor that further complicates music cataloguing is the international scope of music and the music publishing industry. Music is often called the 'universal language' because music notation can be read independently of language by any trained musician, and a musical performance can be appreciated by anyone, regardless of musical training or language. The same musical work, therefore, is often published and recorded in many countries, with title pages and performance notes in the language appropriate to the country of publication. This adds to the proliferation of music resources and presents major problems for collocation in the catalogue. A name or title page in a foreign language will not affect a musician's ability to use the music, but it will affect his or her ability to find that music in the catalogue.

Other contributors to the proliferation of music resources are the age and popularity of the musical work. An emphasis on the standard repertoire of Western art music has lasted over many centuries. When music literature remains popular for extended periods of time, it increases the chance that many manifestations of the work will appear in a variety of formats. For example, a search of the OCLC Connexions database for Beethoven's Symphony No. 9 retrieved 324 scores, 1200 sound recordings, 61 video recordings and 18 electronic resources!

Performance adds still more complexity to music, including the need for performance parts and the dimension of time. Performance of Western music that is not improvised creates the need for performance parts from which each musician can play. The music assigned to each instrument is extracted from the full score and published separately for that instrument. Depending on the musical work, there may be only one instrumental part for a solo performance or dozens of individual parts for a fully orchestrated symphonic work. These music extractions, or performance parts, may be described in the metadata record if the parts accompany the score or they may be described in a separate holdings metadata record that is linked to the score in some way.

Inherent to any performance is the dimension of time. A traditional metadata record includes the overall duration of the work and its individual movements – important information for a musician. This duration metadata is limited in the sense that it can express length textually, but it cannot identify the exact point in time on a recording where a specific theme or scene begins. In other words, it cannot be used as a location tool within the dimension of time.

Another aspect of performance is the concept of the *performable unit*. For example, an aria from an opera can be performed independently of the opera; therefore, the aria is considered a performable unit and as such can be published as a separate vocal work. Another aspect of the performable unit arises from a single opus number that contains several independent works. Beethoven's String Quartets, Opus 59, consist of six separate quartets, each of which may be published separately or together as the complete opus.

It should now be clear that a musical work can have many different and related manifestations. When two or more entities represented in the catalogue are related to one another in some way they are said to have a *bibliographic relationship*. Research has shown that music resources have a much higher incidence of bibliographic relationships than textual resources (Vellucci, 1997). Identifying these relationships and linking the related resources is a major part of music metadata creation.

Practical problems

In addition to the conceptual difficulties described above, there are many practical issues that music metadata creators must consider. Usage is the most important factor, for it influences the approach taken to the metadata content. Music resources are used for different purposes, including recreational listening and viewing, study, rehearsal and performance. Each use requires a different presentation layout, physical format or special music-related details.

With notated music, usage determines the presentation layout. For example, full scores are needed for study and conducting purposes. A miniature score, which includes the complete work but is reduced in size, is sufficient for study, but often inadequate for use by a conductor because of the small size of the print. For rehearsal purposes, it is common for choral musicians to use a piano/vocal score in which the full instrumental accompaniment is reduced for piano. Instrumental performance requires separate parts from which each instrument can play. All of these manifestations contain the same work, but the musical content and layout vary considerably. Presentation information is an essential part of music metadata.

It is also necessary for metadata to identify the specific instruments and voices needed for performance and to indicate if the library owns the full set of parts. These instrumentation details are required for a musician to determine if the appropriate performers and the necessary parts are available for a performance. Other information useful for musicians is the duration of the music and the key in which the work is composed, both of which are critical when planning a performance programme.

Another practical problem that must be dealt with by the metadata creator is musical works with generic, or form titles. Titles like *Symphony* and *Quartet* present retrieval problems if there is no further information to identify the specific work. This can be a problem even when the composer's name is added to the title for search purposes. Additional identifier information needs to be added, such as key, opus number and thematic catalogue number, in order to differentiate, for example, one Haydn symphony from his 103 other compositions in this genre. The library system's application software may hinder the search process if it is not capable of dealing with single character searches (common to key information) and special symbols such as the sharp (#) and flat (♭) signs.

Finally, greater content analysis is desirable in the descriptive metadata for sound recordings. For example, a singer may wish to compare different performances of a song. In order to locate the song on different recordings, the metadata should identify each track on the recordings. Similarly, performance dates are also important for comparison purposes, but dates can be confusing. Does the date represent the date the performance was recorded, the date the recording was issued, or the date it was digitally remastered? This type of problem indicates the need for specific identifier codes or qualifiers to clarify some types of data.

Some of these issues and problems are not unique to music, but are found with much greater frequency in music catalogues, thereby creating a complex music metadata environment. A new data model developed by an IFLA (International Federation of Library Associations) task force helped clarify the confusion and confirmed the conceptual model used in music cataloguing. The IFLA model identified four states of a resource as outlined in the *FRBR (Functional Requirements of the Bibliographic Record)* (IFLA, 1998). These include the *work*, the *expression*, the *manifestation* and the *item*. It is generally agreed that the *work* and *expression* exist in an abstract state, while the *manifestation* and the *item* exist in a tangible state. A Mozart symphony can serve as an example. The musical ideas expressed within the symphonic structure, and the development of those ideas, is considered the *work*. The *expression* of Mozart's symphony can occur as a musical performance or as music notation. A *manifestation* might be a specific performance by the Berlin Philharmonic Orchestra issued by Deutsche Grammophon as a compact disc or the manifestation could be a music score published by Bärenreiter Verlag. Finally, the individual *item* acquired by a library could be represented by a specific copy of the CD or the score.

The current issues and problems confronted when organizing music resources fall into two categories: creating music metadata and using music metadata. The discussion in this section includes both metadata categories, but the bottom line is that music metadata is only as useful as the capabilities of the integrated library system (ILS) or database that contains it. Database structures, encoding syntax, and collocation and display of retrieval sets all play an important role in the success of a metadata system to meet user needs. The FRBR data model allows new catalogue structures to be developed that can make more efficient use of metadata to identify and link related works and aid in the development of unambiguous, clustered screen displays for large retrieval sets of metadata records. This is especially important for searching musical works with multiple manifestations in a library consortium's union catalogue such as Music Libraries Online (Duffy, 1998). The FRBR model would allow the user to search at the work level, sort the results into scores, sound recordings, video recordings and electronic resources at the expression level, and select a specific edition, recording or file by viewing metadata records at the manifestation level. This multilevel search and display capability would improve both recall and precision for music catalogue searchers. Some vendors are beginning to restructure their catalogue databases to experiment with the FRBR relational model, but it is still early days (VTLS, n.d.).

Current music metadata solutions
Music metadata in libraries: AACR2R and MARC

In the English-speaking world, the AACR2R (*Anglo-American Cataloguing Rules*, Second Edition, Revised) and the MARC (MAchine Readable Cataloguing) communications format are the primary metadata systems used in library catalogues. These two standards govern the content and structure of a metadata record. They provide a data-rich description that offers both advantages and disadvantages for the creation and use of metadata for music resources.

AACR2R codifies rules for describing a resource, selecting appropriate name and title access points, determining the form of access points and creating cross-references. The rules for descriptive cataloguing incorporate the ISBD (International Standard Bibliographic Description), which provides AACR2R with a systematic structure for content and order of data. Specifically, Chapter 5 'Music' uses the ISBD PM (for printed music) and Chapter 6 'Sound Recordings' uses the ISBD NPM (for non-print materials). The AACR2R section on choice and form of access points helps determine main entry for the item, a tricky and controversial issue for sound and video recordings. This section also provides guidance for authority control of names and an extensive section on the formulation of music uniform titles in Chapter 25.

The MARC format was developed with its own encoding syntax as a communications structure to exchange bibliographic data electronically. The content of a MARC metadata record is governed by AACR2R and other standards for description such as controlled vocabularies. In addition, MARC provides for content that is not specified by AACR2R. The latest edition of MARC – MARC21 – has a single bibliographic format that can be modified for various types of material (books, scores, sound recordings, video recordings, etc.). This allows metadata records for all types of resources to be exchanged and integrated into one catalogue.

Over the last 30 years, AACR2R and MARC have accommodated the issues and problems discussed above more or less successfully. Chapters 5 and 6 of AACR2R provide for the special details necessary to describe the different formats of music scores and sound recordings, including such data as the type of score, medium of performance, type of music notation, duration of performance, playing speed, number of sound channels, and sound reproduction characteristics. The collocation of multiple related versions of a work is achieved with authority control methods that rely heavily on uniform titles. Included in the music uniform title are distinguishing details, such as performing forces, key, opus or thematic catalogue numbers and language. Additional information is also supplied in the notes area of the metadata record and might include information about individual tracks on a sound recording (i.e. a contents note), names of performers and reissue data.

In addition to the traditional name, title and subject access points prescribed by AACR2R and controlled vocabularies, the MARC format provides for the current and future searchability of other music-related data elements. Some of this information is encoded, including the Form of Composition (008/18-19), Format of Music (008/20), ISMN (International Standard Music Number)/ISRC (International Standard Recording Code) (024), Publisher, Plate or Matrix Number (028), Date and Place of Capture (033), Type of Musical Composition Code (047), Number of Instruments/Voices Code (048) and Duration (306). Other information is given as text, including the Musical Presentation Format (254), Duration (500), Performer Notes (511) and Date and Place of Capture Note (518). Again, the ability to search on this data is determined by the catalogue's application software.

Current issues

One criticism of the MARC format is that there is a great deal of redundancy in the record, with the same data in both encoded and text form. Ironically, the strength of the MARC record is the amount of music-specific detail that it accommodates, especially when compared to other metadata schemes like the Dublin Core.

Additional criticisms of MARC focus on structure. Designed for flat files, MARC has limited capabilities for external linking with related metadata records, a serious problem for music resources with multiple manifestations. Internal linking capabilities are also limited; for example, the MARC structure cannot link specific performers in the bibliographic record to specific tracks on the recording listed in the same record. Relator subfield codes can be used, however, to indicate the relationship of the entry to the item. For example, in the following added entry heading the subfield 4 code 'prf' indicates that the Alban Berg Quartett is the performing group on the recording:

    710 2   Alban Berg Quartett. ‡4 prf

At the request of the RISM (Répertoire International des Sources Musicales) Libretto project, a number of music-specific relator codes were added to the list, e.g. dancer (dcr), vocalist (voc), instrumentalist (itr). The new codes are used for music resources when the broader term performer (prf) is too general.

The data-rich MARC21 metadata records are labour-intensive and expensive to create. With the proliferation of digital music resources, cataloguing agencies looked for ways to create simpler metadata that adhered to the high standards set by AACR2R and MARC21. This led to the development of core bibliographic records for music and sound recordings by the Library of Congress' PCC (Program for Cooperative Cataloging) and the Bibliographic Control Commission of the IAML (International Association of Music Libraries) (PCC, 2002; IAML Bibliographic Control Commission, n.d.). Core records contain data elements judged to be essential for both identification and access of music resources. These records are designed to be dynamic and can be enriched with additional information as needed. What distinguishes core records from minimal-level cataloguing is that all access points are under authority control and are represented by records in the national authority file. Despite the moniker, core records for music and sound recordings are relatively rich in data content.

The effectiveness of the AACR2R and MARC21 metadata standards for resource discovery and retrieval is also dependent on the structural design of the catalogue's database. These databases are designed to accommodate MARC records and, therefore, perpetuate the linear structure that resulted from the transfer of card catalogue concepts into the computer environment. This continues to limit access to much information in the music metadata record and perpetuates collocation and screen display problems for large retrieval sets of related music resources.

Keyword searching made elements of the uniform title accessible and information in the notes area searchable as uncontrolled data; but keyword searching does not address the need for direct links among related metadata records. The growing interest in relational database structures focused attention on the role of relationships and the possibilities for linking metadata records beyond the flat file structure. To compensate for the lack of relational architecture, linking fields (76x–78x) were added to the MARC format. Although these linking MARC fields provide connections among related metadata records, they are mostly used for serials and are not commonly found in music metadata records.

The introduction of web-based catalogues allowed cataloguers to incorporate hypertext features to overcome some of these shortcomings. The 856 field was added to the MARC format to accommodate a digital resource's online location information and enable direct hyperlinks between the metadata record and the actual resource. The Z39.50 search protocol was developed to further enhance cross-platform searching of library catalogues over networks. The protocol includes a set of data attributes that identifies specific access points and maps them to the corresponding MARC fields, or the elements of other metadata schemes to facilitate database-searching interoperability. However, the standard Z39.50 Bib-1 attribute set, which was designed primarily for searching metadata for text-based documents, did not include some important access points for music metadata retrieval. The UK's Music Libraries Online project developed a Z39.50 music profile that identified 24 additional music-specific search attributes necessary for a fully functional, interoperable virtual union music catalogue (MLO, n.d.). This Music Materials Attribute Set is now a superset of the Z39.50 Bib-2 Attribute Set and includes such specific access points as thematic catalogue number, music key, performer, duration and instrumentation.

Extending MARC for music

The music incipit – a melody fragment represented as music notation – is accepted internationally as a unique way to identify works contained in music manuscripts. During the 1930s as part of a US WPA (Work Progress Administration) project, librarians were hired to add music incipits to the catalogue cards for music scores in the New York Public Library. These incipits helped the user accurately identify a musical work from the major themes notated on the metadata record, but because of the limitations of card catalogues, they could not be used for retrieval purposes. In 1975, the Cataloguing Commission of IAML published guidelines for including music incipits as part of the rules for cataloguing music manuscripts in the *Code International de Catalogage de la Musique* (Peters, 1957–83, 29–31). Music incipits continue to be an essential component in music bibliography, but the practice of adding them to catalogue cards was largely discontinued in the cataloguing community because of the expense involved.

Research in MIR (music information retrieval) has renewed interest in music incipits. Incipit data can be entered into an automated system either as an image or as an encoded set of data, but only in the latter case will the data be available for indexing and searching. Early alpha-numeric encoding systems for music notation – such as the Plaine & Easie Code or the DARMS (Digital Alternate Representation of Musical Scores) code – were adopted by music bibliographers to represent a music incipit for thematic catalogues. The IAML Cataloguing Commission recognized the potential usefulness of music incipit data in MARC records, and submitted a proposal to the Permanent UNIMARC Committee of IFLA to add new music-specific data fields to UNIMARC. Among the approved fields, field 036 contains music incipit data that includes clef, key signature and time signature as well as the encoded notation.

Both RISM and SBN (Servizio Bibliotecario Nazionale) – two of the largest existing automated catalogues containing music manuscripts – use the Plaine & Easie Code to represent music notation. Representatives from RISM are now preparing a proposal for additions and changes to MARC21 to accommodate RISM's music-specific information. Among the fields under discussion is a musical incipit field similar to the one adopted by UNIMARC. The ability to derive metadata, including music incipits, from the existing RISM database, convert it to MARC and render it searchable in the library catalogue would greatly enrich current MARC21 music metadata records.

New directions for music metadata

An integrated environment is certainly the immediate future for discovery and retrieval of music resources. In this integrated model, the descriptive metadata in library catalogues links directly to the distributed music resource that it describes, i.e. music scores, sound files and visual recordings. Many librarians, reluctant to abandon the huge investment in the MARC format, continue to use the descriptively rich MARC records in this new distributed online model. In some cases the MARC record is hyperlinked directly to the object. In other instances, the data from the MARC record is converted to a markup language format such as XML and then linked to or embedded in the music resource. Several music projects that experimented with integrating MARC metadata with digital music resources will be discussed later in this chapter.

The rapid growth in the number of digital music resources in the distributed network environment started a conceptual shift in the approach to information organization. Many think MARC records are too detailed, time consuming and expensive for use in this volatile digital environment. Now that the digital music resource, its descriptive information, and the organizational system for identifying and retrieving it all exist in the same electronic milieu, metadata is no longer limited to residing in a file separate from the music resource; it can also be embedded in the digitized object. Information organizers are experimenting with new organizational systems that can harvest metadata and assemble descriptive information at the time of query. Freed from the constraints of the MARC record format, many subject- and format-specific communities seized the opportunity to create customized metadata schemes that would better serve their specific users (such as art, archives, education, museums, etc.). The music community did not immediately choose that route. The multiple formats and complex characteristics of music make it difficult to develop one music-specific metadata set. Instead, current efforts in the music library community focus on evaluating the effectiveness of a variety of schemes for music resources.

Dublin Core Metadata Element Set

The DCMES (Dublin Core Metadata Element Set) is the most widely used and supported general metadata scheme in the library community and an obvious choice to consider for the description and retrieval of music resources. The PADS (Performing Arts Data Service, www.pads.ahds.ac.uk/), a division of AHDS (Arts & Humanities Data Service) in the UK, took the lead in evaluating DCMES for music (PADS, n.d.). The PADS project examined the feasibility of using DCMES for describing both scores and sound recordings and raised several practical and theoretical issues of importance to the music community.

The practical problems addressed the level of specificity and amount of detail needed to identify and retrieve the appropriate music resource. A tension has always existed between the two catalogue functions of resource discovery and description. In order to discover or retrieve all relevant resources, i.e. to obtain high recall, a music resource must be described at a high state, usually at the level of the *work* or the *expression*. But in order to find the exact resource required, i.e. to obtain high precision, the resource must be described at a much lower state, usually the *manifestation* or *item* level.

The DCMES is designed for high-level resource discovery, i.e. high recall. As a simple core set it contains only 15 basic elements considered common to most resources. Clearly, once the music resource is retrieved at the work or expression level (e.g. an audio recording of the Beethoven *Missa Solemnis*), searchers need more detailed metadata that provides an accurate description of the resource for efficient selection of the desired object (e.g. Which orchestra? Which conductor? Which choir? Date of performance? CD or MP3?). One faction of the Dublin Core community argues for few and simple data elements to obtain the best recall and maintain a high level of interoperability, while another part of the community calls for more detailed descriptions to obtain the best precision, even though this may mean sacrificing some interoperability. Element qualifiers that add specificity and identify standards are one solution to this problem, but search engines must be able to ignore unrecognized qualifiers and match on the primary data element alone in order to maintain interoperability and high recall.

The Music Library Association is currently examining the list of recommended DCMES qualifiers to determine whether Dublin Core can be used effectively for the discovery and retrieval of music resources. When completed, a list of element qualifiers will be submitted to the Dublin Core Metatdata Initiative for approval as music qualifiers. Data refinements such as composer, arranger, performer, date of performance, etc. are currently being considered. One specific Dublin Core element, DC.Relation and the Type qualifiers associated with it, is of particular concern to the music community because the known incidence of bibliographic relationships in music materials is high. The Music Library Association has charged a working group to compare the DCMI approved list of relationship types with those already identified by previous research in music relationships. Additional relationships such as 'IsPerformanceOf' and 'hasPerformance' are being considered for recommendation.

Originally the DCMES was syntax independent, but as projects began to adopt the scheme for use in the web environment, use of HTML (HyperText Markup Language) became common. The more recently developed XML (eXtensible Markup Language) allows for more detail and greater flexibility. Coupled with the RDF (Resource Description Framework), XML has become the preferred syntax for use with Dublin Core.

Dublin Core metadata projects

Several digital music projects use the DCMES for description and retrieval. Among them are the Duke World Wide Web (DW3) Classical Music Resources project, the MusicBrainz Metadata Initiative and MusicAustralia.

The DW3 Classical Music Resources site is a 'comprehensive collection of classical music resources on the Web with links to more that 3,000 carefully selected, non-commercial pages and sites in over a dozen languages' (DW3, 2003). The DCMES is used to create an entry in the Duke University Library site index and to provide more specific information for external search engines. Standard unqualified DC elements are used for description, including title, creator, publisher, date, type, format, language and coverage. Scheme qualifiers are added for subject and identifier elements. HTML META tags (author, description, keywords and robots) are also added to provide basic data and instructions for external search engines.

Metadata is also used by individuals outside the library environment to generate and exchange audio playlists. The MBMI MusicBrainz Metadata Initiative (MusicBrainz, 2003) is the reincarnation of the CD Index, a user-maintained community music metadatabase (2003). The goal of the MBMI group is to enable non-ambiguous communication about music free from recording industry marketing bias. MBMI volunteers are defining a music metadata standard for audio and video recordings. The MBMI uses some basic Dublin Core elements along with additional, locally defined elements, including Comment, Lyrics, SyncEvents, SyncText, Signature, PurchaseInfo, Genre and TrackNum. The Resource Description Framework is the underlying structure for the database, which is composed of the MBMI website, the MB Web Service/Client Library of metadata and the MB Tagger. The tagger generates an acoustic fingerprint of a user's MP3, WAV or OGG/Vorbis files. It then finds the appropriate metadata in the metadata library, and writes new metadata tags to the user's audio files.

MusicAustralia, (MusicAustralia, 2002) is another ambitious digital music project that uses the DCMES. Begun in 2001 by the National Library of Australia in collaboration with ScreenSound, the Australian Music Centre and the Australian Council for the Arts, the goal of the MusicAustralia project is to provide integrated access to historical and contemporary Australian music resources. When fully developed, MusicAustralia will enable users to search for music resources from a wide range of institutions, access the music in multiple formats (image, audio, visual) and link to a variety of information sources. Metadata records in several formats (including MARC, MAVIS (Merged AudioVisual Information System) and non-library records) from participating institutions are converted into a pre-determined qualified Dublin Core Element Set (Holmes, 2002). Many qualifiers are music specific, like the DC.Contributor element qualifiers that include principal role, composer, lyricist, librettist, musician, group, arranger, conductor and singer. Once converted to DCMES the records are stored using XML syntax and indexed for searching by a database application.

Other metadata standards

Dublin Core metadata will continue to be useful for high-level retrieval and data exchange, but many digital music projects find it does not provide the necessary level of detail. It is not uncommon for a project to use DCMES in combination with other metadata schemes that provide greater specificity, a hierarchical structure or temporal definition more appropriate for a specific type of music project.

The Encoded Archival Description (EAD) is a metadata standard designed to display and index electronic finding aids for archive and manuscript collections (EAD, 2002). The EAD is one of the most heavily used schemes in music libraries since hundreds of music projects involve the digitization of archival music collections and their finding aids. A key feature of the EAD is its hierarchical structure that allows easy yet sophisticated navigation among multi-level collection descriptions. At the single item metadata level the user can link directly to the digital object. Currently, there is no official DTD (Document Type Definition) standard for music materials in EAD and most music archives use the standard EAD DTD elements. The EAD does allow the development of DTDs for specific projects, however, and a working group of the MLA will examine the feasibility of developing music-specific DTDs for EAD. In order to get a handle on the proliferation of music finding aids, the IAML Working Group on the Registration of Music Archives is developing a database that will record and describe the many international digital music archives (1999).

A quick glance at a few music finding aids shows that the collections range from broadside ballads and silent film music to Benny Goodman archives, ballet music and Jewish songsters (*New York Public Library Music Finding Aids List*, n.d.; *Berkeley Music Library Finding Aids List*, n.d.; Sibley Music Library, n.d.; *Library of Congress Finding Aids*, n.d.; Harvard University Music Library, n.d.; University of Louisville Music Library, n.d.; and the UCLA Music Library, n.d.). By far the most ambitious digital project in the USA is the American Memory Project (AMP, 2003). Available on the Library of Congress's web page, this group of over 90 digitized collections contains at least 21 collections with music or music-related materials from the Library of Congress and other institutions (AMP, 2003). The EAD is the primary metadata standard used for the finding aids. In addition to the text, sheet music, photographs, sound recordings and motion pictures available for many music resources in the project, each AMP collection provides information on the technical specifications of the collections and the methods used to catalogue or index the collections. Among the collections included in the AMP are 'Fiddle Tunes of the Old Frontier', the American Folklife Center's 'Omaha Indian Music' and the William P. Gottlieb collection of photographs from the golden age of jazz.

Expanded metadata functions

The digital environment has expanded the functions of metadata beyond description and retrieval to include structural and administrative data. Both functions are critical for music resources and many of the new and developing metadata schemes rely heavily on both. Structural metadata describes the internal organization of the files that comprise a music resource. This information plays a major role in track sequencing for sound recordings and linking descriptive metadata to the correct sound track. Identifying resource structure is a key metadata function for digital music libraries and e-commerce music services that provide playlists and access to specific tracks on a recording. Structural metadata is also important for enabling page turns with music score images and for synchronizing audio tracks with the correct measures in a digital score.

Administrative metadata has several components important for music resources. In addition to the technical details about the digitization, storage and retrieval process, administrative metadata provides information on rights management and preservation. Concerned about the ease with which digital resources can be accessed, modified and duplicated, the publishing and recording industries are working in conjunction with newly developing multimedia metadata to incorporate rights management systems into the schemes. Preservation concerns are a factor for libraries and commercial industries alike. New data models like the OAIS (Open Archival Information System) have identified data elements necessary for preserving both the content of the resource and the longevity of the digital object (2003).

Multimedia metadata

Although multimedia metadata is beyond the scope of this chapter, music in some form is often a component of multimedia projects and, therefore, music metadata specialists should be aware of its potential uses. MPEG-7, officially named 'Multimedia Content Description Interface', incorporates descriptive, administrative and structural metadata and is a most ambitious standard in its attempt to improve access to AV (audio-visual) materials (Multimedia Content Description Interface,

2002). Unlike its MPEG predecessor standards (MPEG-1, MPEG-2 and MPEG-4) which provide coded representation of audiovisual content, 'MPEG-7 focuses on the metadata representing information *about* the content, not the content itself' (Hunter, 1999). The standard is a comprehensive set of AV descriptions that contain standard bibliographic data, semantic data about the object or event and structural information about an image or sound. The MPEG-7 standard includes audio description tools such as melodic contour description that will enable 'query by humming' and instrument similarity description that will enable 'query by example'. Both of these tools move beyond metadata into the realm of MIR. Additional audio description tools include speech recognition description and sound effects description. MPEG-7 uses XML schema as the markup language of choice for description, thus promoting interoperability with other standards such as Dublin Core. Applications of this standard might include setting-up audio archives, retrieving audio files from the internet, and indexing sound effects and spoken word audio content. At present the MPEG-7 standard is used primarily in the commercial sector, but offers digital music libraries powerful new ways to search on multimedia content.

Eventually MPEG-7 will feature in the MPEG-21 multimedia framework, which is still under development (MPEG, 2002). MPEG-21 is designed to be an open framework 'based on two essential concepts: the definition of a fundamental unit of distribution and transaction (the Digital Item) and the concept of Users interacting with Digital Items' (MPEG, 2002). The standard will define the technology needed for users to interact with digital items in an efficient, transparent and interoperable way. A major part of the MPEG-21 standard is rights management metadata and it seems likely that most digital audio resources in the future will be part of the MPEG-21 multimedia framework.

Ongoing research projects are examining methods to create an integrated multimedia metadata environment that will index, archive, search, browse, retrieve and manage complex structured documents containing temporal, spatial, structural and semantic relationships among the components (MAENAD, 2002). The MAENAD project, www.dstc.edu.au/Research/maenad-ov.html sponsored by the DSTC (Distributed Systems Technology Centre) in Australia, is developing a data model and suite of hardware and software tools that will enable resource discovery, preservation, delivery and rights management across domains, across metadata schemes and across various media types (2002).

Major music library metadata projects

The selection of an appropriate metadata scheme depends on the resource collection and its users. In music libraries, the most common materials being digitized and mounted on the web are archival sound collections, public domain scores, sheet music collections, and audio collections. Many of these projects involve multimedia and use a variety of metadata schemes to accommodate different media types. Various websites are available that list and provide access to the many digital music and multimedia projects. These include the International Music Metadata Projects Working Group (IMMP, n.d.), the Register of International Projects Relevant to Development of MusicAustralia (RIP, 2003) and University of Washington's Digital Projects and Developing Technologies in Music & Media (2003).

Several digital music projects integrate the use of MARC metadata. These include the VARIATIONS Digital Music Library project at Indiana University (Dunn and Mayer, 1999), the (ADMV) Archivio Digitale Musicale Veneto (Massina, 2000), the OMRAS (Online Music Recognition and Searching) project, www.omras.org/ (Dovey, 2001) and the IRCAM (Institut de Recherche et Coordination Acoustique/Musique) Digital Library project (Fingerhut, 1999), to name a few. The VARIATIONS DML and the IRCAM libraries are among the earliest projects, while ADMV and OMRAS are more recent.

The VARIATIONS Digital Music Library project at Indiana University was originally designed to provide online access to digitized listening assignments. The sound files are accessible either from a course reserve list web page, or by searching the IU catalogue and following a link on the MARC bibliographic record. The metadata for this project is currently divided into three types: descriptive, administrative and structural. Descriptive metadata is used for resource discovery and identification and is currently provided by data in the MARC bibliographic records. Administrative metadata supplements the descriptive metadata and provides information for managing the resource, including information related to its creation and use (i.e. digitization details, intellectual property rights, access rights). Structural metadata is used to assist in the display and navigation of a particular resource and includes information on the internal structure of the file to allow access to specific segments of the resource. A separate metadata track file exists as a locally defined ASCII text file. This separate metadata file also includes structural information about the individual tracks on the audio file, including the titles and corresponding start times. These data provide the user with the same level of track access as the original recording (Dunn and Mayer, 1999). The second phase of this project, VARIATIONS2, continues music metadata research, extends access to include score images, and is developing multiple interfaces for specific user applications, including synchronized navigation and playback in the music library and the classroom. A new music domain-specific metadata model is being developed that maps descriptive data from the MARC record to the new XML metadata structure, identifies additional descriptive elements and establishes meaningful relationships between the music resource and the descriptive, administrative and structural metadata.

In the mid-1990s IRCAM undertook a major renovation of its facilities and received funding to create a digital multimedia library. The goal was to add online access to the IRCAM audio recordings, a collection of documentary movies on contemporary music, and a database of information on contemporary composers and their works, and to present all this with integrated access to the existing print collection. The project began by converting all bibliographic records from their local proprietary database to the UNIMARC format commonly used in Europe. HTML and the Z39.50 standards were used for the general interface. Since metadata concepts and schemes were still in their infancy when this project was undertaken, the IRCAM staff developed their own metadata concepts for the project. 'Self-describing' compact discs were created for the IRCAM concert recordings. These included a text file as the first track, which provides a detailed display of the CD contents. A separate file of structural metadata was created for commercial recordings, similar to that used by the VARIATIONS project. All digitized texts included embedded descriptive metadata in a format similar to HTML META tags, which did

not exist at the time. A URL was added to the UNIMARC record to allow
direct linking from the bibliographic record to the digitized document it
describes, to link bibliographic records for scores to an online musico-
logical text about the work and to link authority records for composers
to online biographical information about the composer. In addition, the
IRCAM project used the URL fragment identifier extension to link from
a web page to a single track on a compact disc. At present, the IRCAM
library is studying various new types of metadata, including Dublin Core
and MPEG-7, to take advantage of external library systems and provide
more powerful search and access tools.

Current research in Italy is examining the interaction between an
encoded incipit and its corresponding sound file for retrieval purposes.
Ongoing projects like the ADMV are experimenting with an integrated
service model for searching, consulting and accessing documents that
contain music scores, in order to enable users to link directly from the
metadata record for a score to its digitized image, and its corresponding
digitized sound-document, through systems offering online distribution
of images and sounds (Massina, 2000). The ADMV project will define
standards and necessary metadata for a meta-OPAC search using the
Z39.50 interface as a gateway.

Finally, the OMRAS project bridges the gap between library metadata
and MIR. OMRAS combines the use of text-based searching on MARC
metadata with retrieval using the musical content itself. While some MIR
systems provide content 'query by humming', the OMRAS project also
takes advantage of the descriptive data found in the MARC record. Music
content in various formats ranging from encoded scores to digital audio
is contained in a database separate from the MARC catalogue records.
Because of the nature of the Z39.50 search protocol, a Z39.50 proxy
server can be added between the standard bibliographic Z39.50 server for
the music library catalogue and a Z39.50 client (e.g. a web interface).
Searches can include textual metadata terms, musical phrases as query
terms, or both. The query goes to the proxy server, which passes textual
queries to the library catalogue and music phrase queries to the music
content database and retrieves the appropriate results. A unique identifier is assigned to the music and its corresponding metadata record, so
depending on the type of search, the corresponding data or music will

also be retrieved (Dovey, 2001). The OMRAS project brings music metadata a step closer to the field of music information retrieval, where a wide variety of music content query systems are under investigation.

New perspectives on music access and retrieval

The 'best practice' music metadata system would have to provide information about and access to textual metadata, audio files, image files and encoded notation. In addition, it must be capable of synchronicity to provide access to time-based information and ideally it would have a non-textual means of access. The ideal music metadata system, therefore, would incorporate description, access and retrieval techniques developed in the music library community, the computer science community and the scholarly music community.

While libraries use textual metadata for resource discovery and retrieval, the comparatively new interdisciplinary area of MIR is conducting research on retrieval using the music *content* rather than a description of the content. In order to understand the many difficulties and possibilities for music content retrieval, it is necessary to understand the inherent facets of music. In an excellent MIR literature review article, Downie illustrates that music contains up to seven facets that are inherent to a musical work or phrase (2002). These are pitch, duration, harmony, timbre, editorial content, textual content and bibliographic information. Each of these facets may be represented in a variety of different ways. MIR researchers are developing methods to retrieve music information directly on the musical content using each of these music facets in either notated or aural form. If a system is designed using each of the seven facets for retrieval, and multiple representational possibilities for each facet are accommodated, the complexity of designing a MIR system becomes obvious.

MIR systems fall into two categories: analytic/production MIR systems and locating MIR systems (Downie, 2002, 309). Again the distinction focuses on the intended use. Analytic/production MIR systems strive for the most complete representation of the music, including the symbolic notation and other editorial content. These systems are designed for use by musicologists, music theorists, music engravers and composers in the creation, analysis and production of music. Locating MIR systems are designed for the identification, location and retrieval of a musical work and can be notation based and/or audio based. Some locating systems do not provide a complete representation of the music (e.g. an incipit is a truncated form of a melody). This incompleteness helps the less musically sophisticated user because the user does not have to input a complete music query. Other MIR locating systems are 'full text' in the sense that the music incipit is not truncated. The primary goal for users of MIR locating systems is to locate and use the musical work retrieved, not to manipulate the various facets of the music in the musical content (Downie, 2002, 309–13).

Early work in MIR viewed music retrieval as more of an analytic/production system and therefore as a computer language problem. Since the 1960s hundreds of codes for music have been developed. MIDI is probably the best known and most limited of the codes designed for a computer environment. Early notation codes were developed in ASCII or binary formats. The two codes mentioned earlier in this chapter – Plaine & Easie Code and the DARMS code – are both ASCII codes. Others of the better known ASCII codes include GUIDO, Humdrum-Kern, MusicTex, Musedata and Nightingale. Binary code formats include MIDI, Sibelius, Finale, SCORE and NIFF. More recent music notation codes have been developed for the web environment using the XML markup language, while several of the older codes have been converted to XML. Among these XML-based codes are MNML (Music Notation Markup Language), MML (Music Markup Language), ScoreML, MusicXML, GUIDO XML, MDL (Music Description Language), SMDL (Standard Music Description Language) and X Score (eXtensible Score Language). (See Selfridge-Field, 1997 for a comprehensive review of many of the pre-XML codes.) Gerd Castan (2003) maintains an up-to-date website for music notation at www.music-notation.info/.

A detailed discussion of MIR research is beyond the scope of this chapter, but one of the more mature music query systems must be mentioned here. Meldex (MELody inDEX) is an important early MIR locating system that has set the standard for symbol-based locating systems (2003). Developed at the University of Waikato in New Zealand, the system contains more than 10,000 music notation files and 100,000 MIDI files (McNab et al., 1997). Meldex is now part of the New Zealand Digital Library and provides retrieval on both the pitch and temporal facets of the music. This allows a variety of search possibilities, including 'query by humming', interval contour matching, and matching with or without the use of rhythm. The system accepts acoustic input from the user, transcribes the input into music notation, then searches the database for tunes that contain the same melodic pattern (McNab et al., 1997). The acoustic input may be uploaded from a recording of sung or played notes or by entering a URL for a recording (McPherson and Bainbridge, 2001).The retrieved music can be in score notation or in a variety of audio file formats. A new version of the Meldex system has been integrated with the Greenstone suite of software and is now in alpha-testing. Greenstone offers the user software for building and distributing digital library collections on the web (2003). Metadata is an integral part of the software and is used for browsing indexes. The metadata may be associated with each document or with specific sections within the documents. The collection builder may create the metadata, or it can be derived from another source. The DCMES is the preferred metadata scheme, but the software will also accommodate other metadata schemes.

Meldex is just one of dozens of projects based on melodic similarity. Other MIR projects are experimenting with the timbral facet to automate classification and genre identification (Tzanetakis, Essl and Cook, 2001), the harmonic facet to extract the melody from a polyphonic work (Uitdenbogerd and Zobel, 1998), and the editorial facet to tag and retrieve performance and analytic information about the music (Roland, 2002), to cite only a few of the research projects being conducted worldwide.

Conclusion

The complexities of music information organization and retrieval are compounded by the many metadata options available today. It is possible that a music-specific metadata scheme will be developed in the future, but it is just as possible that the music community will continue to use a variety of existing metadata schemes and adapt them to their music needs. Advanced computing has opened new doors for the scholarly music and library communities; it has also presented many challenges for computer scientists. Interestingly, the traditional methods of organizzing music resources, i.e. AACR2R and MARC, are still flourishing. The rich descriptive detail offered by these standards is still useful in the new digital environment as several digital music library projects have shown. The new technology allows information specialists to push the boundaries of the music catalogue in new directions and offers new opportunities to collaborate creatively with music and computer researchers. A coupling of textual metadata with music content retrieval techniques would provide greater precision in the search and retrieval process and offer imaginative search options for music users to explore.

References

American Memory Project (2003), http://memory.loc.gov/.

Berkeley Music Library Finding Aids List (n.d.),
   http://dynaweb.oac.cdlib.org/dynaweb/ead/berkeley/music/.

Castan, G. (2003) *Music Notation Links*, www.music-notation.info/.

Dovey, Matthew J. (2001) Adding Content-Based Searching to a Traditional Music Library Catalogue Server. In *International Conference on Digital Libraries: Proceedings of the First ACM/IEEE Joint Conference on Digital Libraries held on 24-28 June 2001*, New York, ACM Press, http://portal.acm.org/portal.cfm.

Downie, S. (2002) Music Information Retrieval, *Annual Review of Information Science and Technology*, **37**, 295–340.

Duffy, C. (1998) Music Libraries Online, *Ariadne*, (January), wwwariadne.ac.uk/issue13/music/.

Dunn, J. and Mayer, C. (1999) VARIATIONS: A Digital Music Library System at Indiana University. In *DL '99, Proceedings of the Fourth ACM Conference on Digital Libraries held in August 1999, Berkeley California*, New York, The Association for Computing Machinery, 12–19.

DW3 (2003) *Classical Music Resources*, www.lib.duke.edu/music/resources/classical_index.html.

Encoded Archival Description (2002) Homepage, www.loc.gov/ead/.

Fingerhut, M. (1999) The IRCAM Multimedia Library: a digital music library, *Baltimore IEEE Forum on Research and Technology Advances in Digital Libraries*, http://mediatheque.ircam.fr/articles/textes/Fingerhut99a/.

Greenstone Digital Library Software (2003), www.greenstone.org/.

Harvard University Music Library, (n.d.), http://hcl.harvard.edu/loebmusic/.

Holmes, R. (2002) MusicAustralia: a digital strategy for music. In *The Proceedings of the International Association of Music Libraries Annual Conference held on 4 August 2002, Organised by the International Association of Music Libraries(IAML), Berkeley California*, www.nla.gov.au/nla/staffpaper/2002/iaml8Aug02.html.

Hunter, J. (1999) MPEG-7: behind the scenes, *D-Lib Magazine*, **5** (7), www.dlib.org/dlib/september99/hunter/09hunter.html.

International Association of Music Libraries Bibliographic Control Commission (n.d.) *Core Bibliographic Record Standards*, www.cilea.it/music/iaml/cbdmsrsu.htm

International Association of Music Libraries Working Group on the Registration of Music Archives (1999) *Newsletter*, www.cilea.it/music/iaml/news/wgarchiv.htm.

International Federation of Library Associations and Institutions Study Group on the Functional Requirements for Bibliographic Records (1998) *Functional Requirements for Bibliographic Records: final report*, Vol. 19, Munich, K. G. Saur.

International Music Metadata Projects Working Group (n.d.) *Music Metadata Projects*, www.lib.ox.ac.uk/immpwg/projects.asp/.

Library of Congress Finding Aids (n.d.), http://lcweb.loc.gov/rr/perform/fabiblgds.html.

McNab, R. J. et al. (1997) The New Zealand Digital Library MELody inDEX, *D-Lib Magazine*, (May), www.dlib.org/dlib/may97/meldex/05witten.html.

McPherson, J. R. and Bainbridge, D. (2001) Usage of the MELDEX Digital Music Library. In Downie, J. S. and Bainbridge, D. (eds), *Proceedings of the Second Annual International Symposium on Music Information Retrieval, Bloomington, Indiana*, 19–20, http://music-ir.org/gsdl/ismir2001/index_start.html.

MAENAD (2002), www.dstc.edu.au/Research/maenad-ov.html.

Massina, M. (2000) The Project of a Digital Archive of Veneto Music, *Biblioteca Marciana Newsletter*, **3** (Autumn), http://marciana.venezia.sbn.it/news3/eng/3-05e.html.

Meldex (2003), www.nzdl.org/fast-cgi-bin/music/musiclibrary.

Moving Picture Experts Group (2002) *MPEG-21*,

http://mpeg.telecomitalialab.com/standards/mpeg-21/mpeg-21.htm.

Multimedia Content Description Interface (2002) *MPEG-7*,
http://mpeg.telecomitalialab.com/standards/mpeg-7/mpeg-7.htm.

MusicAustralia (2002), www.musicaustralia.org/.

MusicBrainz (2003), www.musicbrainz.org/.

Music Libraries Online Project (n.d.), www.musiconline.ac.uk/Annrep2.htm.

New York Public Library Music Finding Aids List (n.d.),
http://digilib.nypl.org/dynaweb/ead/music/@Generic__CollectionView/.

Online Music Recognition and Searching Project (n.d.), www.omras.org/.

Open Archival Information System (2003),
http://ssdoo.gsfc.nasa.gov/nost/isoas/.

PCC Core Record Standards (2002),
www.loc.gov/catdir/pcc/bibco/core2002.html

Performing Arts Data Service, www.pads.ahds.ac.uk/.

Peters, C. F. (1957–83), *Rules for Cataloguing Music Manuscripts*, Frankfurt,
Commission Internationale du Code de Catalogage, 29–31.

Register of International Projects Relevant to Development of MusicAustralia (2003),
www.musicaustralia.org/info/internationalprojects.html.

Roland, P. (2002) The Music Encoding Initiative. In Haus, G. and Longari, M.
(eds), *Proceedings of the First International Conference on Musical Application
Using XML*, Washington, IEEE Computer Society Press.

Selfridge-Field, E. (ed.) (1997) *Beyond MIDI: the handbook of musical codes*,
Cambridge, MA, MIT Press.

Sibley Music Library (n.d.), www.rochester.edu/Eastman/sibley/.

Tzanetakis, G., Essl, G. and Cook, P. R. (2001) Audio Analysis using the
Discrete Wavelet Transform. In *Proceedings of the WSES International
Conference on Acoustics and Music: Theory and Applications (AMTA 2001)
Skiathos, Greece*, www.cs.princeton.edu/~gessl/.

UCLA Music Library (n.d.), www.library.ucla.edu/libraries/music/.

Uitdenbogerd, A. L. and Zobel, J. (1998) Manipulation of Music for Melody
Matching. In Smith, B. and Effelsberg, W. (eds), *Proceedings of the 6th ACM
International Conference on Multimedia '98, September 12–16, Bristol, England*,
New York, ACM Press, 235–40.

University of Louisville Music Library (n.d.),
http://library.louisville.edu/music/.

University of Washington Digital Projects and Developing Technologies in Music &

Media (2003), www.lib.washington.edu/music/projects.html.

Vellucci, S. (1997) *Bibliographic Relationships in Music Catalogues*, Lanham, MD, Scarecrow Press.

VTLS, www.vtls.com/.

4

Metadata and the arts –
the art of metadata

Simon Pockley

Introduction

Access to structured metadata in the arts is a radical idea. It can be compared to the challenge of building a nation out of a group of warring
states, where assembly is characterized by friction and tension. When
those who create it do not share the values residing in its use and distribution, metadata becomes unreliable. In a federated repository, it
becomes useless. Understanding the importance of such cultural values
may be as important a step in building a sustainable back-of-house infrastructure for generating quality metadata, as building the front-of-house
services that can understand it. A general discussion about metadata in
the arts is illustrated from research into collaborative metadata production conducted at The Australian Centre for the Moving Image (ACMI).
The research demonstrated how the values of the various practitioners
can have a significant impact on the quality of metadata and hence an
organization's ability to participate in an arts cluster or a cultural network. These values reach into the fabric of how ideas and thoughts are
expressed in an electronic environment. They also play an important role
in the durability of artistic expression. Ultimately, they point towards the
development of a poetic for the art of metadata.

Is art information or is information an art?

> You say neither and I say neither
> Either, either neither, neither
> Let's call the whole thing off.
> George and Ira Gershwin, 1937

This fragment of a Gershwin song embodies many of the themes of this chapter. It was found on the web by using Google and the search term 'you say tomato', then refined by a reference to Gershwin in a blog. It was selected from a larger body of transcription and then downloaded without a thought to seeking permission or paying a royalty. Both the font and layout have been changed to suit a new purpose. It is a fragment of an artist's creative expression that has been thoroughly appropriated without shame. There was no structured metadata involved in this process, although metadata advocates would have us believe that the search could have been more effective if metadata had been deployed and Google had understood it. This might have resulted in a choice of formats such as audio files from sound archives or moving image segments from the film 'Shall We Dance?'. It may have triggered alerts to rights issues and there may have been more contextual information available. Metadata may even have prevented or restricted its use.

In its new context the fragment illustrates the way that:

- a work can find multiple expression
- meaning can be derived from the use of expressive qualities that are not easily captured by basic forms of metadata (in this case text transcription)
- conflict can arise when people have different cultural values. This may not be something that is peculiar to the arts but is the basis for the central argument of this essay; that the culture of metadata has different values from those found in the arts.

Without stretching this too far, Gershwin is saying that coming together is a conditional motion, easily upset by small things that can influence major choices. While the original song could be seen as belonging to the arts or being contained by them, a quick scan of its use in Google illustrates that it has escaped from custody and is now free to become a form of cultural currency in other domains.

Just as the 'arts' is a very broad term that defies precise definition, so there are a variety of more distanced terms that are used to combine the artsy and non-artsy things to which metadata can be applied in the arts. Terms such as assets (cultural), resources, works (of art), material, content, objects, stuff are used regularly and are fairly interchangeable. But they give clues to the values residing in metadata practice.

Arts in custody can be found within the diverse domains of museums, galleries, libraries and private collections. Here the majority of works (not on display) are gathered together to hibernate in keeping places ranging from storerooms with (or without) controlled atmospherics to the humming 'comms rooms' where digital surrogates and new media works reside on the disc drives of servers.

Across the physical and networked world, proponents of networked technologies are arguing that access to these cultural assets should be extended beyond the exhibition spaces. They believe that economies of scale can be achieved by implementing a variety of proposals for clustering the supporting infrastructures of the collecting agencies. The agencies are grouped as 'memory institutions' or 'cultural networks' and terms such as 'gateway' and 'portal' are regularly used. These are terms that imply unrestricted entry and access. They also imply collective agreement to distribute and share within unbounded spaces where all who enter are free to consume their cultural inheritance.

It is assumed that works of art can be treated in the same way as resources without artistic intent, as digestible chunks of information to be retrieved from a 'datascape' of notations, texts, pictures and sounds. All produced and recombined within an electronically mediated world where the separation between information about the work (metadata) and the work itself is no longer as clear as it was in the physical world.

Proponents of the need for common descriptive frameworks in a federated environment usually base their models on the expectation that significant resources should be allocated to the production of high-quality, structured metadata that will not only expose the ideas manifested by these works to cross-collection discovery and access, but will also create value around and about them.

Federating projects seeking to aggregate structured metadata have as a core value a desire to set information free.

But federation is not an end. In the arts, it is a radical idea to federate cultural assets. It is an activity involving assemblage, negotiation, realignment and the accommodation of differences and tensions so that all the inhabitant energies of its participants can produce something dynamic and inventive, something greater than the parts (Gibson, 1998).

If metadata is to act as an effective expressive medium for federating communities to exchange ideas, then understanding why and how these differences arise may be as important a step in building a sustainable back-of-house infrastructure for generating metadata as building the front-of-house services that can understand it.

With hindsight, it was no coincidence that the initial enthusiasm for sharing knowledge in borderless information spaces coincided with the explosion of web-based initiatives anchored in the values of sharing. As the networks matured and the dotcom hype contracted, resistance to these values began to arise from separated domains and communities of interest that had reinvented their identities and their separateness within these spaces. There may be parallels with the way in which the forces of globalization are encountering fierce points of regional resistance.

While there have been many artistic challenges to the fact that expressions of Art are by nature bounded or contained – for example, Christo's wrapping and fencing of buildings and landforms and the use of containers by new media artist Lynette Wallworth in 'Hold Vessel'– artworks themselves become contained as they become objects of trade, interpretation, study and desire. Borders are important to the arts because temporal and spatial location creates meaning through context and display.

Similarly, metadata standards give syntactical expression to a form of wrapping paper or markup in containing the notions that we use to order, categorize, classify and group similar ideas. In the arts, the various patterns of critical interests that have drawn on Aristotelian poetics as a way of aggregating works into types have achieved their status not because they fit together into any preconceived system or taxonomy, but simply because they recur constantly and independently. Arts-related metadata production occurs within communities of interest that apply common terms as a pragmatic convenience where the act of categorization has occurred within a tradition of continuous redefinition.

Metadata fits this purpose because it is extendable, repeatable and infinitely mutable or transformable. As XML, it can be expressed in a modular form where element and attribute values can be recombined without restriction in any order for any purpose. It is a shadow world of essences where metadata deployments can be orchestrated to create substance. In such a world, a richly nuanced record of an individual work may extend across domains and contain such a variety of links to contextual or interpretive resources that it becomes difficult to know where the record, and by extension, the actual work, begins and ends.

At a collection level, the orchestration of metadata schemas occurs through the mixing and matching of schemas into application profiles. However, the blurring of the borders associated with the adoption of application profiles within aggregated metadata repositories can be seen to compromise the borders of the collections and the collecting institution that acts as the rights- or licence-owning custodian of an artist's work.

Most arts organizations also have legacy collections of metadata in the form of condition reports, legal agreements, requirements lists, exhibition layouts, classification schemes, financial records and insurance valuations, etc. These organizations take pride in their custodial, even proprietary, relationship to the works in their care. In such an environment, a desire for interoperability with similar organizations (even at a minimal level) is regarded with suspicion unless there are clearly defined borders. The values that seek to cross these borders can be misinterpreted as intent to make everything available to everyone, regardless of confidentiality or cultural or corporate sensitivity.

It is often assumed that a collaborative production environment will facilitate the collaboration that is implied by having shared metadata outcomes. Following a two-year experiment in collaborative metadata generation, conducted at the Australian Centre for the Moving Image (ACMI), collaborative metadata production was abandoned. This chapter does not describe the experiment in detail but draws observations from it that have been crosschecked with other arts agencies and found to resonate within the arts community in general. Perhaps they may apply to other communities.

Although the primary reasons for collaborative failure started with the values of the various practitioners, they also reach into the fabric of how ideas and thoughts find expression in an electronic environment. In this sense they do not just belong to the arts. However, if the complex works of cultural expression are to be accessed outside physical and restricted exhibition spaces or to be in any way durable, it is in the arts that the most difficult deployments of metadata are required.

What are the values of the metadata creators?

The visibility and durability of the assets and resources of an arts agency are largely dependent on having a store of information (metadata) about them. While some forms of metadata can and should be generated by machines, there are other forms that have to be hand crafted and checked. Even the action of machines requires some form of human instruction. The description by Nardi and O'Day (1999, 80) of the key species inhabiting an information ecology is a useful framework for describing a metadata production environment. There are at least seven kinds of key character species within the overall information ecology at ACMI. They all play an important role in the creation of metadata:

1   *The Creatives*: includes artists and curators who want to provide an interpretive and contextual experience of individual works of artistic expression. They treat these works with reverence – as bounded entities, not as material to be re-purposed, re-used and re-presented.

2   *The Educators*: includes public programmers of events and workshops who encourage their audiences to experience these guided moments but, concerned that the Creatives might seek to control their programmes, create works in progress until the moment of completion when they are too busy working on the next one to describe the last.

3   *The Cataloguers*: who are often library trained and highly skilled in some aspects of metadata creation but protective of their skill base and resistant to expanding beyond the accepted borders of their bibliographic expertise through which they are able to offer up data for

information's sake, as whole, or fragment, or component part – whatever matches the query.

4 *The Technologists*: IT experts who exert control and authority over the deployment of hardware, software, networks and applications. Overloaded with arriving at IT Helpdesk solutions, they have strong views that support proprietary systems and are contemptuous of open standards and open-ended development projects.

5 *The Administrators*: rely on the hardware and software set up by the Technologists and generally use Word and Excel. They keep their files in order and usually rely on paper as authority and archive.

6 *The Hacktivists*: not necessarily a sinister force but low-profile file sharers and MP3 downloaders and gamers who are able to bend software applications to suit their personal needs but prefer complete technical control of their own projects.

7 *The Metaphiles* (metadata advocates): promote metadata standards with a view to creating a united and integrated information ecology with a global perspective. Keen on open-ended web-based projects, distributed searching, fragmentation and a culture of proliferation and sharing.

These are broad groupings and it should be noted the actions of these characters are by no means exclusive to their titles. Some species have several characters.

Faith, hope and promises – what the metaphile believes

The metadata production experiment at ACMI began with the Metaphiles making the argument that scarce resources should be realigned from supporting locally controlled, venue-centric and inward-looking (proprietary) exhibition and programme information environments to outward-looking (non-proprietary) distributed or shared metadata environments that would require a devolution of control and (more importantly) a significant act of faith.

Clearly, these are quite distinct cultures. The argument was neither won nor lost but fell between the interests of the Technologists and the interests of the Creatives. It was an argument that required demonstration and proof. In order to show how the various characters interacted with the Metaphiles' vision, it is important to describe what they were hoping for and where they put their faith.

At heart, the ACMI metadata experiment was based on the concept and values of the ACMI Metadata Standard. This was an application profile based on an expanding, evolving and flexible schema that included Qualified Dublin Core and a variety of ACMI specific schemes. It mapped to a legacy database of over 90,000 titles with a view to migrating its content into a new integrated system built on an XML server as a data store.

After various naming attempts that began with 'title-record database', it was the name 'Meta4' that stuck (Figures 4.1 and 4.2). There was an expectation that it would act as the underlying content engine for XML outputs to the website, to didactic screens associated with the works in exhibitions, to printed flyers and brochures, to online catalogues, and more importantly, to external systems that would require access to component parts of the title records. In addition, it contained a contacts database based on V-card with the facility to manage biographies, filmographies, etc. as well as the tools needed for content management includ-

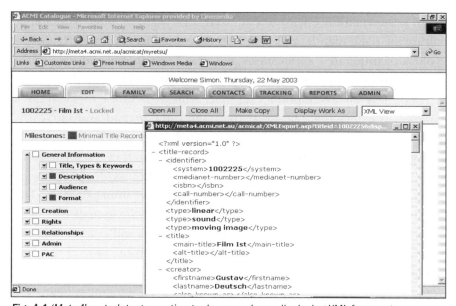

Fig. 4.1 'Meta4' metadata generation tool screen-dump displaying XML fragment

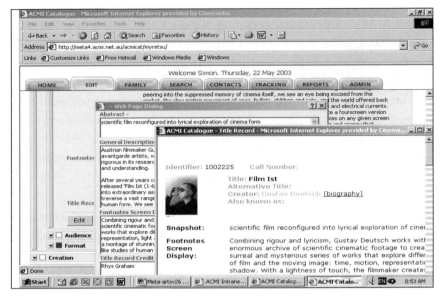

Fig. 4.2 'Meta4' screen-dump showing entry screen and HTML display

ing a tracking and administrative module. It was flexible, configurable and based on an open source technology.

It was anticipated that it would be an important step in transforming ACMI's information environment from an inward-looking paper-based culture of data islands and duplicated systems to an outward-looking ecology of integrated applications and workflows that would lead to the production of metadata conforming to international standards.

There was an assumption that once this structured metadata was exposed to external applications that could understand and harvest it, then (internal and perhaps even external) service providers would emerge to process this information and add value to it in the form of services that ACMI needed, used and might even pay to be part of. Examples might be rights management or video-streaming services. This was the act of faith that unpins most attempts to conform to one or more metadata standards, the hope that business models will emerge that will repay and even drive an investment in metadata production.

The short-term promise was that conforming to metadata standards would assist in the interoperability necessary for exchanging information with other organizations that would access and interpret a metadata repository. The hope was that the metadata created would be of high enough quality to be useful for building and maintaining distributed collections.

However, with exceptions relying on fairly primitive (minimal) element sets, for example Picture Australia (www.pictureaustralia.org/), there are few readily accessible examples to point to as possible models that might make such expectations credible. Those that do exist appear to be being undermined by the uncomfortable reality that the benefits are not as visible as they should be:

- Commercial search engines do not take much notice of structured metadata and are evolving business models that either sell position in search results or generate revenue from advertising.
- The adoption of standards is often compromised by differing interpretations of elements as well as local and deployment-specific terms.
- The metadata can be of such poor quality that service functionality falls short of text searches yielding better results.
- Data-aggregating technology concepts such as Total Information Awareness could override the need for metadata standards as information or data containers.
- There is a vibrant, naturally occurring culture of data exchange within file-sharing networks that does not use metadata.

A gap between vision and reality can (in the short term) be bridged by faith if there is sufficient strength of will but when a vision is founded on values that are not shared, it is difficult to attract participants.

Currier and Barton (2003) have identified five reasons for the absence of interest in how metadata should best be created:

- the original ethos of the internet, for which a basic tenet has been that anyone can post information to be openly and widely shared, unmediated by controlling authorities
- an assumption that rigorous metadata creation is too time consuming and costly, a barrier in an arena where one of the benefits is supposedly saving time, effort and cost
- a belief that only authors and/or users of resources have the neces-

sary knowledge or expertise to create metadata that will be meaningful to their colleagues

- an assumption that, given a standard metadata structure, any problems associated with metadata content can be solved by machine
- the fact that metadata is too often seen as a tedious but necessary evil rather than the key that unlocks resources.

Metadata islands in a culture of separation

The competitive and divisive behaviours that can emerge from the complex hierarchical ecologies within an arts domain will be recognized by anyone who has experience within it. Competition for scarce resources can also be a contest between short-term and long-term strategic values. The short term is imbued with a sense of urgency where resources are rapidly directed towards mounting public (blockbuster) events or exhibitions, whereas the long term appeals to the methodical values of process and procedure where works can attract a provenance and a history. Most people will find the time to do what they consider to be important. When values are not aligned, time for activities that are not considered important gets harder to find. For this reason, the Metaphiles heard, 'We don't have time. We understand the need for it but this is critical. We'll give it to you when we've finished. It's just not important at the moment, we've just got to get this done. We'll look into developing this later.' Just as frequently, but more importantly, the Metaphiles also heard, 'This does not fit what we do.'

The conflict of values and interests at ACMI has resulted in the development of quite separate information environments where the same metadata content is regularly re-keyed or cut and pasted (often in spreadsheets or Word documents) as signage, print catalogue, marketing or programme flyer, website and search catalogue. This is hardly an efficient or effective production environment, but once identified, the phenomenon creates an opportunity to demonstrate where the economies in metadata production might lie.

The more metadata can be re-used, the more cost effective it becomes to produce. However, the economies of multi-purposing can only be delivered through integrated applications, processes and planning. This is an outcome that is as dependent on technical integration as on cultural integration. They must go hand in hand. Technical integration is a waste of time without cultural integration because it will be seen as a form of totalitarian control and lead to the emergence of data islands. Cultural integration will quickly dissolve without technical integration because separate systems rapidly create separate cultures.

In as far as structured metadata facilitates external discovery, the very notion of search and browse creates an expectation of availability or accessibility and this can be a contentious value. While most text and even audio and image-based resources are often regarded as carriers of information, even cultural memory, as soon as they enter the domain of the Creatives, the nature of the experience is a value that must be carefully orchestrated within an interpretive space (physical or virtual). In such spaces, distributed values arising from proliferation, re-use, re-purpose, re-presentation and even fragmentation are anathema to the moral rights commonly associated with artistic integrity.

The experiment at ACMI might serve as a cautionary tale for anyone planning a significant metadata initiative in the arts. It illustrates how values can have a significant impact on an organization's ability to participate in an arts cluster or a cultural network.

From the beginning, the Technologists were opposed to the experiment. Nevertheless, after developing the web-based metadata generation tool that displayed different outputs of the content from an XML schema (Figures 4.1 and 4.2, pages 73–4), the Metaphiles tried a variety of strategies to involve the Creatives, the Educators and the Administrators in metadata production. These strategies included:

- providing one-to-one training and assistance
- renaming the display of element fields to suit the terms understood by the users
- providing configurable drop-down menus of terms to choose from
- adding displays of the outputs (HTML views, submission forms, etc.)
- developing a more graphic coloured interface to fit the users' workflows
- adding borrowing services so that reference copies of titles, masters, etc. could be tracked

- allocating specific tasks during an 'adopt-a-record' month
- creating different views of the input screen to suit the users
- making the creation of title records mandatory.

But there was little enthusiasm for the task:

- Metaphiles made the mistake of assuming that metadata creation would be unambiguous and that non-specialists would understand the wider purposes and uses of descriptive metadata and therefore be careful and diligent when creating it.
- Metaphiles had difficulty accepting the desire by Creatives, Hacktivists and Educators to 'own' and control the metadata content. XML containers built for re-using and multi-purposing metadata content made it hard to accommodate the interweaving of display-specific values (font sizes, emphasis, case) with meaning.
- Cataloguers were accustomed to using a command-line-driven (legacy) system without a GUI. The high level of skill and training that the use of this legacy system required conferred a level of expertise that was compromised by the notion of collaborative metadata production. Although library orientated, they were reluctant to embrace the distributed values of multi-purposed metadata and were unexpectedly resistant to the value of producing rich metadata records that reached beyond their traditional sphere of influence and library training.
  N.B. Cataloguers do *not* always become metadata specialists or Metaphiles.
- Administrators readily accepted training but preferred the comfort of using their own filing systems and working outside Meta4 in Word or Excel. This meant that any data entry was often a duplication of work and for this there was little or no time.
- Hacktivists were called upon to work on either games-related projects or on technical projects such as transcoding and format checking. They wanted total control over their information environment because they configured it to suit themselves. This resulted in the creation of separate databases and standalone applications.
- Creatives were exacting in their production of interpretive metadata and what is called 'didactic' metadata, but in practice, they preferred

to keep this information out of the metadata management system (Meta4) so that formatting of the texts and images could be carefully controlled in PDF documents.

- Creatives (by training) either saw the act of cataloguing as an act of accession outside of their influence or perceived the need for incisive and very specific information as tedious and irrelevant to the spontaneous flexibility that can accompany less defined notions of look and feel. Creatives were generally not good at the kind of objective or distanced language that makes for good discovery metadata creation (cataloguing).

- Creatives exerted the same control over web environments as they did over exhibition environments and did not consider access to information about art works a priority other than through these controlled spaces or through printed catalogues which became arts objects in themselves.

- Creatives considered that a significant proportion of contextual and interpretive material was not metadata but part of their profession property and not for general consumption. Both creative and legal workers had deeply entrenched paper-based work practices and fiercely defended claims over the 'ownership' of information about art works.

- Technologists could not understand why the organization would want to exchange information with other organizations. They viewed the exposure of metadata via web protocols as a significant security risk and took Meta4 off line. Technologists opposed the development of non-proprietary applications and moved the XML structured metadata into a relational database where rapid development ceased.

- Educators felt that their event-based programmes (cinema screenings, talks, workshops, performances) did not fit comfortably with the framework that suited titles that were being acquired by the Creatives. They were uneasy about having their programmes taken over by the Creatives and preferred to keep the details of these programmes in their own systems (spreadsheets).

- Educators were aware of the concept of re-usable learning objects and associated standards but they did not understand how their own processes and procedures could be harnessed to create and distribute such objects through metadata repositories.

- Creatives and Educators (by training) tended to paint with different brushes from those used by Cataloguers and saw themselves as interpreters where contextual and interpretive metadata (bio, artist's statement, genre) was raw material for interpretive texts that took precedence over descriptive (discovery) metadata (subject headings, keywords, type, classification).
- Creatives and Educators did not understand the multiple uses and purposes of metadata and had difficulty seeing beyond the scope of their immediate needs because they were usually working to exhibition or event deadlines. Any desire to 'tidy up' afterwards was quickly replaced by a desire to begin work on the next exhibition or event.
- Creatives and Educators had little or no interest in applying significant resources to producing conformant metadata, which was perceived to be the behind-the-scenes province of registrars and cataloguers.

The collaborative metadata production experiment continued for just over two years and resulted in the creation of over 2500 records of unreliable quality. When difficulties in tracking new titles arose, 35% of the digital works in the tracking and registration systems were found to have little or no metadata. At this point the Metaphiles and the Cataloguers abandoned collaborative metadata production and embarked on a quality assurance programme to put things right. Quality was significantly compromised by spelling mistakes, typos and incorrect data and, more commonly, by empty or misunderstood fields or elements.

The quality assurance programme at ACMI is now ongoing and involves a team of cataloguers checking, verifying and locking each record. A thorough analysis of the shortcomings of these records is currently under way.

Cataloguers are finding that cleaning up metadata records is taking nearly twice as long as generating them from scratch. It is therefore likely (even with effective metadata generation tools) that quality assurance will become a major issue within the domain of metadata standards. Collaborative metadata production is recommended by Currier and Barton (2003) but it is unlikely to be cost effective without first supporting it with an integrated technical architecture and a collaborative culture.

Is metadata harmful?

The shape of the container inevitably influences the way content is both produced and consumed. This can create discontinuities between different data stores and their production environments. There is a big difference between the containers needed to hold the kind of atomized data that fits into relational databases and the kind of information that doesn't fit neatly into boxes because it tolerates recursive structures and the re-use of content along with mixing up the container with the contained. As a container, XML generally fits this model by having labelled hierarchically structured containers with a general separation between content and processing expectations, whereas RDF (expressed as XML) creates interlocking assertions that combine to make statements (St Laurent, 2003).

At ACMI the Technologists have little interest in exploring the values associated with using these containers. Their primary concern is that the applications are installed and function according to specifications. They assume that users will adapt their practices to the hardware and software 'products' and are not at all open to adapting and shaping these products to suit the users. When the Technologists took control of the XML data store they attempted to move it into a relational database but found managing the information modelled in XML extremely complex, difficult and unsatisfactory. Rather than persevere with new technologies that support the simplicity of storing data in XML, the Technologists have opted to isolate the metadata production environment at ACMI and contain it within a proprietary collection management system.

It is worth acknowledging the intuitive resistance to metadata containment by the Creatives and to consider some of the ways that different values can be embedded in both the semantics and the syntax of metadata. Although the terms used to describe the elements in a standard such as Dublin Core have been developed through a consensus designed to facilitate cross-domain consumption, arts practitioners are not nearly as willing to adapt their terminology beyond their field of interest.

If metadata can be understood as information at one remove from the object it describes, or structured information about something – even itself – then there are values residing in the linkage between the idea described and who or what is describing it. As digital technologies evolve to handle formats other than text, metadata is moving into the fabric of the works themselves. MPEG-7 (Martínez, 2002) provide an example of the ways that metadata can move from simple referencing of the title as an entity, to sequence, shot, frame and even pixel with the frame. In these forms metadata can be embodied and embedded in markup. This kind of markup is a sequential and hierarchical meta-language that might not only be different for different domains but also can enforce structure on expressions that are not always structured in sequential and hierarchical ways.

An example (see Figures 4.1 and 4.2, pages 73–4) is an artwork by Austrian film-maker Gustav Deutsch entitled 'Film Ist' and currently on display at ACMI as a four-screen work (Gibson, 2003). It contains repetitions and overlapping instances of quite random associations and interconnections from which meaning might be experienced before it is understood. The conjunctions of images that appear, both in linear sequences on any given screen and spatially aligned from one screen to another, create sparks of meaning and energy that enliven the way we experience the work (see 'Re-presentation in an endangered present', below).

Those that question the impact of digital formats on the expressions of existing analogue works are sometimes branded as being reactionary. Nevertheless, in the digital domain the challenge is to find durable techniques for describing and even addressing material at a byte level without contaminating or misrepresenting the material with structural values. Nelson (1997) is credited as being the first to raise these issues in relation to embedded markup (HTML). While Nelson's theories of 'transculsion' have yet to find popular application, his three-layer reference model is a useful way of approaching the kinds of metadata that interest arts practitioners and could be included in an organization's metadata schema. It is a similar approach to the preservation strategy proposed by Hunter and Choudhury (2003) (see 'Re-presentation in an endangered present', below):

- a content layer
- a structure layer
- a special effects or realization layer.

One of Nelson's solutions to the problem of contamination by metadata is to deploy parallel markup (sometimes called standoff or out-of-line) in which the object and the metadata are treated as separate parallel entities.

This raises the problem of how multiple instances or overlapping hierarchies of metadata can be associated with the same object without confusion. It also raises the possibility of creating metadata at a distance from the object. It could be used as a form of remote appropriation similar to the practice of web content scraping by content aggregators. If there is an accessible resource pool, it could mean that art objects could continue to find expression in multiple locations and contexts outside the control of either the creator or the custodian.

If distributed standoff metadata facilitates the same unashamed appropriation exhibited in the Gershwin download at the beginning of this chapter, then there will need to be a reassessment of how the values of arts practitioners can be accommodated. The historical connection between the advance of electronic technologies and the erosion of cultural memory is cause for reflection. The impact of the train following the telegraph lines in Central Australia in the 1870s is a poignant example. According to Daisy Bates (1945, 194–5) the effects were devastating.

> With the railway began the extermination of the Central native groups. Each group through whose territory the track was passing saw its waters used up, the trees and bushes were destroyed for firewood and fence posts, the whole country turned to strange uses. They thought that the train and its people would go away, and leave them the things to play with. They were mesmerised by the trains, the trains became their life, the rhythm of their days.

The delivery of the benefits imagined or promised by a technology can also create a profoundly different receptive environment in which good and bad can change places according to your point of view. This duality is visible in the changes that networked technologies have made to the value of the objects themselves. The change is so far-reaching that it is creating a new economy, the economy inhabited by the Hacktivists.

Networked challenges to the arts economy

The business of the arts relies on the economics of copyright where recognition combines with scarcity to drive price. The economics of the network, on the other hand, is founded on ubiquity where recognition combined with availability drives access. When these values intersect, the values that champion availability and underwrite the production of high-quality metadata collide with the values that foster a sense of the rare and the precious. Qualities that assist arts custodians justify their acquisitions and attract audiences.

When Marshall McLuhan articulated his prescient insight that 'new media makes old media content', he did more than anticipate the ease with which old media (film) would be transferred to new (at that time, video). He provided an insight into the way in which resources could be absorbed by a technology and re-purposed beyond the scope of the licences and agreements that governed their use. It is important to understand the origins of this change in the concept of value because it represents a significant barrier to metadata production.

At ACMI there is occasional anxiety about the extent to which the logo of another agency can be displayed. The patronage evident in the attachment of logos to electronic and paper resources harks back to the status of the author when manuscripts were mass-produced by copyists. Prior to the 16th century an author could only gain recompense for his efforts by obtaining a powerful patron. His rights were not defined or protected.

The profession of author grew out of the communications revolution that was born with the invention of the printing press. But it took several hundred years before a system of royalty payment could evolve. Publishers began looking for fresh material when the supply of ancient texts started to dry up. Authors found themselves in a stronger position and it became common practice in the 17th century for the publisher to buy a manuscript outright. But as the printing industry expanded, there was widespread dissatisfaction with this arrangement among authors all over Europe. Eventually, a French decree in 1778 recognized a form of perpetual copyright whereby an author had the right to sell and distribute his work and to assign this right in whole or in part – even for a period after death.

Advocates for this form of copyright protection have argued that such a system provides incentive for creative work. Copyright confers a time-limited form of monopoly or control over the supply of a resource. Capitalist societies are wedded to the notion of property because the value of property (in the markets of an analogue world) is largely derived from scarcity. The market control that a monopoly implies usually means that value can be generated by restricting supply.

Over the last 50 years the broader global concept of 'intellectual property' has been applied to many forms of the expression of ideas. However, in Australia (and other countries), piecemeal applications of this wider protection have led to inconsistencies and significant barriers to the free flow of information and ideas, as well as to the distribution of creative work.

The widespread adoption of communications technology has led to the growth of an information economy largely dependent on the free flow of data. In the context of a society's 'total information system' the restrictive practices inherent in existing forms of copyright control are now being questioned because (in practice) they impede the effective distribution and expression of innovative ideas.

The earliest forms of electronic communications technology opened the doors to a new notion of value in which significant streams of revenue could be derived from resources that were ubiquitous or had proliferated. For example, a telephone or a means of sending e-mail only has value because other people have access to it too. A single telephone has no value. Value is added by increasing supply.

As various electronic communications infrastructures have evolved, so has the form of the material they carry. The shift from analogue to digital is having profound implications on how this material can be accessed, managed and used. A digital expression of an idea is unlike an analogue expression because:

- It requires the action of mediation by machine(s) in order to be accessible.
- A copy can be identical to an original.
- It can be transmitted or reproduced without degradation.

- It is easy to manipulate, transform or recombine (significant in a culture of fragmentation).
- Its preservation is dependent on long-term accessibility.
- It may also be a system that generates other expressions such as an online gaming environment.

These qualities have led to the development of networked transmission infrastructures that are rapidly absorbing the expressions of human thought and make almost every analogue management and preservation strategy (including copyright), problematic if not obsolete.

The provision of both short- and long-term access to resources, generated as a consequence of this interaction, will be compromised if we do not move away from the restrictive practices that surround these expressions as fenced-off property. One has only to look at the information economy around us today (notwithstanding the merchandizing of CDs and DVDs), to see that it is already access and use, rather than ownership, that we are prepared to pay for (if we pay at all).

These networked and distributed values have actually facilitated the production of new forms of sound collage (Hip Hop, Gabba, Skratch or Turntable music), built almost entirely of 1970s music samples. Such forms are beginning to generate significant revenue through the merchandizing of analogue material. Ironically, they often make use of the more advanced production and distribution technologies which, when discovered by the traditional industry, may compromise their sources, if existing copyright restrictions are enforced.

Similarly, a generation raised on film and television is now using samples of sound and image from file-sharing downloads to forge a new genre of iconographic digital film making. The re-use, re-purposing and re-presentation of moving image sequences, sounds and gaming engines have considerable cultural significance. Yet to suggest that the collecting agencies within the arts domain should share these values and build a significant presence within these unrestricted domains is dismissed as a heresy.

Re-presentation in an endangered present

There are many eloquent speculations on the future of the museum, the gallery and the containers of art that have become the 21st-century cathedrals. As the buildings themselves become less fortress and more sieve, it is important to consider the impact of more open forms of gathering and collecting. This will inevitably alter the notion of what might be considered to be the 'original' work. It will change the way distributed collections are managed and require new procedures for identifying works of significance and works requiring archival intervention.

Just as the chances of most digital art works surviving for more than ten years in their current formats are slim, so the life cycle of a title record or a piece of structured metadata is even shorter. Not only will these 'chunks' of data change so rapidly that it might be more useful to consider them as dynamic streams, but sooner or later someone will need to migrate this metadata. It is worth acknowledging this from the outset and ensuring that there is an infrastructure to support:

- a flexible data model with a mechanism for keeping track of it
- a non-proprietary and non-carrier-specific approach to future-proofing metadata as it transforms from one schema into another
- a culturally integrated approach to access (short-term or long-term)
- dynamic outputs generated from metadata components that will keep the data live and visible.

A tangible and profound illustration of these issues comes from the interstellar outreach programme. It was only 25 years ago that Carl Sagan at NASA recorded some metadata about the Earth to send into the future aboard the Voyager Outreach spacecraft (Rudd, 1997). Using the technology of the day, the metadata was recorded on to 12-inch gold-plated copper phonograph records encased in protective aluminium jackets. The records (encoded in analogue form) contained astro-spatial data about the planet along with sounds and images from many of the world's vanishing cultures. It was a remarkable and prescient exercise, as much a communication with an endangered present as it was a journey through space and time. It will be 40,000 years before Voyager 1 and 2 come within a light year of a star and millions of years before either reaches any other planetary system. It is quite possible that this metadata may become the only evidence of our existence. Back on the ground, the (mainly aural) metadata has become increasingly inaccessible and a prime candidate for migration into some more accessible and non-proprietary format.

The imagined future implied by the interstellar outreach programme took little or no account of the endangered present. Short-term accessibility is important in setting up the cultural values that are necessary to ensure the long term.

When it comes to managing digital resources, the provision of access is so interconnected with the development of archival strategies, that preservation is really the challenge of providing either short-term or long-term access. In this role, the distributed values of the network are the values that may facilitate the long-term. The best chance electronic information has of being accessible in the long-term is that it is used or available for use – continuously.

Digital artworks can be expensive to produce because they often involve combinations and arrangements of different media in complex spatial and temporal configurations. They often employ bespoke or proprietary software and have unusual technical dependencies that rarely conform to standards. At ACMI we try to insist that moving image content is delivered on Digital Betacam even though a variety of encoding formats may be employed in realizing the work within our exhibition spaces. This is to ensure that content can be re-encoded to suit the delivery and display systems.

There are a number of initiatives relating to the preservation of the arts. The Variable Media Initiative at the Guggenheim Museum (www.guggenheim.org/variablemedia) provides a metadata structure that questions whether artists want their work re-presented. However, artists are not a reliable source of information (Banks, 2001, 84). Emulation software (Granger, 2000) may accommodate standard formats but is unlikely to be effective with bespoke systems. Migration not only enforces structural values on works but assumes that the less stable expressive qualities (previously described) can be mirrored.

Hunter and Choudhury (2003) have recently proposed an optimum preservation metadata schema for artworks that find expression as complex multimedia objects. This is based on the Metadata Transmission and Encoding Standard (METS) combined with the use of the Synchronised Multimedia Integration Language (SMIL) for specifying spatial and temporal structure. Their paper, 'Implementing Preservation Strategies for Complex Multimedia Objects', provides a thorough analysis of the current status of arts-focused preservation. However, while the proposed solution may have theoretical merits, it takes little account of either the practical realities of metadata generation within arts agencies or their will to allocate sufficient resources and skilled staff to the task.

At ACMI we can observe trends that will compromise long-term access to works of significance:

- Artists working in the digital domain sell multiple manifestations of their work (in limited editions) where content is struck from masters retained by the artist. This has the effect of reducing the sense of responsibility that an organization might possibly accept for ensuring long-term access to the edition in custody.
- Creatives accept commissioned works from artists that are in highly compressed or redundant formats requiring bespoke software that runs on obsolete equipment.
- New media artworks are often akin to performances as a result of their dynamic responsive or streaming qualities. A pragmatic approach to access would suggest that they might best be captured as snapshots in time.

Clearly there are new types of conservation skills urgently required to manage access to digital artworks effectively. As the prices and profiles of new media artwork rise, it is only a matter of time before high-profile works become publicly and embarrassingly irretrievable. Perhaps this will serve to focus the arts on the true value of metadata of high quality. However, even if the values of the practitioners converge and the creative practitioners call for help from the Metaphiles, we are a long way from the collaborative solutions that are needed.

Conclusion

The development of a healthy metadata ecology involves a complex inter-play of technologies, values and cultures. In the arts, it needs to be rec-ognized that conflict and tension will take place in an environment of constant negotiation, re-assembly and re-alignment if all these energies are to be harnessed.

Within such a fluid environment, there are significant changes in thinking required before the values that revere bounded entities in care-fully controlled spaces can be reconciled with the values of fragmenta-tion, unrestricted distribution and proliferation that reside within structured metadata standards.

As metadata enters the fabric of the artworks themselves, these values are becoming critical to the durability of the works. Not everyone wants to set art or information free, or to contribute to an infrastructure where there might be a choice about what to make available.

A checklist for a healthy arts metadata ecology is as follows:

- a culturally integrated approach to access and distribution (short-term or long-term)
- a flexible and fluid data model with a mechanism for keeping track of it
- a non-proprietary and non-carrier-specific approach to future-proofing metadata as it mutates and transforms from one schema into another
- dynamic outputs generated from metadata fragments that keep the metadata live and visible
- the continuous re-use of metadata anywhere possible (web output, fly-ers, catalogues, etc.)
- a presence within file-sharing networks and a proliferating mentality
- a conservation literacy that reaches into the fabric of digital content management and celebrates transformation through fragmentation and experiments in re-presentation such as SMIL (2001).

Without all or most of these attributes, metadata production is likely to be marginalized within an arts organization. Quality will be compro-mised and resources dissipated. At first glance the barriers to cultural integration appear to be irreconcilable. Yet this checklist could also characterize the kind of approach to material that deserves the status of being called art. They are qualities that anyone embarking on a metadata project should understand belong to the concept of structured metadata, qualities that are anchored in a need to send ideas through time and space.

Just as the production of feature films has been characterized by the concept of assembly or montage, so we could consider metadata production to be the result of the combined efforts of quite separate skills. Perhaps it is time for the Metaphiles to talk more about the art of metadata, about how images and sounds can also be metadata and about the new literacy of this emerging form of expression.

> If truth is that which lasts, then art has proved truer than any other human endeavour. What is certain is that pictures and poetry and music are not only marks in time but mark through time, of their own time and ours, not antique or historical, but living as they ever did, exuberantly, untired.
>
> Jeanette Winterson, 1995

References

Banks, G. (2001) Preservation Metadata for Electronic Artworks. A case study of 'Turbulence: An Interactive Museum of Unnatural History'. Unpublished thesis, University of Canberra.

Bates, D. (1945) *The Passing of the Aborigines*, Melbourne, Oxford University Press.

Currier, S. and Barton, J. (2003) *Quality Assurance for Digital Learning Object Repositories: the power of metadata*, Draft 0.2, posted to DC-General Fri, 28 March 2003 14:05:18 (to be published in ALT-C 2003 proceedings), as well as personal correspondence.

Gibson, R. (1998) *A Curatorial Philosophy*, www.acmi.net.au/dctypeproposal/GibsonCurosophy.html.

Gibson, R. (2003) *Exhibition, Remembrance: the persistence of vision*, www.acmi.net.au/remembrance/site.html.

Granger, S. (2000) Emulation as a Digital Preservation Strategy, *D-Lib*

Magazine, **6** (10), www.dlib.org/dlib/october00/granger/10granger.html.

Hunter, J. and Choudhury, S. (2003) *Implementing Preservation Strategies for Complex Multimedia Objects,* http://metadata.net/newmedia/pres_meta.pdf.

Martínez, J. M. (2002) *MPEG-7 Overview,* http://mpeg.telecomitalialab.com/standards/mpeg-7/mpeg-7.htm.

Nardi, B. A. and O'Day, V. L. (1999) *Information Ecologies: using technology with heart,* Cambridge, MA, MIT Press.

Nelson, T. H. (1997) *Embedded Markup Considered Harmful,* www.xml.com/pub/a/w3j/s3.nelson.html.

Rudd, R. (1997) *Voyager's Greetings to the Universe: interstellar outreach programme,* http://voyager.jpl.nasa.gov/mission/interstellar.html.

St Laurent, S. (2003) *The (Data) Medium is the Message,* www.oreillynet.com/pub/wlg/3139.

Synchronised Multimedia Integration Language (2001) Version 2.0, W3C Recommendation, www.w3.org/TR/smil20/.

Winterson, J. (1995) *Art Objects – essays on ecstasy and effrontery,* London, Jonathan Cape.

Part 3

METADATA IN GOVERNMENT

5

Metadata and taxonomy integration in government portals

Eileen Quam

Introduction

The history of government websites is not pretty. Like many early sites, they started out decentralized, static and infrequently updated. Navigation was a concept of the future and taxonomies were still relegated to the animal kingdom. Eventually, enterprise-wide search engines helped bring together these distributed sites, and gateways came into being that directed users to the many separate websites that made up governments' outpouring of digital information. In recent times there has been considerable progress in navigation and design. The portal concept has revolutionized how governments organize and present information. Taxonomies are flourishing, making click-through navigation a comfortable and workable reality. Search engines can be designed to recognize and weigh metadata. Web page creators are learning that their creative efforts are part of a whole, not just individual pages on specific topics. Application developers are beginning to respond to the notion of integration, so that the many pieces that make up a complete website can speak with each other.

However, some work still remains to be done. Integration is far from commonplace and the very basis of information organization has been largely ignored. This chapter will look at portal components including search engines and content management software. It will discuss and define portals, metadata, controlled vocabularies such as taxonomies and thesauri, and related topics in the field of discovery of web information. Beyond that, the chapter will discuss what is missing in the current climate from a user as well as a provider perspective, and make recommendations on directions application developers can take to improve the current offerings. Throughout there will be references to what works and what does not, using the State of Minnesota portal and other sites as examples.

The chapter is organized into the components of a comprehensive information architecture, including:

- metadata
- controlled vocabularies, including thesauri and taxonomies
- portals
- content management solutions.

The remainder of the chapter is centred around the integration of these parts and lessons learned.

Metadata

Ah, metadata! The obsession of the library world – our contribution to getting a handle on the glut of electronic information – and the bane of web page creators not endowed with cataloguer personalities. Despite the obvious problem that metadata requires an extra step in page creation, great progress has been made in the organization of information utilizing metadata.

Metadata is more than a condensation of descriptive information extracted from a resource. It is, as Stephen Abrams said at the 1999 Internet Librarian conference, 'the story that tells the story'. This definition offers a more comprehensive look at what metadata can do. Metadata does the basic task of identifying author, title, subject and description of a resource. But it can also offer information about the metadata fields: meta-metadata, if you will. The Dublin Core Metadata Element Set (DCMES) (http://dublincore.org) is the most adaptable and advanced example of this capability. Table 5.1 illustrates the 15 basic Dublin Core elements arranged according to function. These elements make up 'simple Dublin Core'. Each of the elements can have qualifiers that offer further information about the element, the content of the element, or the format of the element. This extended view of elements is 'qualified Dublin Core'. The three types of qualifiers are:

- *Modifiers*: this type of qualifier is an element refinement, which makes the meaning of the element more specific. Examples of this are the Dublin Core date modifiers that identify what kind of date is being encoded, such as creation date.
- *Schemes*: this type of qualifier identifies schemes that aid in the interpretation of an element value. An example of a scheme is a controlled vocabulary from which the subject element is populated.
- *Web links*: this qualifier is directly related to the scheme and gives the web location where the scheme resides.

Table 5.1 *Dublin Core Metadata Element Set*

Content	Intellectual Property	Instantiation
Coverage	Contributor	Date
Description	Creator	Format
Type	Publisher	Identifier
Relation	Rights	Language
Source		
Subject		
Title		

The Dublin Core metadata standard (ANSI/NISO standard Z39.85 and ISO standard 15836) has the following goals:

- simplicity of creation and maintenance
- commonly understood semantics
- international scope

- extensibility.

Other web metadata sets include:

- Global Information Locator Service (GILS) – in use by a number of state governments (www.gils.net/)
- local community metadata standards intended for access to specific types of resources on portals dedicated to those resource types
- standard metadata – uncontrolled HTML metadata elements, which are largely ignored by internet-wide search engines.

Regardless of the metadata standard, business purposes include providing:

- descriptive information about a resource
- accurate and reliable identification
- logical searching and improved resource discovery
- consistency in metadata element and scheme application
- reduction of ad hoc home-grown metadata sets
- increased reliability and fewer errors in metadata content
- re-use of metadata information in taxonomy development.

Controlled vocabularies

Controlled vocabularies are the foundation of a good information architecture. If the portal developer pays close attention to choosing and/or creating quality sets of controlled vocabularies for the several places in the architecture that they are employed, the site will fulfill its promise. It will be easily navigable from various user perspectives, the search engine will provide relevant results, and the user will find comprehensive, targeted access to the important topics on the site.

Controlled vocabularies are listings of terms that serve several purposes. They

- provide unambiguous language for specific concepts
- provide synonym control to avoid false hits or incomplete search results

- offer related topic terms
- provide current terminology as well as terminology specific to the site.

There are several types of controlled vocabularies, including:

- *controlled term lists*: lists of preferred terms, usually alphabetical
- *uncontrolled term lists*: simple lists of terms without structure
- *classification systems*: not usually natural language, often employing a coding system
- *authority files*: controlled lists of the preferred form of proper names; naming conventions
- *thesauri*: lists of preferred terms with hierarchy and cross-references
- *taxonomies*: a system for naming and organizing things; hierarchical.

Of these controlled vocabulary types, we will be primarily concerned with the last two: thesauri and taxonomies.

Thesauri

The controlled vocabulary in the form of a thesaurus brings together like concepts, synonyms and related terminology, which can assist the user in selecting appropriate search terms that may not have been envisioned at the onset. Such assistance takes the form of two types of cross-references:

- 'See' references lead users from a synonym to the preferred terms or phrase for a concept, or variant spellings of a name or title.
- 'See also' references suggest related concepts that are not precisely synonyms yet bear a close connection to the chosen term.

A true thesaurus will provide hierarchical views, allowing for broader and narrower ordering of concepts. A thesaurus can provide a world view on a particular domain or discipline by organizing concepts and subject matter, and creating a comprehensive, logical understanding of the entire knowledge area. A further advantage of a thesaurus is the ability to share the vocabulary. If other similar projects use the same vocabulary, cross-domain searching is facilitated. Using the same set of terms for similar concepts brings coherence and consistency to searching. The thesauri used for the subject field in cataloguing such as the Library of Congress Subject Heading List are familiar to the library world.

Taxonomies

Taxonomies are conceptually broader than thesauri in that they include both the terminology as well as the infrastructure that fuels the taxonomy. Taxonomies are typically hierarchical in nature, but can also be expressed in alphabetical or other navigational formats. An example of a multiple-format taxonomy is on the Montague Institute website (www.montague.com:8080/Public/indexes.htm), where the searcher can find articles on topics via the A–Z index, the thesaurus, the click-through browsable topics on the search engine, or other listings such as people and organizations.

The thesaurus and the taxonomy have some common ground. The taxonomy can be built from thesaurus terms, thereby making direct re-use of the terminology for the user. An example of this is the 'search topics' on Minnesota's North Star portal (www.state.mn.us/cgi-bin/portal/mn/jsp/search.do?action=easysearch&agency=NorthStar). The topics listed are terms taken from the state thesaurus, which is adapted from the Library of Congress's *Legislative Indexing Vocabulary* (www.loc.gov/lexico/servlet/lexico). Another approach is to build the taxonomy structure from a user-centric perspective, utilizing terminology that may or may not be in the thesaurus. Yet the thesaurus terms can still be fed into the taxonomy via a set of rules that matches thesaurus terms to topics in the taxonomy. An example of this is also on the North Star portal, but in the 'themes' that run across the top navigation bar, which were named with the portal customer in mind. This approach is explained below, in reference to the integration diagram.

Portals

Portal is a term generally used to describe a website that serves as a gateway or major jumping-off point for accessing a defined set of websites.

The Library and Information Technology Association Portal Interest Group ((http://litaipig.ucr.edu/index.php) defines portal as a service (and related systems and approaches to organization) that facilitates organized knowledge discovery through the internet.

Common services provided by portals include:

- content management software
- taxonomy management
- personalization and authentication
- instant messaging
- workflow or collaboration software
- directory services
- security components.

Portals can take on different forms. General portals include Yahoo! or AOL (America Online). Community- or topic-specific portals include webMD.com and Orbitz.com. Organization-specific portals, whether internet or intranet, are in high demand by corporations, educational institutions and governments. These latter types of portals fall under the description of enterprise information portal (EIP). An EIP serves as a gateway to an organization's information and knowledge base for employees, customers, business partners and the general public (Kauth, 2003). The one common necessity when designing any of the different kinds of portal is that they should be customer-oriented and intended to reflect and respond to the needs of their audience.

One highly visible way to design for the audience is to create a customer-centric taxonomy, based in part on the metadata and the controlled vocabulary or thesaurus. Such a taxonomy may take the outward form of themes on a website, or browsable categories on a search page. Building a customer-centric taxonomy calls for an organized approach informed by:

- *domain analysis* – who are the user groups?
- *user studies* – what do they want to know?
- *process analysis* – how does the information arrive?
- *organizational structure* – where is the information gathered and

stored?
- *controlled vocabulary* – how does the thesaurus define the topics? Can the terminology be adapted or mapped to the taxonomy?
- *usability studies* – now that it's built, are users finding what they need?

Content management solutions

Portals typically include content management software to control and publish the content created by the page authors. Content management systems provide an end-to-end solution that manages all types of business content, whether in XML or native format, throughout the life cycle from design, creation and management through publishing and distribution. Most content management systems include workflow functionality to set up and track business processes. Also included are content creators that allow authors to create new content and stylesheets (Kauth, 2003). The benefits include:

- streamlined content creation and publishing
- integration of content with other portal elements such as themes, portlets (a way to interface with other applications through a single web interface), workflow
- self-management by business users
- IT operational efficiency
- ease of administration
- security and control of content.

The State of Minnesota's portal, North Star (www.northstar.state.mn.us) is a portal and content management system (BroadVision) that integrates the state's search engine (Verity Ultraseek) and its add-on, the Content Classification Engine (CCE) (www.verity.com/products/ultraseek/classification.html) into the theme management and other taxonomies. This was not realized without effort. The search engine that came with the portal solution did not offer the kind of tuning needed for leveraging the state's metadata. Developers put in weeks of effort to program the integration of Ultraseek (then Inktomi) with BroadVision and ensure that the themes and other taxonomies functioned correctly.

The integration of the content management, search engine, metadata,

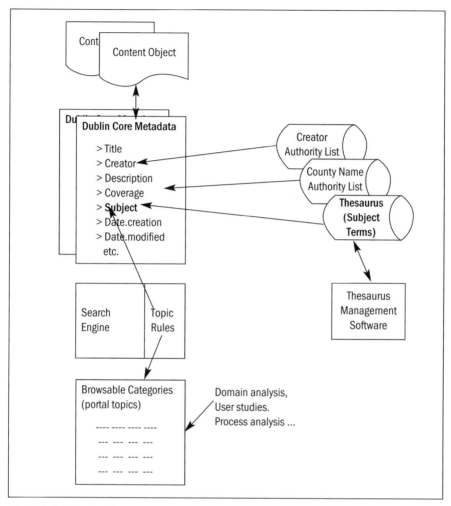

Fig. 5.1 *Integration diagram*

controlled vocabulary and browsable categories (themes/taxonomies) is illustrated in Figure 5.1, about which the followin points should be noted:

- The diagram starts at the top with a resource, or *content object*.
- Metadata is linked to this object, as indicated by the *Dublin Core Metadata* box. This linkage can come through the content manage-ment software, as it is in North Star, via a custom-designed template that requires certain elements to be entered.

- The template offers appropriate *controlled vocabularies* for certain elements, as indicated by the cylinders to the right of the metadata box in the diagram. One such controlled vocabulary is the state's thesaurus, LIV-MN, which offers terminology to be used in the *Dublin Core subject* element.
- The diagram shows a double arrow from the thesaurus to *the thesaurus management software* that runs it, in this case Lexico.
- An independent task is to set up the *browsable categories* in the search engine add-on, CCE. This is shown at the bottom of the diagram.
- Behind those categories, which include the themes at the top of the North Star pages, are *rules* that tell the *search engine* how to populate the topics.
- The *search engine* draws on the Dublin Core *subject* tag, according to the *rules*, to provide dynamic search results to the themes and subtopics and other *browsable categories*.

The diagram is intended as a general illustration of the process and does not rely on specific solutions or brands. Not all state agencies are hosted by the portal, and a different metatagging solution is available to them (HI Software's TagGen Dublin Core edition (http://hisoftware.com/fact_sheetcc.htm)). Similarly, the search engine add-on could alternatively be managed through the content management solution, in which case the rules would reside within the content management rather than on the search engine side.

That said, it is important to employ a search engine that can be tuned to prefer the Dublin Core metadata fields, and to leverage the subject element for re-use in the topic hierarchies.

What's missing

While the State of Minnesota and other portals have successfully cobbled together a suite of solutions that satisfies their business needs, it is a cumbersome and time-consuming process. Since such integration is not built into the offerings by vendors (despite their claims) problems continue to crop up that require ongoing programmer time. Here are some items on the 'what's missing' list.

Understanding

Most developers do not properly credit the importance of metadata, and the world standard Dublin Core metadata in particular, when creating or upgrading their applications. Most content management solutions have rudimentary metadata fields, often intended for the simple use of identification. When the developers are asked about Dublin Core, the answer is that the templates are customizable. This does not begin to address qualified Dublin Core.

Controlled vocabularies seem to be a distantly remembered concept to application developers. While most can understand parent–child relationships from a database perspective, they have rarely built such a tool into content management solutions. And where they have, they are simple hierarchies that do not allow the kind of sophisticated relationships that thesaurus management software provides. One wonders where the thesaurus management software vendors are on this issue. Those solutions, that provide excellent offerings – such as Lexico (www. pmei.com/lexico.html), Data Harmony's Thesaurus Master (www.dataharmony.com/tm.htm), Open Text's BASIS (www.opentext. com/basis/) – are still primarily standalone systems. Those that are building out their software to include a more comprehensive approach to content management are far from the integration diagram in Figure 5.1.

Integration

Primarily this comes down to integration issues. Vendor awareness in the fields of content management, search engines, metadata management and thesaurus management could use a big boost. There are great pushes in development in tunable search engines, browsable categories, Dublin Core metadata templates and embedded vocabularies, but not in integrating among them. Large customers, whether government or corporate, have caches of data stored in many ways, often with multiple search engines and taxonomies in place. A crossover solution that could bring them together without throwing out everything that has been employed to date would easily woo these customers.

User perspectives

From a government portal perspective, search tools and metadata revolve around the following topics:

- ranking
- matching of terms
- advanced search/custom searches.

Taxonomies are very important in portals at the moment. As defined above, this is the dual solution of topic navigation (often in the form of browsable categories) and the applications that give it functionality. As a glance through articles on the Montague Institute website (www.montague.com/review/971001.htm) shows, this is a very hot topic and one that merits the close attention of both information architects and developers.

From a content provider perspective, the following topics are critical:

- metadata application
- controlled vocabulary application
- topic creation and management
- search engines, including tunings and advanced search customizations.

These two perspectives show the similarity of issues and correlate directly to what is missing or needed from current offerings.

Conclusion

Ideally, a portal or gateway will offer the following components:

- taxonomies
  - well-organized and logical
  - based on thesaurus or controlled vocabulary
  - user-oriented
  - current and customizable
- metadata

- co-ordinated, standardized effort
- based on controlled vocabularies
- complete metadata application tool
- training options
- business case
- search engine
  - tunable to metadata
  - integrated into the content management solution
  - integrated with the taxonomy creation tool
- content management system
  - metadata creation tool
  - thesaurus management tool
  - integrated with the search engine
  - including other standard offerings such as workflow, authentication, etc.

And finally, a portal needs people who care about these things, who understand the concepts and can offer training or mentoring.

While it is true that libraries have offered excellent access to bibliographic information for a long, long time, their influence on the creation of highly usable websites is not great. The nature of the internet is that it is self-monitoring, which often means no monitoring at all. For large repositories of information, such as governments provide, this home-grown approach is rapidly becoming untenable. Government agencies need to look beyond their specific customer base and hoard of documents and look toward a more co-ordinated effort in providing access to users that could easily come from anywhere in the world. This broader approach to accessibility allows for better search and discovery, a greater level of taxonomy development, and a more customer-oriented approach to website navigation. At the same time, autonomy is important to consider, as each agency or division presents its unique offerings to the world.

A good suite of applications that work together can offer the benefits of co-ordinated effort that result in cost savings and consistency of application. Such a system can also give the individual agencies the capability to customize the solution to their needs and their users' expectations, enhancing their individuality. Current solutions have much to offer. With attention to the power of metadata and controlled vocabularies, they could really give the portal creator the tools needed for highly sophisticated sharing of information.

Reference

Kauth, J. (2003) *What is a Portal?*, St Paul, MN, Minnesota Office of Technology.

6

Metadata and the UK archives network

Bill Stockting and Louise Craven

Introduction

For over 20 years archivists in the UK have been looking at the use of the tools offered by information and communications technology for the management of a core function, that of the creation, storage and presentation of metadata about our holdings: a process often simply known as cataloguing. Urgency in this area, however, only really began with the arrival of the internet. There was a concern that archives would be left behind by our 'bigger' partners in the cultural heritage sector, libraries and museums, in taking advantage of the possibilities for offering wider access to our material.

An influential report commissioned by the National Council on Archives (NCA), called *Archives On-line*, published in 1998, started the ball rolling. It reviewed the issues facing the archive profession in order to achieve 'the goal ... that a researcher anywhere in the world who has access to the Internet should be able to contact a common gateway, submit a single enquiry and receive a single integrated response, listing the relevant source materials housed in all UK archive repositories' (NCA, 1998, 2.8). In the intervening period a number of strands of this National Archives Network (NAN) have developed online catalogue services. These strands are both regional and sectoral, reflecting the availability of funding.

Archive repositories in the higher education (HE) sector are represented by the Archives Hub (www.archiveshub.ac.uk/), which covers the whole of the UK, and other regional services such as AIM25 (www.aim25.ac.uk) representing greater London and the Gateway to Archives of Scottish Higher Education (GASHE, www.gashe.archives. gla.ac.uk/) and Navigational Aids for the History of Science, Technology & the Environment (NAHSTE, www.nahste.ac.uk/) in Scotland. Outside the HE sector the strands are mainly national. There are the catalogues of the national institutions such as the Public Record Office Online Catalogue (PROCAT, http://catalogue.pro.gov.uk/) and National Register of Archives (NRA, www.hmc.gov.uk/nra/nra2.htm) at the UK National Archives, and the Online Manuscripts Catalogue (MOLCAT, http://molcat.bl.uk/) for the British Library. Online catalogues of the National Archives of Scotland and the Public Record Office of Northern Ireland are in development. There have also been a number of regional programmes dealing with the catalogues of local repositories. There is Access to Archives (A2A, www.a2a.pro.gov.uk/) for England, the Scottish Archive Network (SCAN, www.scan.org.uk/) and a similar service is in development in Wales.

The metadata presented in these online catalogues is of two types. There is the data that describes the archive materials themselves as well as that used to access these descriptions, which usually takes the form of authority-controlled names and subject terms. There follows a discussion of the standards relating to each type of metadata and the major related issues facing archivists in the development of the online services making up the NAN. A constant theme in this discussion is the particular nature of archives and its effect on archival metadata.

Metadata for archival description

The creators of the NAN have to contend with a basic fact about archives, that the informational value in them is found not only within each individual document but also in the relationships between documents. This means that archival descriptions are by nature hierarchical and this is reflected in both content and technical standards. It also raises questions about the depth and quality of the data provided to users by the strands of the NAN as well as how we fulfil the NCA's goal and bring these strands together in a single archive gateway.

The nature of archival descriptive metadata

To understand the nature of descriptive archival metadata (and what makes it different from those of bibliographic materials, for example) it is necessary to understand the nature of archives themselves.

Archives are the documents produced as part of everyday human interactions or transactions. They hold evidence of these transactions and, therefore, have an evidential value, which is not only to be found in each separate document but also in the relationships between documents. When arranging and describing archives, this value as evidence has to be kept in mind in order to avoid its loss. This is achieved by adherence to two related principles: provenance and original order.

The principle of provenance states that the archives of a particular body or individual must be kept together as a whole, this grouping often being referred as a *fonds*. By keeping the records of a particular creator together the context of the archives will be preserved and the evidential value with it. Contextual information about creators and records creation is not only important in relation to the body as a whole, but also within it. Particular parts, offices or individuals, for example, will have had particular functions and created records accordingly. All these relationships need to be preserved and described. Physically, this is achieved by adherence to the principle of original order, which states that documents should be kept in the order established by their creators. Intellectually, this is achieved by the creation of metadata structures that represent these contextual relationships.

Metadata structures for archives, whether called finding aids, catalogues or lists, are then different from those for bibliographic materials. The latter usually contain information about separate objects with no information about the way any one relates to any other. When developing a typology of finding aids Heaney, therefore, contrasts such 'analytic' structures from archival catalogues (2000, 5.5.3 and 6.7). These are classified as 'hierarchic', as they have to represent the relationships between documents in order to ensure that the context in which they were created is evident to the user (Heaney, 2000, 5.5.2 and 6.8). These relationships are represented hierarchically and there may be three broad levels of description in an archive catalogue. At the top will be information about who created the documents and why. This will be followed by information about an individual document's relationship with other documents. Finally, the individual documents themselves will be described.

The hierarchic, or multi-level, nature of archival catalogues is fully recognized by the International Council on Archives' *General International Standard for Archival Description* (ISAD(G)). This standard states that the levels described above should be clearly labelled (*fonds*, series, and files and items) and defines rules, which are necessary to consistently describe the relationships between levels. The standard also deconstructs the content description of archives into 26 elements that may be used at all levels. These data elements are broken down into seven areas as follows:

- identity statement
- context
- content and structure
- conditions of access and use
- allied materials area
- notes
- description control area.

The standard does not claim that all data elements are necessary, or even desirable, at all levels in all catalogues. It specifies a set of elements that 'are considered essential for international exchange of descriptive information' (ICA, 2000, i.12). These elements come mainly from the first two of the above areas; they are particularly important in the context of the development of the NAN and will feature in the following discussion. They are:

- level of description
- reference code
- title
- creator
- dates
- extent and form of materials.

A question of level – 1: collection-level or multi-level catalogues?

A major question facing archivists contemplating the provision of online access to archival catalogues is the depth of description to be provided. While archivists would agree that multi-level finding aids as defined by ISAD(G) provide the best representations of archive material, the call for access to archival information online has led to arguments that finding aids at collection level are useful in certain circumstances. The concept of collection-level description is, however, problematic for archivists.

Collection level is the term often given to descriptions containing information about a collection as a whole, rather than about the individual items it contains. Such descriptions have been described as unitary finding aids (Heaney, 2000, 5.5.1 and 6.6). In this case collection is being defined loosely as any aggregation of items (Johnson, 2001). As we have seen above, an aggregation of archives is known as a fonds rather than a collection. Traditionally the term collection has only been used by archivists to refer to groupings of documents that are not linked by provenance (Proctor and Cook, 2000, 14; Powell, 1999). In archival terms such collections are seen as artificial accumulations often gathered together by an individual on the basis of topic. They are, therefore, the result of collecting rather than being the organic by-product of the business of an individual or organization that properly constitutes a fonds. In the library context such accumulations are often called special collections. When talking about collection-level descriptions in the archival context then, it should be understood that the word collection is being used loosely to relate to an archival grouping as a whole, whether it is strictly a fonds or an artificial collection (Johnson, 2001, 4).

Can such a collection-level description properly be classed as an archival description at all? Many archivists in the UK would agree with the Manual of Archival Description when it states that, 'Archival descriptions should normally be written at two or more levels, a higher and a lower level' (Proctor and Cook, 2000, 19). As multi-level finding aids give a more detailed representation of the materials described, it is recognized that users are better served by them than by collection-level descriptions (NCA, 1998, 4.14; NCA and NANURG, 2002, 6). It can be argued that the latter are at too high a level of abstraction and users will have greater difficulties relating such descriptions to the actual documents being described. Furthermore, it is in the descriptions of individual documents that users actually find the information they require. The largest archive user group in the UK, for example, is family historians, and collection-level descriptions will not give them reference to the information about individuals they need. The lack of data in collection-level descriptions also diminishes the potential for automated searching online as, to put it crudely, if the data is not there it can not be retrieved. The force of these arguments is such that some of the strands of the NAN, such as PROCAT and A2A, have been mainly concerned to put multi-level catalogues online.

It has long been recognized, however, that descriptions of fonds as a whole are useful, particularly in the context of published guides. The ICA's Committee on Descriptive Standards, therefore, accepts them as legitimate archival descriptions (ICA CDS, 2002, Appendix A; ICA, 2000, i.8 and 1.1). A number of strands of the NAN have found themselves producing collection-level descriptions rather than converting pre-existing multi-level catalogues as the result of a number of factors. First, such descriptions are seen as better than having no description at all. The volume of uncatalogued archives is such that cataloguing to collection level is seen as an essential first step (NCA, 1998, 4.14; NCA, 2000, 5.1.2; CHC, 2002, 2.8). Second, the provision of basic descriptions of holdings is seen as a way to give users a comprehensive view of the archival heritage relating to particular areas or sectors. This can be seen as an extension to the internet of the role of collection-level descriptions in hard-copy guides to records. SCAN is attempting to provide access to descriptions of most archives in Scotland, while the Archives Hub is aiming at such access to archives held in all UK HE institutions and AIM25 has done the same for institutions in the greater London area. Even though most A2A projects have focused on multi-level catalogues, at least one, Yorkshire Signpost, has followed the collection-level route (see www.archives.wyjs.org.uk/base1.html). The perceived need for the Yorkshire and Humberside region was for users to have a comprehensive view of the archive holdings of the region, because of its size and administrative complexity.

The core elements of description for collection-level descriptions being put online by these strands of the NAN are those considered essential for data exchange by ISAD(G) noted above. Most of the projects, however, have asked contributors for additional elements. In order to give the user a full sense of the content of a collection and to maximize the potential of free-text searching online, some content description and administrative history have been made mandatory (Stockting, 2002; Collis, 2003). The need for information that might otherwise be found at a lower level in a multi-level catalogue has also been recognized. Information that may affect how, or indeed whether, researchers interact with the original records has also been specified such as physical characteristics, access restrictions and notes of languages found in the records other than English. Finally, a note of the existence of more detailed finding aids has also been thought useful.

Issues with legacy data

Within the NAN it is accepted that collection-level descriptions may be a useful first step, but the eventual goal is for description to be at file or even item level. Given that multi-level finding aids at varying levels exist describing much of the UK archival heritage in analogue, there is a need to convert this data to electronic form. Estimates of the costs for such retroconversion are, however, large, as there is an estimated 3 million to 3.5 million pages of this material (NCA, 1998, 4.1.6). A programme run by the UK National Archives to retroconvert its own catalogues suggests that rather than each repository setting about converting its own catalogues, programmes of mass conversion would benefit from significant economies of scale (NCA, 1998, 4.1.5; Dunham, Geddes and Thomas, 1999). A2A is one such programme designed to convert the existing paper catalogues relating to archives held by local English repositories.

The catalogues in question are those found on the public reading room shelves of most archive repositories in the UK and are generally similar in form. There is usually an introductory description, often a single narrative block of text, at an upper level, followed by an inventory that lists individual files, volumes or boxes (ICA CDS, 2002, Appendix A, class B). Within the body of the inventory there are often headings representing sub-*fonds* and series levels (for a typical example see www.pro.gov.uk/archives/a2a/markup.htm#comm). In a minority of cases actual items may also be described (ICA CDS, 2002, Appendix A, class C1). Also found may be descriptions on card catalogues that list a single item on a card often without any hierarchical context (ICA CDS, 2002, Appendix A, class C2). Generally the finding aids are typed but a minority are in manuscript. As well as differences in the structure and depth of description, content is also inconsistent. Data elements have not always been clearly defined, particularly at the uppermost levels. Descriptions are also often very brief especially at the central series levels, the only recognizable data element often being a title.

This inconsistency reflects the fact that the catalogues were prepared without reference to standards such as ISAD(G). Without standards the process of conversion is complex and the resulting data is not fit for purpose: it cannot be exchanged or searched, presented or navigated online. A central issue for programmes such as A2A, therefore, is the variant quality of this legacy data.

An initial question is whether such catalogues are actually fit for conversion and public online presentation at all? In discussing the quality of legacy data the Archives On-line report spoke for many UK archivists when it said, 'The need to ensure that data entered on to a national archive network conforms to the key ... standards would appear to require substantial checking and improvement of this inherited data' (NCA, 1998, 4.16). Based on the experience of converting its own catalogue for online presentation 'warts and all', the UK National Archives argued that users are more concerned about access to archival data than its consistency or editorial perfection. If the quality of most of the data concerned was considered fit, however, to what extent did it need to be standardized to make it usable in the NAN?

There was obviously a need for the A2A programme to specify to what extent the paper catalogues contributed would conform to standards. In so doing it was necessary to achieve a balance between the potentially competing aims of maximizing the content created for the NAN on the one hand and the need for a level of consistency, translated into conformance to ISAD(G) on the other. This balance was achieved by asking for catalogues that minimally conform to ISAD(G) in terms of data elements (A2A, 1999). This flexible approach prescribes sets of elements as mandatory at different levels of description. At the uppermost level, the mandatory elements include those considered essential for data exchange by ISAD(G) supplemented by some content description and any negative access conditions. This at least ensures a basic collection-level description for each catalogue. As this level of detail is demanded only once for each catalogue, this also means that the contributing repositories do not have a great deal of extra editorial work to do if content for these data elements does not exist. This is more of an issue at file level where a reference, creation dates and some content description are asked for. Given the online context, this was thought to be the bare minimum that would enable users to understand what was being described and to enable them to gain access to the documents themselves. At other levels only one of the data elements demanded at the uppermost level is asked for. This flexible approach to legacy data has been vindicated and at the time of writing the equivalent of over 600,000 catalogue pages have been made available for searching on the A2A database in three years.

Data exchange: EAD – the glue that holds it all together

As well as considering metadata standards and the depth of description, contributors to the NAN also need to think about the means by which data, once created, can be transmitted to systems for online searching and presentation. In the UK the environment in which such data exchange takes place is affected by government e-strategy, which has at its root the desire that public sector organizations work more closely together. A fundamental policy for this strategy is the e-Government Interoperability Framework (e-GIF), which is designed to facilitate the free flow of public sector information (Office of the e-Envoy, 2003). Adoption of the framework is mandatory for all public sector organizations and includes the adoption of XML and XSL as the primary standards for data integration. In the context of the NAN the requirements of e-GIF relating to XML can be satisfied by the use of the Encoded Archival Description (EAD) data communication format.

EAD is a data structure standard that has been specifically designed to allow for the creation of electronic versions of hierarchically structured archival finding aids that can be electronically maintained and exchanged as well as searched, presented and navigated online. Reflecting its American origins, the standard is jointly maintained by the Library of Congress and Society of American Archivists (see the official website at www.loc.gov/ead/). There was, however, early international input, including that from the UK National Archives, and the standard has become increasingly international in scope (for the working group see www.loc.gov/ead/eadwg.html). EAD has distinct advantages that have led to its adoption in the UK and elsewhere. It is an open standard that is freely available to all. It is also standards based and relates to both technical and archival description standards.

The need to represent the hierarchical structure of archival finding aids led to the early decision that EAD should take the form of an SGML Document Type Definition (DTD), itself an ISO standard (for a history of EAD development see www.loc.gov/ead/eaddev.html). Issues surrounding the difficulty of delivery of SGML documents to users on the internet also led to the decision that the first public version of the standard (EAD 1.0) should be XML compliant. Developments in XML and related technologies since the initial release in 1998 have led to major changes to the second version of the standard (EAD, 2002).

EAD is not a content standard in its own right. Rather it has been designed to map to international description standards, in particular MARC and ISAD(G). While an approximate mapping was possible from EAD 1.0 to the first version of ISAD(G), an exact map is now possible between the second versions of each standard (EAD, 1999, Appendix B; EAD, 2002, Appendix A). EAD, moreover, flags the importance of the elements considered essential for data exchange in ISAD(G) by inclusion of its related elements within the Descriptive Identification wrapper tag (<did>), thereby allowing easy access to the most significant metadata for data exchange. Compatibility with ISAD(G) was a major focus of the EAD Working Group when developing the latest version as a result of both international comments and, perhaps, the fact that the developing North American archival content standard, CUSTARD, will be based on the principles of multi-level description (SAA, 2002).

EAD is a tool designed to work with the data at the heart of the NAN. It is, therefore, used to some extent by a number of the strands of the NAN, including GASHE and NAHSTE as well as A2A and the Archives

Hub. Both the latter programmes use EAD throughout the process from data creation to online presentation, but do so in slightly different ways reflecting the different environments in which they work.

As noted, the Archives Hub has been mainly concerned with online access to collection-level descriptions of archives found in HE institutions. As these descriptions are generally newly created, it has been possible to provide contributors with the facility to create descriptions online using an ISAD(G)-based template (see www.archiveshub.ac.uk/template/new/eadform2.html). Descriptions are saved as EAD files in SGML. With A2A the process is different as the programme is mainly concerned with the retrospective conversion of existing multi-level catalogues. Contributors mark up paper catalogues to indicate levels and elements conformant to ISAD(G) (Flynn, Hillyard and Stockting, 2001, 184–5). Catalogues are re-keyed offshore using a standard EAD template and returned as EAD files in SGML. While each project's process may be different, EAD is being used to successfully capture the data in a standardized manner.

In both programmes EAD is also used as the editing environment for the files once created. Contributors to the Archives Hub can also edit their catalogues online and may have no need to interact with EAD. EAD is quite extensively used by HE repositories in the UK, however, and many have developed an EAD editing environment based on the use of SGML or XML text editors. (An example is the Modern Records Centre, University of Warwick at http://modernrecords.warwick.ac.uk/mrcead.shtml.) Many of the contributors to A2A by contrast have invested in proprietary archival management systems that include cataloguing modules. EAD is not, therefore, their editing environment of choice and they are not offered the option to edit A2A EAD catalogues online. The A2A central team undertakes such editing as is necessary using an SGML/XML text editor.

EAD files are the basis for the systems for online searching and presentation in both programmes. While there are again differences in execution, neither system is a traditional relational database system. The Archives Hub system is based on the Cheshire search engine, has XML as the database format and incorporates a client–server architecture based on the Z39.50 retrieval protocol (Watry, 2001). The A2A database is a customized proprietary XML document manager and search engine utilizing the HTTP protocol (Flynn, Hillyard and Stockting, 2001, 185–188). In both cases the structure in the EAD files, reflecting ISAD(G) compliant data, is that used as a basis for the construction of indexes for searching. For presentation, the EAD XML files of both systems are converted to HTML. The Archives Hub uses GRS-1 syntax for this transformation, while A2A uses a number of XSL stylesheets to present different views of the EAD files.

A2A and the Archives Hub illustrate the use of EAD as a key communication format for the transmission of standardized data from creation to users online. While most of the other contributors to the NAN have systems based on traditional relational databases, EAD can still have a role in data exchange. It is the favoured data format for the import of converted catalogues into contributors' proprietary cataloguing systems, which forms the final stage in the A2A process. These cataloguing systems also have the ability to export, as well as import, data as EAD. The same is true, for example, of PROCAT. In this area, however, the flexibility of EAD has proved to be a disadvantage. EAD offers encoders of finding aids many options, which means no two sets of EAD files will be the same. This hinders data exchange and has led to calls for EAD to be more prescriptive. In response to this, RLG's EAD Advisory Group has developed a set of *Best Practice Guidelines* for EAD designed with technical and user needs uppermost (RLG, 2002). Despite this disadvantage, the fact that use of EAD ensures compliance with e-GIF means that the Interoperability Protocol currently being developed (under the auspices of the National Council of Archives) will require that systems that are part of the NAN will have the ability to import and export data in EAD.

Pulling the strands together – a national archives portal?

While a great deal of progress has been made towards the achievement of this goal set by NCA's Archives On-line report since 1998, in one respect at least current services are lacking. Rather than there being one single gateway, users have seen a proliferation of online databases allowing them to search descriptive archival metadata.

This diversity is due to a number of factors. Different sectors within the UK archives community have different funding environments and it has made sense for each to secure funding for building of content and infrastructure as widely as possible. Different regulatory environments affect systems development and functionality. The need to work within the Public Records Acts, for example, has meant that PROCAT has data structures and functionality not needed by local archives repositories. User needs also differ and affect the scope of services offered.

While there are good reasons for the current diffuse character of the NAN, the question of how the various strands can be brought together has to be asked. Broadly, there seem to be two possible solutions to this question. First, given that most of the metadata in these systems conforms to ISAD(G), could it be brought together in one central server for users to search online? The problems with such an approach reflect the factors favouring diversity noted above. Such a system would require copious and sustained funding and currently no such funding opportunities exist. Repositories have invested heavily in systems that relate to their own needs and would not easily give these up. The provision of exported data to a central server would entail strict version control and regular updating. It is also questionable if any of the current systems would be scalable to the large volumes of data concerned. While users may find such a central service useful, many would also still want the tailored services currently offered by the individual strands of the NAN.

The second option is the distributed searching of the current systems. The leading technical solution for such cross searching is the Z39.50 protocol. While extensively used in bibliographic environments, use of this protocol for archives has been limited. An early test of the potential for the networking of archival metadata using the protocol was the National Networking Demonstrator Project (NNDP), funded by JISC (Sweetmore, 1998). A follow-up to this project is the Archives Hub, which as has been noted uses the protocol at the heart of its system (see above). While the current system is a federated system, development testing is currently taking place of a truly distributed system (Watry, 2001, 6). While the system is designed to link to the constituent repositories to enable them to manage their own data, it may have the potential to provide distributed searching for archives users. More recently there has been the development of another prototype portal, the Archives Network Gateway (ANG) at www.ang.org.uk/ang/index.jsp. This again uses the Z39.50 protocol to search across two strands of the NAN, A2A and the Archives Hub. Finally, the AIM25 project has addressed the potential of the protocol in a cross-domain context by making its database a Z39.50 target to enable cross-searching with library catalogues in the same region. While there are many complex issues relating to the distributed searching of the various databases making up the NAN, these projects illustrate two issues relating to the nature of descriptive archive metadata.

Central to the operation of the protocol is the mapping of the metadata in each system to an agreed profile and associated attributes sets and there has been no agreement about which to use. The developers for the NNDP project attempted to develop a profile for archives which included an 'Archives-1 Attribute Set' based on the Bib-1 attribute set (JISC, 1996). The Bib-1 attribute set is the main set used by the Archives Hub system although other sets based on it have been developed for the distributed system (Archives Hub, 2001). ANG also use attributes based on the Bib-1 set.

Second, there are serious questions about Z39.50's ability to search archival data across any more than a handful of databases and efficiently return results to users within an acceptable time frame. The NNDP report concluded that Z39.50 could successfully be used to cross-search distributed archival datasets and that 'doubts about scalability ... have, to an extent, subsided as a consequence' (Sweetmore, 1998, 4). Concerns have remained, however, and the other projects illustrate approaches designed to provide more targeted searching and, therefore, improved performance. The developers of the Archives Hub note that the broadcasting of search requests to all the servers in a network 'is highly inefficient and unlikely to scale to more than a few users' (Watry, 2001, 6.2). To overcome this problem they have used the Z39.50 SCAN and EXPLAIN services in the distributed search system to harvest key descriptive metadata as well as that relating to the servers themselves. A less dynamic solution has been adopted to deal with the multi-level catalogues making up A2A in the ANG. The EAD versions of these catalogues are in many cases very large: too large for the system to efficiently search and display the data in a timely manner. The original EAD files have been broken down into their component records at all levels. Given the importance of context, metadata about parent levels (title, reference and dates) is also brought into each record. It is these records that are then mounted for searching by ANG.

Cross-searching of the online databases of the various strands of the NAN seems then to offer the best route for the provision of a single gateway to information about the archival heritage of the UK. While the Z39.50 protocol may be the means to this end, we are still faced with issues relating to archival descriptive metadata, which reflect the nature of archives themselves.

Access metadata for archives
What is meant by access metadata in the archival context?

Access metadata in an archival context is the term used to describe those names or terms that searchers can use to gain access into an electronic archival catalogue. The term 'access point' originated in the library profession: it refers to those points of entry into a library catalogue. In the archival context the function of access metadata is to take the searcher to the descriptive metadata of the archival catalogue; the relationship between access metadata and descriptive metadata should be direct and concise. In the NAN these access terms are personal, place and corporate names and subject terms.

The UK archival community has developed its own standards for names and terms acting as access points, which have been available for six years (NCA, 1997). These standards ensure consistency by controlled vocabulary of access points in archival catalogues in the UK. As yet, this is not the case for subject terms, though a recent initiative will present nationally agreed subject terms for use in archival cataloguing in the very near future. In the online context, the advantages of standards for the access metadata of archival catalogues are clear: they bring internal consistency to an archive's catalogue; they facilitate the searching of, and access to, archival catalogues across networks on the internet; and put simply, they help people find things by affording interoperability of terminology (NCA, 1997, 1.2.2).

Archival standards for authority control

In the UK, recognition of the need for standards in this area of archival description led the NCA to look into the feasibility of establishing general rules in the 1990s, when the development of electronic archival catalogues was altering search procedures and needs beyond recognition. A need for separate standards for archives was identified, as there was a need to provide for archaic forms, name changes in the lifetime of an individual, place or corporate body, and for variant names in use over time. These provisions were not fully addressed by current bibliographic standards. All too aware of the advantages of international consistency, however, the NCA IT Committee, were keen to keep departures from AACR2 to a minimum (NCA, 1997, 1.5.1).

The *NCA Rules for the Construction of Personal, Place and Corporate Names* (1997) give general and specific guidance for the selection and format of names commonly used as archival access points. In the case of personal names, the rules define a surname and a forename, giving guidelines as to the inclusion of dates, titles, pre-titles and epithets. They cater specifically, for example, for a medieval name having no established form in English, for names having a patronymic or a toponym, for peerage titles, for women's names, and for royal and papal names. For the names of corporate bodies, natural language order is recommended, as are qualifications sufficient to identify each body, cross-references to conventional or alternative names, and the creation of a new name when a body changes its title. General high-level rules attempt to deal with place names from parish to country, with linguistic differences and Anglicization, with qualifiers necessary for identification, and with name and boundary changes. Throughout, the rules suggest cross-referencing to enable access by names in formats not consistent with the standard.

A standard for subject terms is taking a little longer to develop. The practice of subject indexing, and hence the selection of subject metadata, is relatively new to archivists in the UK. Unlike their counterparts in the library profession, postgraduate archival courses do not include subject indexing in depth as part of the syllabus. Paradoxically, subject searches are one of the most popular types of search enquiry in archives and record offices in the UK (Ashley, Craven and Garrod, 2002, fn.7). Given this, and the changing context in which the archivist now works, there has rarely been a time when subject indexing and subject metadata were of greater importance.

At present, not all archives in the UK have a subject index to their holdings. Archivists in many of those which have, have chosen to adopt the *UNESCO Thesaurus* (1995) or the *Library of Congress Subject Headings* (LCSH, 1997) or other established thesauri, but it is the case that in many record offices in the UK, subject indexes are local, provenance based and often in hard copy.

However, there will soon be a new possibility. The UK Archival Thesaurus project (UKAT) will make available a standard for the subject indexing of archival cataloguing for the first time in the UK. It will be based on the *UNESCO Thesaurus* (1995), but will take terms from other word lists and thesauri used in archival cataloguing. UKAT will be disseminated in two ways: as an online thesaurus available via a website, and, by making the data available to software suppliers, in cataloguing software. Archivists will be able to propose the addition of new terms, and a central editor will process those terms in a manner consistent with peer review and the hierarchical conventions of the *UNESCO Thesaurus* (1995). Terms will then be added on a nationally agreed basis and regular updates of the online UKAT will make added terms immediately available to users.

In the context of the NAN, the presence of UKAT will be extremely valuable in providing the basis of a nationally agreed standard for subject metadata. Additionally, in incorporating terms from subject thesauri and word lists used elsewhere, that nationally agreed standard will have an international dimension. For the first time, subject terms that summarize the content of archival material will be available, on a national basis, to enhance the usability of the archival material itself.

Archival authority records

In addition to access metadata in the sense of names and terms, some strands of the NAN have developed contextual data further: they have created archival authority records in line with the *International Standard Archival Authority Record for Corporate Bodies, Persons and Families (ISAAR (CPF))* (ICA, 1996). This recognizes that archival organizations might have different functions for authority records, and allows for differing information depending on that function. Overall, it requires that each record incorporate an authorized name, parallel names, non-preferred terms and related entries, in a standard format with an identity code which anticipated international data exchange and a declaration of type: person, corporate body or family. It allows other descriptive information to be included as is felt necessary depending on function. A note area allows for identification of the rules or conventions used in creating the record, comment by the archivist and the date of the record's creation.

The second version of ISAAR (CPF), is soon to be published. This much revised and streamlined standard now provides for four areas of description (ICA, 2002, 10):

- *Identity Area*: which identifies the person, corporate body or family and defines a standardized access point
- *Description Area*: allowing for description of the nature, context and activities of the person, corporate body or family
- *Relationships Area*: where relationships with other persons, corporate bodies or families may be described
- *Control Area*: allowing for unique identification and information on the creation and maintenance of the authority record.

Unlike its predecessor, this version indicates which elements are 'essential for international exchange of archival authority information' (ICA, 2002, 11).

The appearance of the second version of the ISAAR (CPF) at this time is most welcome, particularly in the context of the development of the NAN. The creation of National Name Authority Files (NNAFs) along the lines of ISAAR (CPF) has been anticipated by the NCA Rules (1997, 1.3.3) and it seems likely that steps toward the creation of such will be made in due course. NNAFs presented in Encoded Archival Context (EAC) in XML may complement ISAD(G)-compliant archival descriptions in EAD in the network as a whole. In this, they would prove extremely valuable both in supporting a new level of archival consistency and in making the authority records from archives and record offices in the UK available to an international audience of archivists and users. NNAFs based on the second version of the ISAAR (CPF) would support interoperability between the strands of the NAN and invite further national and international development.

The draft of the second version of ISAAR (CPF) also stresses the importance of context to the creation of archival authority records, and provides for the linking of authority records where the archival documents of one creator are held by more than one repository either nationally or internationally. This is a departure from the shared function of bibliographic and archival authority records suggested in Version 1 of the standard, and indeed, the second version clarifies the differences between archival and bibliographical authority records. Where it is the case that:

> Archival authority records are similar to library authority records in as much as both forms of authority record need to support the creation of standardized access points in descriptions. ... Archival authority records ... need to support a much wider set of requirements than is the case with library authority records. These additional requirements are associated with the importance of documenting information about records creators and the context of records creation in archival descriptions and control systems. As such, archival authority records go much further and will usually contain much more information than library authority records.

The standard aims to enable 'access to archives and records based on the provision of descriptions of the context of records creation that are linked to the descriptions of the often dispersed and physically dispersed records themselves'. ISAAR (CPF)'s compilers hope to enhance users' understanding of these differing needs, and the standard itself serves to facilitate 'the exchange of these descriptions between institutions, systems and/or networks' (NCA, 2000, 11).

It may be a matter of debate as to whether or not archival authority records constitute metadata: are they data about data or a reference source in themselves? It doesn't really matter. Archival authority records will be available to the searcher for archival information who sees them as a way to gain access to descriptive metadata, as they will be to the searcher for reference sources, who sees them as information about particular individuals or corporate bodies.

A question of level – 2: the selection of access points

The format, content and authority control for all types of access metadata in UK archives is therefore complete: all the archivist has to do is select. But what and where? The issues of selection and level are not as easy to address as they might seem, and there are no national guidelines for either.

Naturally the creators of documents are to be selected as access metadata on the grounds of provenance: 'the relationship between records and the organizations or individuals that created, accumulated or maintained them in the conduct of personal or corporate activity' (ICA, 2000, 11), but who else? Importance or significance to the process of creation may be the criterion for selection, and a British Standard gives advice on the selection of subject terms, which summarize the documents being considered, or which are relevant to the most significant concepts (BS 2733:1985).

Muddying the water further here is the prickly issue of the multi-level nature of descriptive archival data. Here though, decisions about the level at which access can be made, and at which access metadata can be selected from the text of the archival description, may determine the kind of term to be selected. In the context of subject terms, for example, the higher the archival level, the more general the term and the greater need for that term to reflect a general relevance to the majority of the documents at and below that level. However, in selecting a general term, the archivist is losing specificity, and the user wants the specific rather than general.

The question of level of access has up to now remained one dealt with on an individual repository or collection basis. In the context of the NAN it presents quite a challenge.

Examples from the UK National Archives

How then has access metadata been used in the National Archives of the UK? In both PROCAT and A2A, we subscribe to the *NCA Rules* (1997) to *ISAAR (CPF)* (ICA, 1996) and to the *UNESCO Thesaurus* (1995). The access metadata terms are the creators of archival records, immediate sources of acquisition of those records, and the names of places of deposit of those records, together with those terms selected by the archivist as being highly significant to the process of creation, or which summarize the content of the records.

Access metadata in PROCAT is available via an Index Browser which presents the user with an alphabetical list of all the access terms. An example based on a search for the term 'Churchill' can be seen in Figure 6.1. The user has access from the index term to the authority record for that term, which enables identification as shown in Figure 6.2: 'which Churchill?' 'Yes that one!'. A further click takes the searcher to the relevant descriptive metadata that describes the records about or created by Churchill, which are held in the UK National Archives. PROCAT has also created authority records for places and subjects. Though there is no national or international standard for these records, we have followed the content guidelines of the *NCA Rules* (1997) for place name records

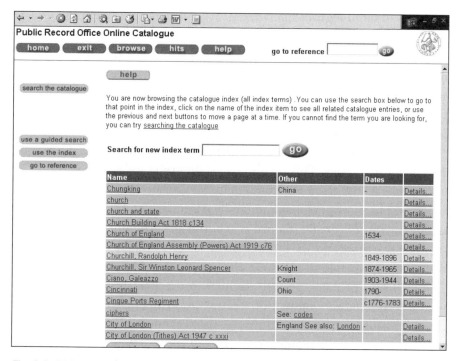

Fig. 6.1 *PROCAT: Search for 'Churchill'*

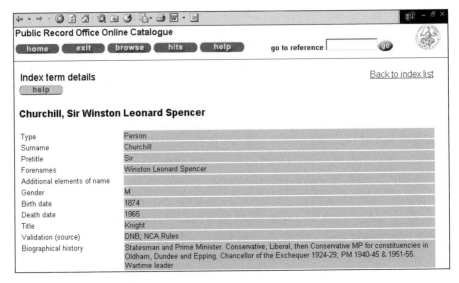

Fig. 6.2 *PROCAT: Archival authority record for Churchill*

and the standard constituents of a subject thesaurus for subject records as can be seen in Figures 6.3 and 6.4. We felt they could help the user in the same way as records for persons, corporate bodies and families.

Before the development of UKAT seemed likely, a number of repositories keen to develop a national consistency of archival terms made their own added terms available to other archivists and members of the public. These included the UK National Archives as well as the AIM25 project, for example.

Of the 17,000 authority records currently in PROCAT, over 13,000 are for corporate bodies. This is contrary to the trend for archives in the UK as a whole, as reflected for example in A2A, where a greater percentage of access points of personal and family names are found. This difference is due to the particular nature of central government and its departmental structure, and we found it necessary to embellish the minimum conformity principle of the *NCA Rules* with regard to corporate bodies. The inclusion of dates proved essential in the British government context where a large number of central government departments may change names frequently and may re-use a name within a short period of time. Here, dates alone enable identification. While dates are suggested as useful to contributors of name access points to A2A, they have not been made compulsory because of the large amount of extra work

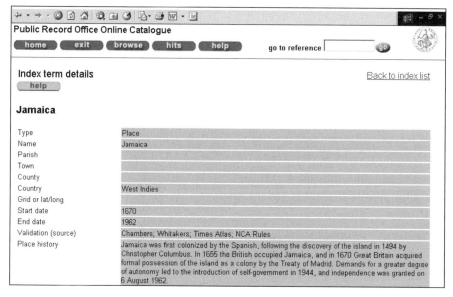

Fig. 6.3 *PROCAT: Archival authority record for Jamaica*

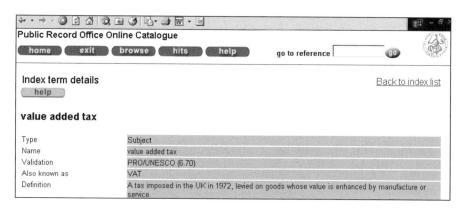

Fig.6.4 *PROCAT: Archival authority record for value added tax*

this would impose in a programme focused mainly on the retroconversion of existing data.

In PROCAT, terms not in standard format, acronyms and conventional names which we know will be used to gain access to the catalogue, are added to the browser as non-preferred terms and are linked by a 'see' reference to the relevant terms. The aim here is to give access to as wide an international audience as possible. As to the appropriateness of the terms themselves, a User Advisory Group comments on the use of language in the catalogue and the terminology used in access points.

In PROCAT, the creator can be at any level, though it is likely to be at series level or above. Other access point terms may be selected from any level to appear as access metadata, though there has been a tendency to focus around series level. This was thought appropriate because series level is where the general functions of a department and the specific functions of a record series come together, and it has been assumed in archival practice that an access point term at series level is indicative of the relevance of all archival levels below, to the subject of the access point.

In A2A a 'Special Interest Search' takes users from the name or term to relevant descriptive metadata. Archival authority records have not been created in A2A, as this would largely be a duplication of the data already found in the NRA. Given the national scope of the A2A database, creator and index terms are mainly found at *fonds* level rather than at series or below and are, therefore, even less specific than in PROCAT. While guidelines and training are given to the repositories contributing catalogues, it has not been possible to have the control over selection of terms possible in a single repository. The result has been inconsistency in selection of terms, which may have a negative impact on the effectiveness of the 'Special Interest Search' for the user.

The differences in the two databases of the UK National Archives indicate the challenge faced in the provision of searching by access metadata as we begin the development of interoperability between these and all the other strands of the NAN.

What's the advantage of all this to the user?

A rough estimate puts the collective resource of the National Archival Network at 100 million records. All contributors have finished or are in the process of creating and presenting archival access metadata. The growth of metadata schema for archives and the related field of electronic records management indicates that metadata is of primary significance in giving the user access to information about archives. The burgeoning number of archival websites (public, higher education and commercial) testify that much information about archives is being presented to the user; and the meteoric rise in users seen in website statistics testify that searchers are using that access metadata. Recent developments indicate there will soon be much more in the government context and in terms of international and cross-sectoral initiatives.

Access metadata terms from UK government archives will soon be made available to government departments through a Government Secure Intranet (GSI). Additionally, recent work undertaken by the Office of the e-Envoy's Metadata Working Party and Thesaurus Sub-Group to provide the UK citizen with online information about the functions which government departments perform and the information they can supply has taken information about the subject access metadata used in PRO-CAT. In the records management context, newly issued guidelines for the access metadata to be provided by the electronic records management systems of government departments accord with e-GIF and with the development regarding subject terms (PRO, 2002). All three initiatives indicate that access metadata in UK government archives will become of greater, not lesser, significance to the UK government in the near future.

The High Level Thesaurus project (HILT) at the University of Strathclyde aims to make possible searching by subject term across a variety of disciplines and sectors. It aims to do so by means of a 'terminologies route map', which will take Dewey Decimal Classification as its spine (Nicholson, 2002). The UKAT project will provide a regular contribution from the archives community, having agreed to supply HILT with terms added to the *UNESCO Thesaurus*.

In the context of archival metadata as a whole then, the user is getting a great deal of data, and is set to get much more. But is this what they want? And what might this mean for the NAN?

In 1998, the Montague Institute for Librarians asked its online readers 'Why is access metadata a hot topic?' and answered 'Because people need better ways to find and evaluate information on the internet'. Is this what archival metadata does? Does it help people find and evaluate information on the internet?

Searchers are introduced to access metadata by and large when they have got into the archival domain that is integrated into the archival network. There are some terms available on the internet about archive resources in the UK, but most are available when the searcher has arrived at the archival catalogue. It might be argued, therefore, that users are being limited at the outset. Should all authority terms be available directly on the internet? When the searcher has got to the NAN, do the terms presented make it easier to find things? Do they take the searcher to the descriptive metadata of the archival catalogue? Is the relationship with descriptive metadata direct and concise?

All we can really say at this stage is that we think so. We know much about our numbers of users, how often they use the sites, their preferences and their ages; but not much at all about how they use archival resources. The NANURG survey (NCA and NANURG, 2002) told us, perhaps surprisingly, that archival networks in the UK are attracting many previous non-users of archives. Recent surveys of electronic resources carried out at the UK National Archives indicate that the typical UK user of archives is interested in family or military history, is as likely to be male as female, and is probably over 45. In the UK as yet, it remains the case that we have relatively little hard evidence about user strategies.

Recent studies of academics and undergraduates in the USA and UK indicate that academics are not impressed by any cross-linking and cross-referencing of archival sources that may be presented to them. 'If you are interested in this, then try this!' doesn't seem to go down well with people who still rely on word-of-mouth recommendation of other sources and actual discussions with students and fellow academics (Anderson, 2003). The needs of students, on the other hand, are quite different from those of scholars or librarians (and dare we say archivists?) with regard, for example, to the precise terminology and the language of library classification. Students are confused by these terms. While not many archivists in the UK use systems of library classification, they do use archive-speak, be it in terms of 'class' or 'series' or the more arcane 'verso', 'recto' and 'rot'. Ninety-one percent of students felt that high quality and accurate information sources were very important, but only 51% felt that available electronic information sources were meeting that need (RLG, 2003, 4–5).

In a context both international and historical, perhaps we have been too keen to compensate for the use of variant English globally with the use of non-preferred access terms, for example railways and railroad (same meaning); typography and typography (different meaning), and to explain the use of medieval Latin in Exchequer records ('annates' cross-referenced with 'first fruits'), and not sufficiently aware of the problems caused by archive-ese. Why do we keep 'rot' anyway?

How else do users search then? Responses to the PROCAT 'usability' survey indicated that free-text searching remains the most popular with all users regardless of ongoing improvements to access metadata. The majority of in-house users, when asked how the online catalogue service could be improved, emphasized the need for fuller and more accurate catalogue descriptions.

Those who used the access metadata searches were content with them, but wanted more access metadata at more levels. We can only conclude here that while the current selection and location of access metadata may be intellectually satisfying to the archivist, and sound to archival principles, the users (being generally unfamiliar with the principles of archival practice, and feeling no compunction as to their observation) remain free to suggest otherwise. In any case, index terms at *fonds* or series level appear to be insufficiently specific to merit a user's concern. Users' comments are changing our policy on access metadata in the UK National Archives. In the context of the NAN this is an issue to be noted.

In terms of the NAN, all this tells us that we have a great deal of work to do. We have, or are in the process of developing, national and international standards for the creation of archival access metadata, but we need to know a great deal more about our users' search strategies before we can be sure that we are helping people who need 'better ways of finding and evaluating information on the internet'.

Conclusion

Since the arrival of the internet in the mid-1990s, a great deal of work has been done by UK archivists in resolving issues relating to the key metadata about their holdings with the aim of providing easy and comprehensive online access to users. We have agreement on international and national standards for content and data exchange and have developed frameworks for dealing with issues such as how to present legacy data and the appropriate depth for new cataloguing and indexing. This has enabled the development of a number of complementary online services offering access to information about archives. With the goal of a single integrated portal in mind, however, the metadata issues resulting from the particular nature of archives and the need to convey contextual information are still apparent. Practically, many of the answers may be technical in nature but more importantly, perhaps we need to be guided to a greater extent than hitherto by what our users actually want.

References

Access to Archives (A2A) (1999) *Cataloguing Standards for A2A*, www.pro.gov.uk/archives/a2a/cataloguingstandards.htm.

Anderson, I. (2003) *Information Seeking Behaviours in the Digital Age: historians in the United Kingdom*, a Powerpoint presentation of initial results from the Primary History project at the Humanities Advanced Technology and Information Institute (HATII), University of Glasgow, www.hatii.arts.gla.ac.uk/research/historians/primarily_history.htm.

Archives Hub (2001) *Distributed Archives Hub*, http://gondolin.hist.liv.ac.uk/~cheshire/distrib/.

Ashley, K., Craven, L. and Garrod, P. (2002) *UKAT, The Case for Subject Indexing in Archives* (document in support), fn.7.

BS 2733: 1985 *Guide to the Examination of Documents and the Selection of Terms*, London, British Standards Institute.

Collis, P. (2003) *Archives Hub Online Template: Data Creation Guidelines*, www.archiveshub.ac.uk/BIG4.pdf.

Cultural Heritage Consortium (CHC) (2002) *Full Disclosure Prioritization Study: Final Report*, www.bl.uk/concord/fulldisc-prior.html.

Dunham, S., Geddes, J. and Thomas, D. (1999) The Retrospective Conversion of the Public Record Office's Catalogues, *Journal of the Society of Archivists*, **20** (2), 223–30.

Encoded Archival Description (EAD) (1999) *Application Guidelines for Version 1.0*, Society of American Archivists and Library of Congress, www.loc.gov/ead/ag/aghome.html.

Encoded Archival Description (EAD) (2002) *Encoded Archival Description Tag Library Version 2002*, Society of American Archivists and Library of Congress, www.loc.gov/ead/tglib/index.html.

Flynn, S. J. A., Hillyard, M. and Stockting, W. (2001) A2A: the development of a strand in the UK National Archives Network, *Journal of the Society of Archivists*, **22** (2), 177–91.

Heaney, M. (2000) *An Analytical Model of Collections and their Catalogues*, UK Office for Library and Information Networking, www.ukoln.ac.uk/metadata/rslp/model/.

International Council of Archives (ICA) (1996) *International Standard Archival Authority Record for Corporate Bodies, Persons and Families (ISAAR (CPF))*, Ottawa, ICA.

International Council of Archives (ICA) (2000) *General International Standard for Archival Description (ISAD(G))*, 2nd edn, Ottawa, ICA.

International Council of Archives (ICA) (2002) *International Standard Archival Authority Record for Corporate Bodies, Persons and Families (ISAAR (CPF))*, draft 2nd edn. Exposure draft, www.hmc.gov.uk/icacds/eng/standardsISAAR2.htm.

International Council of Archives (ICA), Committee on Descriptive Standards (CDS) (2002) *Report of the Sub-committee on Finding Aids, Guidelines for the Preparation and Presentation of Finding Aids*, www.hmc.gov.uk/icacds/eng/findingaids.htm.

JISC (1996) *Z39.50 for Archival Applications: scoping and draft specification document 1996: Fretwell-Downing Informatics*, www.kcl.ac.uk/projects/srch/reports/z3950.htm.

Johnson, P. (2001) An Introduction to Collection-Level Description, Information Paper from the NOF Technical Advisory Service, www.ukoln.ac.uk/nof/support/help/papers/cldintro.htm.

Library of Congress (1997) *Library of Congress Subject Headings (LCSH)*, 20th edn, Washingron, DC, Library of Congress.

Mining the Catalogue (2003) *RLG News*, **56** (Spring), 4–5.

National Council on Archives (NCA) (1997) *Rules for the Construction of Personal, Place and Corporate Names*, www.hmc.gov.uk/nca/title.htm.

National Council on Archives (NCA) (1998) *Archives On-line*, nca.archives.org.uk/online01.htm.

National Council on Archives (NCA) (2000) *British Archives, The Way Forward*, nca.archives.org.uk/brarchs.htm.

National Council on Archives (NCA) and National Archives Network User Research Group (NANURG) (2002) *User Evaluation: report of findings*, www.resource.gov.uk/information/research/respubs2002.asp#nanurg.

Nicholson, D. (2002) *HILT: High Level Thesaurus Project. Final report to RSLP and JISC*,
http://hilt.cdlr.strath.ac.uk/Reports/Documents/HLTfinalreport.doc.

Office of the e-Envoy (2003) *e-Government Interoperability Framework Part One: Framework*, Version 5.0,
www.govtalk.gov.uk/schemasstandards/egif_document.asp?docnum=732.

Powell, A. (ed.) (1999) Collection Level Description: a review of existing practice. An eLib supporting study, UKOLN,
www.ukoln.ac.uk/metadata/cld/study/.

Proctor, M. and Cook, M. (2000) *Manual of Archival Description*, London, Gower.

Public Record Office (2002) *Requirements for Electronic Records Management Systems. 2: Metadata Standard*, www.pro.gov.uk/recordsmanagement/erecords/2002reqs/2002metadatafinal.pdf.

RLG (2003) *RedLightGreen Project: Mining the Catalog*,
www.rlg.org/redlightgreen/mining.html.

RLG EAD Advisory Group (2002) *RLG Best Practice Guidelines for Encoded Archival Description*, www.rlg.org/primary/eadac.html.

Society of American Archivists (SAA) (2002) *Statement of Principles for the CUSTARD Project*, www.archivists.org/news/custardproject.asp.

Stockting, W. (2002) *A2A – Guidelines for Collection Level Description*,
www.pro.gov.uk/archives/a2a/standards.htm.

Sweetmore, K. (1998) *National Networking Demonstrator for Archives*,
www.kcl.ac.uk/projects/srch/reports/ksfinhtmldoc.html.

UNESCO (1995), *UNESCO Thesaurus: a structured list of the descriptors for indexing and retrieving literature in the fields of education, science, social and human science, culture, communication and information*, Paris, UNESCO.

Watry, P. (2001) *Archives Hub System Specification and Architecture*,
sca.lib.liv.ac.uk/cheshire/hubarchitecture3.html.

Part 4

METADATA IN EDUCATION

7

Metadata and the education sector

Stuart A. Sutton

Introduction

The Semantic Web in the domain of education and training will be largely driven by metadata – data about data – of various forms. Even a cursory look at US and international activities such as those of the IEEE Learning Technologies Standards Committee (http://ltsc.ieee.org/), the Schools Interoperability Framework at www.sifinfo.org, and the work of IMS Global Learning Consortium (www.imsproject.org), to name but a few of the major players, reveals that metadata (broadly defined) is the spine upon which the remaining architecture shaping digitally enabled education through the remainder of this century will be built. Metadata permeates every aspect of these challenging initiatives in the form of descriptions of entities of every sort from the attributes of students in the form of the proverbial transcript writ large through the digital resources by which we will teach and learn (treated in a manner that may permit snapping them together like Lego®) to managing transportation schedules and the cafeteria.

In order to keep the problem this chapter addresses tractable, we will look at only a small slice of the domain of metadata in education and training. We will focus sharply on metadata as it relates to educational resources necessary to the teaching and learning enterprise. Even with such a restriction of the domain, the landscape is still vast. Therefore, we will limit our discussion to the processes of resource discovery. Thus we eliminate from consideration metadata (and accompanying issues) surrounding the packaging of resources for delivery and use by learning systems of all sorts. Instead, the chapter will focus on those metadata for describing aspects of educational resources that make them different from metadata describing any other types of digitally available resources. The base premise of the discussion is that while educational resources share common attributes with all other digitally available entities, they also possess attributes that are either unique to, or are in need of unique treatment in, the domain of education and training.

The chapter begins by defining a set of core terms used throughout the text. Definitions are followed by a general discussion of the categories of metadata (or categories of attributes) necessary for various functions in resource discovery, and, to a certain degree, to the use of those resources as teaching and learning instruments. We then focus sharply on those metadata issues that we think are unique to the domain of education and training. Having framed a set of issues regarding the attributes of educational resources that render them somewhat unique, we describe in broad terms the technical architecture necessary to effective metadata generation, deployment and use.

Definitions

As with all areas of discourse in their early stages, domain terms used to describe entities and processes in the generation and use of metadata in the education domain lack consensual definitions and are immensely 'fuzzy' around the edges. This fuzziness frequently leads either to hot debate over meaning or to misunderstanding stemming from assumptions of congruence of meaning where none actually exists. So, the following are the author's definitions. It is not important that the informed reader agree in some universal sense with these definitions if, in fact, we can agree on how the terms are being used in this text. We ask the reader to be more attentive to the semantics – the substance of the definitions – and less attentive to the labels or terms attached to those semantics. In essence, the labels or terms are not significant so long as we operate from consensual meanings.

Educational resource. An educational resource is the principal entity of concern to this chapter. It is any entity that was either purposed for use within an education or training context at the point of creation or was subsequently repurposed for such use. At a minimum, contextualization in this domain takes the form of: (1) identifiable (although not necessarily explicitly stated) learning objectives (i.e. objectives expressing desired or necessary shifts in the cognitive state of the learner through interaction with the resource), and (2) the learning-significant attributes of the learner (i.e. audience characteristics). To avoid repeating the phrase 'educational resources' throughout, we shall simply refer to all of them as 'entities'.

Learning object. In this chapter, we use the term 'learning object' in the sense in which it is used in object-oriented programming. In addition to having an overarching and purposeful objective of supporting one or more processes of learning (thus its characterization as a *learning* object), a learning object is a self-enabled (and usually immutable) entity that consists of both information (i.e. content) and one or more built-in procedures (routines or functions) that operate on that content or manage content brought into the object's ambit in some manner from the outside – e.g. through input from the learner. A learning object is one form of educational resource.

Educationally purposed resources. This category of educational resource denotes: (1) resources educationally purposed at creation, and (2) resources educationally purposed at some point after the creation of the resource.

Metadata as language

It is useful to think of instances of metadata as statements about some attribute of an entity. Thus, we might make the following statement about this text: 'Stuart Sutton is the author of this chapter.' In essence, we are saying that some resource (i.e. this chapter) has an author attribute to which we can assign the value 'Stuart Sutton'. In the end, all metadata (simple or complex) can be thought of as some form of attribute/value pair. As metadata, we usually recast statements such as these in terms of some relatively simple formalism such as: 'Author=Stuart Sutton'. We may go further and syntactically bind the statement in XML (or some other machine-readable binding) in the manner of '<author>Stuart Sutton</author>'.

When we speak of metadata, we are generally talking about a pre-determined, bounded set of statements about the attributes of an entity that some metadata architect has decided will be useful for a prescribed set of purposes – e.g. retrieval of the entity, its management or use. This bounded set of statements is referred to in the metadata community as an element set or a schema. Like all languages, these metadata statements about entities have a grammatical structure – some simple (witness the Dublin Core Metadata Element Set (DCMES) schema) and some complex (witness the IEEE Learning Object Metadata (LOM) schema).

Categories of educational metadata

Gilliland-Swetland (2000) asserts that all entities, regardless of form, have three basic classes of attributes – content, context and structure – all of which find expression in metadata statements. Gilliland-Swetland defines each of these classes in the following language:

- *Content* relates to what the object contains or is about, and is *intrinsic* to an information object.
- *Context* indicates the who, what, why, where, how aspects associated with the object's creation and is *extrinsic* to an information object.
- *Structure* relates to the formal set of associations within or among individual information objects and can be *intrinsic* or *extrinsic*.

We assert that the entities of concern to us here cannot be distinguished from non-educational entities in terms of unique properties that would fall into Gilliland-Swetland's first class of attributes (content). Thus, to the extent that any entity is 'about' something, or contains certain matter that must be described for purposes of identification, educational entities present no unique metadata issues. In similar fashion, the third class of attributes (structure) presents no particularly unique issues when educational resources are viewed as individual entities. Where educational entities present relatively unique issues to metadata architects rests with Gilliland-Swetland's second class of attributes – the context of the entity. For the purposes of this chapter, however, we must extend Gilliland-Swetland's second class of attributes to include matters of 'who, what, where, and how' that are both intrinsic and extrinsic.

Elsewhere we defined the nature of these contextual attributes for educational entities as being threefold (Sutton, 2003):

> Statement classes more-or-less fundamental to metadata for an educational resource include the following: (1) attributes of the explicit or implicit audience for which the resource is intended or useful (i.e. the *audience* attribute); (2) attributes of the resource that address the learning objectives or competencies to be achieved by means of the resource (i.e. the *standards* attribute); and (3) attributes of the explicit or implicit processes by which those learning objectives are achieved (i.e. the *pedagogy* attribute). While the first of these broad classes (audience) is not a characteristic unique to educational resources, we posit that the second and third classes are unique to resources in this domain. Thus, any resource that contains an explicit or implicit learning objective and, optionally, one or more mechanisms for measuring the degree to which that learning objective has been attained is an educational resource within our meaning.

In the following pages of this chapter, we will dwell momentarily on Sutton's audience and pedagogy classes of attributes and then focus more sharply on the standards attribute.

Pedagogy attributes

Pedagogy may be defined as 'the act, process or art of imparting knowledge and skill' (Editors of the AHD, 1995). The *Thesaurus of ERIC Descriptors* (Houston, 2002) simply defines pedagogy as 'instruction' and goes on to define instruction as the 'Process by which knowledge, attitudes, or skills are deliberately conveyed [and] includes the total instructional process, from planning and implementation through evaluation and feedback'. Thus, 'Any metadata statements about the teaching and learning processes that an educational resource explicitly or implicitly supports or requires can be characterized as pedagogical statements' (Sutton, 2003).

Audience attributes

Inherent in any assertion that an education resource is useful for some education or training purpose is the assumption that there is a particular audience that will either assist others in the attainment of the entity's purpose or that the entity will do so without assistance. This implies that the potential audience for any particular entity is of two sorts: (1) *beneficiaries*, those for whom the achievement of the purpose represents a change in a state of understanding, and (2) *mediators*, those who on occasion stand as intermediaries between the beneficiaries and the actual entity or its contents.

The audience class of attributes is rich and complex. Table 7.1 illustrates a non-exhaustive set of attribute classes for the audience of an entity.

Table 7.1 *Attribute classes for an audience*

Audience Characteristics	Description
Achievement Level	Student achievement in terms of some recognized education sector or particular point in such a sector (e.g. specific grade level or an educational sector
Student Aptitude	Level of student aptitude or attainment (e.g. gifted students)
Cultural or Linguistic Group	Membership of the learners in some cultural or linguistic group (e.g. Torres Strait islanders)
Physical/Emotional Disabilities	Physical and/or emotional disabilities of the learner (e.g. visually impaired students)
Linguistic Abilities	Learner's linguistic abilities (e.g. a second language resource)
Gender	Gender of the learner
Chronological Age	Learner's chronological age
Professional/Occupational Status	Professional or occupational status of the learner or intermediary (e.g. apprentice plumber)

'Standards' attributes

It is inherent in the definition of educational resources that such resources have been 'purposed' to achieve some learning goal. Thus, we eliminate from consideration those entities that are merely 'informing' in some way or that might support achieving some learning goal if purposed to do so – or, to phrase it in terms of Gilliland-Swetland's typology, an educational resource is an entity that has been educationally contextualized.

As noted earlier, we extend Gilliland-Swetland's definition of context by noting that the learning objectives that contextualize an educational entity may be characterized as either intrinsic or extrinsic. We characterize intrinsic objectives as those educational goals set by the resource that have no formal external imprimatur of approval. Thus, a learning objective for a particular resource might be for the learner to master braiding twine in the form of macramé. Such an objective may or may not be associated with any formally recognized statement of competence. In contrast, extrinsic objectives represent clearly defined statements or illustrations of what learners are expected to know and be able to do. Usually (but not always), these statements have been promulgated by a government agency or some scholarly or professional organization. While different labels may be attached to these external objectives (e.g. academic standards, frameworks, benchmarks, etc.), they all represent some recognized body's definition of competencies that well educated (or well trained) learners should attain. We shall refer to these external objectives throughout as content standards or CS.

Recent reform efforts in primary and secondary education in the USA such as the federal No Child Left Behind Act (US Department of Education, 2002) have led to the development of CS nationwide. Several of the alleged goals of CS are to provide uniformity and accountability in such education. By identifying what information and concepts are important to students, teachers and parents, content standards are designed to provide clear expectations for learning. We err if we permit our likes and dislikes about measuring student achievement by means of such prescribed academic goals to discolour the fact that good educational resources are created with clear learning objectives in mind and that the systematic articulation of those goals supports teachers and students.

Academic content standards as language

An analogy can be drawn between the evolution of living human languages and the statements of academic standards expressing a society's educational goals. Languages embodying the communicative norms of a culture change over time. Those changes reflect the gradual (and, on rare occasions, disjoint) evolution of their associated cultures and not a purposeful movement toward some absolute state of perfection. In like fashion, a culture's communal statements about the academic goals of its educational system constitute a living sub-language of that culture – i.e. a sub-language expressing what is knowable, or, to be more precise, what 'should be known' as a result of the interaction of the learner with the educational system. Just as cultures' languages live and evolve as the cultures evolve, so their sub-languages expressing what should be known live and evolve. However, in the problem domain addressed in this chapter, the forms of sub-language expression are manifold and take the form of national, state, local and organizational academic standards. They form a rich, complex, intertwined tapestry of what we will refer to here as jurisdictionally based statements of academic goals that are codified into jurisdictionally based academic standards.

Aligning disparate content standards

It is clear that the level of investment in time and expertise necessary to create metadata correlating educational resources to academic standards precludes one-to-many correlations – i.e. precludes the correlating of one resource to many standards. If the goal is to be able to discover and retrieve educational resources that share common learning objectives even though correlated to disparate standards, then one (or both) of two infrastructure mechanisms must be in place. Semantic relationships among various standards may be achieved either: (1) through the traditional mechanism of a vocabulary cross-walk – i.e. a many-to-many semantic alignment, or (2) a many-to-one semantic correlation of resources to some form of intermediary, reference or 'switching' statements embodying the common semantics of the many standards that form the domain of concern.

A human cross-walk mechanism is a massive, and perhaps largely intractable activity given the large (and growing) number of standards and the fact that each of them is a more-or-less living, dynamic aggregation of statements about learning objectives. Figure 7.1 illustrates the

problem of creating semantic many-to-many cross-walks among promulgated content standards.

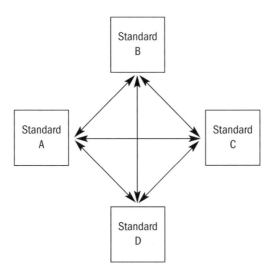

Fig. 7.1 *Academic standards cross-walk*

So, the target content standards to be cross-walked are moving (and
increasingly numerous) targets presenting a maintenance problem that
cannot scale to manage correlations of millions of resources to potentially thousands of such standards.

While the second mechanism – creation of intermediary or reference
statements (i.e. creation of a set of meta- or pseudo-standards) – achieves
a result similar to the first mechanism, it does so in a more efficient, economical manner. Figure 7.2 illustrates this many-to-one alignment process.

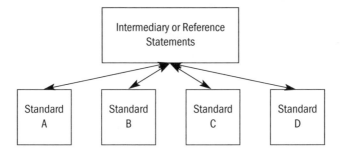

Fig. 7.2 *Academic standards intermediary statements correlation*

The creation of the intermediary statements supporting such efficiency and economy are currently achieved only through the human distillation of the associative semantics among the various standards that make up the domain of concern. Thus, individual standards must be used to both derive the reference statements and then be individually aligned to those statements by a knowledge expert. As the various standards of the target domain evolve, so must the distilled reference statements and their associated alignments. As a result, even though the alignment-to-reference-statement mechanism is more efficient and economical than the many-to-many cross-walk, the scale and dynamic nature of the standards domain may result in nearly as intractable a problem for both mechanisms – intractable, that is, where the alignment activity must be carried out by human experts. However, advances in natural language processing and machine learning promise to make the problem tractable using either or both mechanisms in a manner that will automatically support the generation of the various standards associations and the evolution of those associations over time.

Correlating educational resources to standards

Given the two mechanisms for generation of a knowledge base of standards associations described above, there are three forms of alignment methods that may be employed in correlating an actual educational resource to that knowledge base (JES & Co., 2003). Table 7.2 summarizes these methods, defined below:

Table 7.2 Standards alignment methods

Type	Input	Output
Direct	State or nationally recognized standard or benchmark	The same state or nationally recognized standard or benchmark
Indirect/Forward	Intermediary or reference statement	One or more state or nationally recognized standards or benchmarks
Indirect/Reverse	State or nationally recognized benchmark	One or more different state or nationally recognized standards or benchmarks

Direct. An individual resource is aligned to a specific, 'official' set of standards (a state, national or local set of academic standards) by a subject matter expert or other process (e.g. by NLP processes) designed to provide specific authoritative alignments.

Indirect/Forward. A resource is directly aligned to an intermediary or reference statement which is, therefore, logically linked functionally, symbolically or semantically to the various 'official' CS by a subject matter expert or other process (e.g. by NLP processes). Figure 7.3 illustrates how various semantically equivalent standards have been aligned through mapping to intermediary or reference statements.

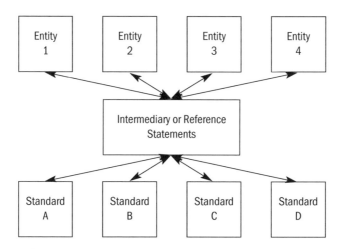

Fig. 7.3 *Correlating resources to intermediary and machine 'cross-walk'*

Similarly, various educational resources at the top of the figure have been mapped to the statements as well. These mappings make it possible for individual standards through a single mapping to be linked with disparate resources and, through the logical connections inherent in the mappings to be aligned with other standards.

Indirect/Reverse. An individual resource is aligned to a specific, official state, national or local set of academic standards) by a subject matter expert or other process (e.g. by NLP processes). A look-up is performed to an intermediary or reference statement which is then used to infer logical alignments to various official standards.

Since the working environment in the education domain will include educational resources and services that rely on all three forms of correlation noted above, an automatically generated, and dynamically maintained, knowledge base (with related communications schemas and protocols) will be needed to ultimately meet resource and discovery goals.

Academic Standards Network Architecture (ASNA)

The technical services outlined here might well form an Academic Standards Network Architecture (ASNA) needed to achieve the goals described in the previous section. Figure 7.4 illustrates the three services that make up the proposed ASNA architecture: (1) repository services, (2) alignment services, and (3) network communication protocols and schemas. In the following paragraphs, we will describe each of these three service components.

As illustrated simply in this figure, the Protocols and Schemas services layer provides the mechanisms that allow a set of agents – metadata gen-

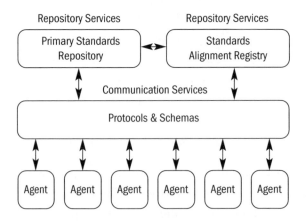

Fig. 7.4 *Academic Standards Network Architecture*

eration and search tools and services – to communicate in a standard way with registries and repositories. The arrows in the figure represent those communications. Thus agents may communicate with one or more repositories of state, national and organizational content standards (Repository Services) and/or with one or more services that align standards in the repositories with one to another.

Repository services

Education resource providers in the USA, such as publishers and content aggregators, have responded to the call to correlate their educational objects to content standards, but the manner in which the information is made available to the end-user is problematic. Both resource providers and resource consumers struggle with implementations that have high learning curves, limited (or no) access and no interoperability. Similarly, colleges and universities, foundations, professional organizations and content providers are conducting research to understand the relationship of standards to teacher effectiveness and, ultimately, student outcomes. Each organization typically collects and develops its own version of state and national standards at considerable duplication of cost and human resources.

This class of information is ideally suited for incorporation within available metadata tools and services. A significant barrier to use of the available elements for academic standards or benchmarks within applications using the metadata schemas of Dublin Core, GEM, IEEE LOM and MARC exists, however: lack of a common agreement on the appropriate choice of element qualifiers and a standardized approach to encoding element values precludes effective use.

Although the text of the benchmark might appear to be a logical and open approach, the lack of consistency in printed versions of state documents, the lack of meaningful notation or codes, and the need for basic additional identification information such as declaration of the state or district, grade level and hierarchy position within the state standards documents make them far from transparent.

Publishers, content aggregators, commercial cataloguers and research centres have resorted to proprietary representations of state academic standards and benchmark data for in-house systems designed for alignment, correlation and other curricular and cataloguing uses. Because this represents a significant investment of funds and because these databases often contain other valuable intellectual property such as alignment and correlation data, owners of these databases have been reluctant to expose any portion of them for public consumption.

Although it would be possible to code academic standards and benchmarks within a catalogue record to a private key that could be used to tie back to the proprietary database for the value-added information, the value of the resulting catalogue record is minimal for general consumption beyond the context for which it was originally intended. Most publishers and other content providers want their potential and active customers to have alignment information on their resources, but they rightfully want to protect the intellectual property and proprietary processes that were used to achieve the result.

The most practical approach to resolving these issues would be to treat the collection of state academic standards and benchmarks, along with their immediate identification metadata, as a form of controlled vocabulary. These vocabularies would be maintained by a non-commercial consortium or non-profit standards body and made available in a common, agreed-upon format at the lowest possible cost that would initially fund the collection effort and provide for continued maintenance and updating. Ongoing access to the information would be through a subscription model with subsidization of educator, non-profit and public school use by higher commercial fees. State academic standards and benchmarks are public documents and although there is value in the process of collecting and managing a repository, there is no intellectual property issue per se in the content of such standards. Figure 7.5 illustrates this repository function.

Standards alignment services

While the repository service component of the proposed architecture

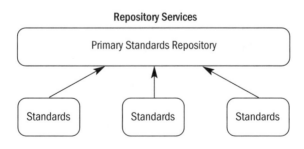

Fig. 7.5 *Standards aggregation*

maintains canonical versions of the primary CS documents in a machine-addressable format, a logically separate service creates the alignments that relate semantically similar CS to one another. Exemplars of such services exist in the USA – e.g. McREL through its Content Knowledge database (www.mcrel.org/standards-benchmarks/) and the Align to Achieve Compendix knowledge base (www.aligntoachieve.org/AchievePhaseII/basic-search.cfm). Similar in technical structure, both the McREL and the Align to Achieve knowledge bases have created their intermediary or reference statement (see Figure 7.3 above) by analysing and distilling learning objectives from recognized CS. Thus, the intermediary or reference statements are themselves not standards in any formal sense of the term but rather are meta-standards that embody the meaning of the CS from which they are derived. Since Align to Achieve also maintains a repository of US state CS, it performs both logical services noted so far in the ASNA – the repository service and the alignment service. However, nothing in the ASNA dictates that either of these services must be performed by single agencies. In fact, all evidence indicates that, at a minimum, the alignment services may be provided by any number of agencies. The same is likely to be true for the standards repositories.

It is through the alignment services that it becomes possible for an educational resource to be correlated once using a *direct correlation* to a recognized, conventionally promulgated CS – e.g. to a mathematics standard defined by the US National Council of Teachers of Mathematics (http://standards.nctm.org/document/) – or an *indirect correlation* to an intermediary or reference statement such as one from the Align to Achieve knowledge base. Since the CS used in the direct correlation would also have been aligned to the reference statement, the alignment service can be used to determine that resource's correlation to any other conventionally promulgated standard through the alignment mappings.

It is tempting to think that once complete repository and alignment services are in place that the major task of building the registry components of the ASNA would be finished. Unfortunately, that is not the case. As noted above, CS are like other human languages, they are dynamic and evolving. Experience with organizations such as Align to Achieve indicates that between 13% and 15% of state CS in the USA change annually. In periods of heavy educational reform, it is highly likely that the rates of change would be even higher. Thus, as CS are updated and sometimes even replaced in the primary standards repository (or repositories), adjustments must be made in the alignment service mappings.

Network communication services

The utility of the repository and alignment services will hinge on the ability of metadata tools (generation and search) to discover and communicate with them effectively. The protocols and schemas needed to support such communications are emerging. For example, the CEN/ISSS Learning Technologies Workshop Project group on vocabularies and the ISO JTC1/SC36 WG1 Vocabularies represent but a few efforts toward standardization of the supporting mechanisms. It is likely that existing standards such as UDDI (Universal Description, Discovery, and Integration) and WSDL (Web Services Description Language) may provide the means for supporting the deployment of the ASNA architecture.

ASNA use scenarios

The recognized benefits of a sustainable repository of state, national, international and organizational CS across the school curriculum that have been aligned to one another are not new – see for example, Align to Achieve (www.aligntoachieve.org/about_a2a.html). However, any such initiative must confront the scale of the initial expenditure of funds and effort to create such a comprehensive knowledge base. While the initial creation of such a knowledge base is no small task, the real issues of sustainability come into play as result of the facts noted earlier: (1) the number of CS is growing and, most likely, will continue to do so as the number of ever more fine-grained CS develop within jurisdictions (i.e. district-level CS within state CS, etc.), and (2) the living, evolutionary nature of all effective CS.

Scenario 1: CS alignment organizations

Being able to automate the ongoing process of CS alignment and ongoing maintenance of aligned CS knowledge bases by organizations principally focused on such activities will greatly enhance the survival potential of such organizations. Such organizations currently support goals synergistic to those of digital libraries in that they provide the means for supporting the rational development of CS across jurisdictions and the development of services resting under the remaining use scenarios described below.

Scenario 2: Publishers and other collection holder correlations

As demands for accountability in the nation's educational systems increase, educational resource providers from both the public and private sector will address such accountability by correlating their resources to relevant CS. To date, the mechanisms for alignment noted in this text (direct, indirect/forward and indirect/reverse) have been extremely costly, and, therefore, activities only sustainable for the top levels of the commercial sector. Automated means as well as open access to knowledge bases will likely lower the barrier to more sectors being able to correlate their resources to standards.

Scenario 3: Cataloguing applications

In a fashion similar to the publishers in the preceding use scenario, cataloguing tools such as the US Department of Education's GEMCat4 cataloguing tool will rely on networked machine accessibility to CS. While such tools will support the correlation of resources to a particular CS, such resources will be catalogued based on the understanding by the architects of the metadata that the simple direct correlations can be used through the direct/reverse interactions of a registry service for query expansion.

Scenario 4: Networked search applications

As noted in Use Scenario 3, search services can rely on the CS knowledge base to perform query enhancement through look-up. Such a CS knowledge base service could be integrated directly into the technical infrastructure of such search applications or be handled through standardized communications schemas and protocols with remote service such as those described in this proposal's section on sustainability.

Scenario 5: Educator personalized work spaces

Portals serving the education community are emerging worldwide. In like fashion, state after state in the USA is creating jurisdictionally bounded portals (e.g. the Washington state Digital Learning Commons). Advanced teacher/client personalization services of these portals will inevitable include applications that permit the teacher to personalize a digital workspace that includes the controlling CS of the teacher's jurisdiction that will then be dynamically and continuously wedded to resources and assessment instruments that address the competencies expressed in the CS. Such portals will ultimately be networked, making it possible for a teacher to move from one jurisdiction to another – even moving to a different state while taking the underlying personal portfolio 'across state lines' and having the knowledge base re-compute the resource base of the old jurisdiction in terms of the new. The project proposed here provides a powerful substrate for such portal services.

Scenario 6: CS jurisdictional developers

One of the original purposes of Achieve.org (the parent of Align to Achieve, founded by the USA states' governors) began as an endeavour to share information about evolving CS across USA jurisdictional boundaries in the hopes that some semblance of a national view of what 'should be known' might emerge from a set of educational systems rooted in local and state values. This desire was a principal motivator in the development of what has emerged as the Align to Achieve Compendix knowledge base. Just as Use Scenario 1 outlines the potential application of the work proposed here, this use scenario illustrates the base functionality of aligned CS in shaping education policy in the USA through knowledge sharing.

Global applications

One might legitimately ask whether the ASNA just described has any applicability outside the USA where so much current emphasis is being placed on school accountability as measured by how well students meet given sets of objectives. Clearly, not all nations have followed the same path as the USA with regard to defining content standards in their school educational systems – although many have pursued a similar course. However, even though many nations have not established a prescribed set of content standards to guide their educational systems, it defies logic to assume that: (1) those nations use educational resources that are not framed in terms of educational objective since all education *has* a purpose; and (2) at a sufficiently abstract level, all modern nation states pursue similar learning goals for their children.

Conclusion

Useful metadata for educational resources requires substantial effort and expertise in the generation. In addition to metadata statements regarding the content and structural relationships of the entities, educational resources must be contextualized in order to be useful in the processes of teaching and learning. Contextualization requires that careful attention be paid to the learning objectives of the resource being described in relation to the resource's audience. As pressures for accountability in USA schools increases, this push for ever deeper contextualization will increase in importance as well. The successful addition of metadata to entities reflecting their learning objectives will require substantial investment in the network architecture and services needed to build and deploy knowledge bases of the required content standards.

References

Editors of the American Heritage Dictionaries (1995) *Roget's II: the new thesaurus*, 3rd edn, Boston, Houghton Mifflin.

Gilliland-Swetland, A. J. (2000) Setting the Stage, In Baca, M. (ed.), *Introduction to Metadata: pathways to digital information*, Getty Research Institute, www.getty.edu/research/institute/standards/intrometadata/index.html.

Houston, J. E. (2002) *Thesaurus of ERIC Descriptors*, 14th edn, Phoenix, AZ, Educational Resources Information Centre and Oryx Press.

JES & Co. (2003) *Data and Metadata Relating to Academic Standards and Benchmarks*, www.jesandco.org/.

Sutton, S. A. (2003) Principled Design of Metadata Generation Tools for Educational Resources. In Mardis, M. (ed.), *ERIC Clearinghouse on Information and Technology* (in press).

US Department of Education (2002) *No Child Left Behind Act of 2001*, US Public Law 107–10, 115 Stat. 1425, www.ed.gov/offices/OESE/esea/index.html.

8

Educational metadata in transition: an Australian case study

Jon Mason

More than ever, we live in an economy that values and rewards
knowledge
> Thomas Davenport, in Beerli, Falk and Diemers, 2003, ix

Introduction

This paper is presented in two parts, as two aspects of an evolving context. Firstly, it discusses the development and application of metadata standards as a feature of the evolving requirements of the Australian education and training sector as it harnesses the capacities of the internet. Secondly, and more conceptually, the notion of value creation in the development of metadata standards and knowledge-based economies is explored. This latter discussion is informed by the experience associated with the first, given that knowledge-driven work practices depend upon a technical infrastructure. This range of topics is brought together with a view to discussing the wide and complex context in which metadata standards are developed and utilized for learning, education, and training. There is an ongoing challenge in balancing a current pragmatic need while also contributing to an evolving discourse that will shape the development of next generation metadata standards. Thus, pragmatics demands that current and next generation metadata standards require simultaneous application and development, with outputs from each informing the other. Within both of these scenarios attention is given to the notion of value – a key organizing principle in managing information and knowledge. In the digital domain, value is developed in numerous ways characterized by a meshing of recursive relationships between data, information, and knowledge.

In recent years the discourse developing within the Australian education sector concerning metadata has suffered from confusion and an emerging inertia regarding what constitutes best practice in the application of metadata schema to the tasks of describing and managing digital resources. There are a number of identifiable reasons for this. There is also significant effort under way to rectify the situation and to determine a pragmatic way forward.

Within Australia the political terrain has been characterized by the differing requirements of each of the formal education and training sectors: school education, vocational education and training (VET), and higher education. Developing a national approach has always looked like a tall order despite the major achievement during 1998 of some collective voice expressed in the development of the EdNA Metadata Standard, an extension of the Dublin Core, for cataloguing online resources (primarily websites). Moreover, the development phase can be characterized as theoretical – in practice, the EdNA Metadata Standard was only minimally applied. Furthermore, each sector has fiercely defended its unique identity and requirements, though both the schooling and VET sectors have put effort toward developing sector-wide application profiles within a standards framework. In the case of higher education its inherent unwieldiness has made whole-of-sector co-operation on metadata a very challenging exercise.

From a resource discovery perspective one of the more significant reasons for the absence of direction in whole-of-sector metadata application has been the success story of Google as a useful search engine. Google's immediacy, simplicity, and high yield in terms of quality results has influenced many users including developers of large portals. In short, Google is seen as providing the answer for everyday resource discovery. However, for many users there is no understanding that Google doesn't reach into the deeper web of well catalogued, though often repository-bound, collections of educational and research material.

These challenges arise from the ongoing transformation of learning, education and training made possible by the web. But the challenges are not all political and educational. There is also a significant range of technical issues to deal with as the applications infrastructure develops in sophistication. On the upside, there is now a growing appreciation for the complexity involved in both modelling the problem space and in implementing systems that demand runtime interactions within a distributed networked environment.

The underlying assumption throughout this chapter is that context always shapes knowledge and our capacity to understand and manage information. Thus, while there are many theoretical and practical challenges identified there are also some achievements and milestones. With the first generation of metadata standards providing a stable reference point for application there is now an opportunity to scope out the complexity of online interactions as they evolve in educational settings. The next stage of discourse surrounding metadata that best serves learning, education and training will be essential before the delivery of next generation of standards.

Historical context

Ever since the 1950s Australia has developed a reputation as a leader and innovator in distance learning, utilizing mainstream communications technologies such as radio (e.g. in operating the School of the Air), television (e.g. through Open Learning Australia) and the internet and web, initially through AARNet (the Australian Academic and Research Network). Since the 1970s it has likewise earned a reputation in early adoption of new technologies, not just for educational applications. For example, in recent decades it has consistently demonstrated high levels of per capita expenditure on ICT devices. It currently has over 45% of its population owning a mobile phone and the IMF has recently ranked only Sweden ahead of Australia in its spending on technology. This background context has been important in shaping policies and programmes that have been aimed at exploiting the benefits of the internet for learning, education and training.

It is now nearly a decade since the web first began to affect education and training in Australia, although there had already been significant leadership provided by the academic and research communities in pre-web internet years through AARNet. The ongoing impact of the web is now well documented (and accessible via the web), particularly through the proceedings of annual conferences organized by ASCILITE and AusWeb. Similar to its enthusiastic adoption elsewhere around the world, the web has also been commonly characterized as unleashing organizational, economic and pedagogical turmoil while providing a rich new set of tools that stimulate innovation and the transformation of work and learning. And while providing new information management tools the web has also exacerbated the complexities of information management in networked environments.

Internationally, this context has also been shaped by key international metadata specifications and standardization efforts led by the Dublin Core Metadata Initiative (DCMI), the IEEE (Institute of Electrical and Electronics Engineers) LTSC (Learning Technology Standards Committee), the IMS Global Learning Consortium and, more recently, the ISO/IEC JTC1 SC36, the international standardization body for IT in learning, education and training. Because of the tension between current real-world needs and the development of a sustainable interoperability framework each of these organizations has had differing views on what is required. This has caused some difficulty for implementers who have often tried to 'solve' the problem by choosing between a general purpose metadata schema for resource discovery (DCMI) and a more specific schema for learning object management (IEEE LOM). In an effort toward minimizing the confusion, representatives of each group jointly published a key paper on metadata principles and practicalities (Duval et al., 2002). With the recent international standardization of both schema – IEEE 1484.12.1-2002, Standard for Learning Object Metadata (LOM) and ISO 15836 (the Dublin Core Metadata Element Set) – there is now a new opportunity to move forward.

Some key policy responses

Among the many responses to the opportunities provided since 1995 has been a series of government-sponsored programmes aimed at fostering a collaborative approach to 'maximizing the benefits of the Internet for education and training' (EdNA, 2003). Apart from the economic benefit of minimizing duplication of effort during the early stages of an emerging industry, other identified benefits have included networked information and knowledge sharing. This has clearly been evident in the development of EdNA (Education Network Australia, www.edna.edu.au) and its various advisory bodies, and more recently with the formation of AICTEC (the Australian Information and Communications Technology in Education Committee, www.aictec.edu.au). Both these initiatives have been primarily sponsored by DEST (the Commonwealth Department of Education, Science and Training) and its organizational forerunners. Both involve well developed consultation processes and both have visible outputs in the implementation of portal and related web-based information services while also supporting the emergence of an agenda shaped by interoperability standards.

At the level of government policy Australia also benefits from activities undertaken under the auspices of the National Office for the Information Economy (NOIE), a cross-portfolio agency established in the mid-1990s. A number of NOIE initiatives have involved close collaboration with the education and training sector, principally through EdNA, AICTEC and state educational authorities. Thus, in 1998, a NOIE ministerial report identified online content development as a strategic area for public-funded stimulation of the information economy. By early 2001 this had translated into a major project servicing the schooling sector funded under the Commonwealth Government's *Backing Australia's Ability: innovation action plan* (Australian Government, 2001; TLF, 2003).

Emerging from this context there has also been a growing discourse and policy direction focused on developing a 'national information infrastructure' that is designed for interoperability, can support and stimulate an 'innovation culture', provide better access to scholarly information, promote knowledge management practices appropriate for a knowledge economy, and thereby ensure a strong economic outlook (McLean, 1997;

DETYA, 1999; CAVAL, 2000; Houghton, 2000; Australian Government, 2001; McLean, 2003).

The following five initiatives, all requiring metadata specification and application at some stage of their development, have all been supported by government funding.

EdNA – Establishing some foundations

After a lengthy stakeholder consultation process encompassing a period of around 18 months, Version 1.0 of the EdNA Metadata Standard was published in August 1998 (EdNA, 1998). Strictly speaking this document was not an official standard developed through Standards Australia processes – it served more as an agreement between representatives of the education and training sectors that enabled the aggregation of content on portals such as EdNA Online. A minor update was ratified as Version 1.1 by the EdNA Standards Sub-Committee (now known as the AICTEC Standards Sub-Committee) in December 2000 (AICTEC SSC, 2000).

The EdNA Metadata Standard comprises a set of guiding principles together with a set of metadata elements based upon the Dublin Core Metadata Framework. Its development was motivated by both resource discovery and information management needs. In facilitating targeted resource discovery and the retrieval of evaluated and classified online educational resources it was also seen as a positive response to the growing concern on the part of both the education sector and the broader community at the problems associated with younger students stumbling across offensive content while surfing the web. EdNA stakeholders at the time considered that building a quality collection of resources was preferable to identifying content for on-the-fly filtering. And as we all know, it seems that the spammers continue to keep themselves a step or two ahead of the rest of us!

In order to manage its collections of educational resources and accommodate sector needs, EdNA stakeholders extended the basic Dublin Core Metadata Element Set with elements that describe the intended audience of purpose-built content as well as vocabularies that specify the type of educational resource. Added to this were a number of administrative elements that enable the automatic harvesting of websites from authorized sites.

Parallel to the development of the EdNA Metadata Standard were a number of other key activities: the development of AGLS (Australian Government Locator Service), another Dublin Core-based metadata schema which has since been standardized as an Australian Standard (AS 5004); the public release of a specification for Learning Resource Meta-Data by the IMS Global Learning Consortium (IMS, 1998); and the establishment of the DC-Education Working Group as the first domain-specific working group within the Dublin Core Metadata Initiative (DCMI, 1998).

In order to recognize the significance of these other events the EdNA Metadata Standard also made explicit that alignment and interoperability with other metadata schema needed to be a guiding principle and long-term goal. As a consequence, EdNA representatives (and others) provided input into both the IMS and AGLS consultative processes. The input into both forums was that a pragmatic approach and minimalist specification was favoured.

Other principles specified by the EdNA Metadata Standard included a commitment to maintaining consensus on a national approach to a metadata framework utilizing authoritative Australian classification schema where possible, while also accommodating local requirements. This has proved increasingly difficult to achieve, particularly with the growing interest in and projects associated with re-usable 'learning objects'. This can be seen when considering a current snapshot of key projects within the Australian education and training sectors – where the initial interest in knowledge sharing and resource discovery soon spawned a stronger interest in developing quality educational content.

The Le@rning Federation

Enabled by five-year funding announced by the Howard Government in 2001 and matched by State education authorities, the Le@rning Federation was established as a joint venture of two other government agencies: the Curriculum Corporation (providing expertise in curriculum content development) and education.au limited (providing expertise in online systems development). Its aim is to develop a shared national pool of quality online learning content for Australian schools. For such an initiative to be successful, a standards framework was identified in the early scoping and has now been specified. Central to this framework is a metadata specification required to support the access, search, selection, use, distribution, trade and management of learning objects.

In addressing its metadata requirements the Le@rning Federation has developed an application profile that references a number of other standard metadata schemes or 'namespaces' (such as Dublin Core and IEEE LOM) while also including custom metadata elements that accommodate state-based curriculum vocabularies. Referencing these namespaces has been done with a view to providing a pragmatic approach to local extensibility and interoperability while maintaining the potential for further interoperability presented by those metadata schemes in their original form (Friesen, Mason and Ward, 2002).

The notion of a 'learning object' has now become commonplace within much of the discourse associated with e-learning and is central to developing a pool of shareable content. However, there is no commonly accepted simple definition of what a learning object actually is. For its purposes the Le@rning Federation has defined learning objects as components of online content (e.g. text, graphics, animations, video clips, URLs or aggregations of such resources) that have an assigned educational integrity that can be applied in a range of contexts (Friesen, Mason and Ward, 2002). As such, versatility of digital content can be understood as the bottom-line assumption in driving expectations regarding re-use and modularity of learning objects.

One of the key features of the Le@rning Federation application profile has been the need to consider requirements beyond simple resource discovery, such as the management of learning outcomes and teaching approaches associated with learning objects; accommodating the flexible application of these learning objects, enabling aggregation, re-use, and disaggregation; and the tracking of intellectual property rights. While further detailed description of the application profile is well documented elsewhere (Friesen, Mason and Ward, 2002) it is worth highlighting the grouping of its metadata elements under the five categories of Management, Technical, Educational, Rights, and Accessibility.

Early prototyping of learning objects and the exchange infrastructure enabling their distribution has not yet fully tested the application profile as a workable implementation. Probably the most difficult category of metadata concerns the assignment and tracking of rights associated with the creation and re-use of learning objects and in the first phase of development this challenge has been avoided by distributing the content on a free basis. As the exchange develops, enabling trade will very much depend on Rights metadata being effectively implemented.

In sum, the Le@rning Federation metadata application profile combines all the key requirements specified by stakeholders. However, in terms of enabling optimum interoperability with other web-based portals and services its utility is as yet unproven.

Australian Flexible Learning Framework

Administered by the Australian National Training Authority (ANTA) and initiated in 2000 the Australian Flexible Learning Framework (AFLF) is also an initiative funded for a five-year period. It is similar to EdNA, AICTEC and the Le@rning Federation in being an exercise in knowledge sharing. However, its sole focus is on flexible learning and promoting its take-up within the vocational education and training (VET) sector. Each year, AUD$20 million is allocated to projects that range from the development of flexible learning content to professional development programmes.

One of the key projects initiated in 2000 was the VET Preferred Standards project in which six areas of technical standards development relevant to online training were identified and profiled: learning management systems, groupware, web protocols, multimedia, resource locator technologies and hardware (VPS, 2000). The project produced both a set of recommendations on preferred standards for current application and emerging standards requiring further attention as well as a set of operational guidelines. These outputs were signed off by ANTA in May 2002 and are still being disseminated throughout the VET sector.

The VET Preferred Standards project has also informed a number of subsequent projects involving development of learning object repositories, toolboxes that enable the development of online training packages, collaborative technologies, interoperability standards, and resources for teaching, learning and assessment.

Projects within the AFLF have also informed the development of state-based activities within the VET sector concerning metadata application. For example, the TAFE NSW Online project specifies a metadata application profile that supports the use of learning objects, improves access to online materials and enables more effective use of existing video and graphic resources in creating new online course materials for both schools and TAFE (technical and further education).

From a content management perspective several states (New South Wales, South Australia, Western Australia and Victoria) have also identified the SCORM (Sharable Content Object Reference Model) profile of e-learning specifications as an important de facto 'standard'. SCORM brings together specifications for learning object metadata, content packaging and runtime interactions through referencing specialized work already completed by other standards organizations. As with the Le@rning Federation the underlying assumption for the application of SCORM to VET online materials is that high-quality learning content should be developed in ways that optimize its re-use and portability.

AEShareNet

The VET sector in Australia also is served by AEShareNet (www.aesharenet.edu.au), originally an ANTA-funded project but now constituted as a non-profit company. The broad aim of AEShareNet is to facilitate the sharing and licensing of Australian training materials, of which some may be only accessible online. From its early conception this initiative has been heavily dependent upon metadata and its emphasis upon streamlining the use of copyrighted materials is its distinguishing feature.

AEShareNet has developed its metadata scheme based on the EdNA Metadata Standard but adds VET-specific qualification levels, coding systems and controlled vocabularies that support the local system software that registered participants need to use in order to interoperate with others and exchange materials. It currently has approximately 20,000 training materials registered in its database. All materials are well catalogued according to the defined scheme.

Early in 2003 AEShareNet also began the process of involving private providers of training materials. The response to date has been largely enthusiastic. However, as this is a diverse and generally unsophisticated sector (with some businesses being sole traders) many issues of quality, price and access have arisen.

COLIS

Initiated in 2001 the COLIS (Collaborative Online Learning and Information Systems, www.colis.mq.edu.au) initiative involved a consortium of five Australian universities (Macquarie, Newcastle, Tasmania, the University of New England and the University of Southern Queensland) and five software vendors (Computer Associates, Fretwell Downing, IPR Systems, WebCT and WebMCQ). The key objective was to develop an enterprise-wide interoperability architecture that could inform future e-learning infrastructure development for higher education. As such, a standards framework was an essential consideration as was the practical development of a 'demonstrator' prototype – and ultimately, interoperability needs to be demonstrable.

In terms of a standards framework the COLIS project provided substantial input into the development of the IMS Digital Repositories Interoperability specification, publicly released in February 2003 (IMS, 2003). It was also informed by other IMS specifications (such as Content Packaging) and it aimed to test the interoperability of IEEE LOM and DC metadata records through using query protocols such as Z39.50 and XQuery. It further aimed to test how best to implement the expression of digital rights associated with learning objects. For this, a specification developed by IPR Systems known as ODRL (Open Digital Rights Language) was used (Iannella, 2002). In this regard some similarities in requirements with AEShareNet are apparent.

A key achievement of COLIS has been to widen the interoperability debate and to place it within a service model framework. In this framework content is understood to be comprised of 'information objects' and 'learning objects' – this dual classification being a simplified view of the diverse and heterogeneous content that is routinely accessed within educational settings, through diverse access methods (portals, learning management systems, student administration systems and library information services). From recently documented accounts the COLIS project has been very successful. Moreover, the experience gained has also provided insight into understanding the complex interactions involved in the 'learning object lifecycle' (Dalziel, 2002).

Metadata in the digital domain

Having discussed a range of activities that have utilized metadata in the evolving context of web-enabled education and training in Australia, the following discussion now adopts an abstract perspective on the role of metadata. The assumption for doing so is motivated by a growing world-wide discourse that suggests that 'Phase 1' of e-learning infrastructure development – the 'cottage industry phase' – is now moving toward 'Phase 2', characterized by a strong interest in systems interoperability, learner-centred architectures and knowledge management systems, and a growing interest in the de-coupling of instructional context from learning resource materials (Berild, 2003; Mason, 2003; McLean, 2003; Norris, Mason and Lefrere, 2003; Nilsson, Palmér and Naeve, 2002; Perriault, 2003; Petrides and Nodine, 2003). Thus, the following theoretical discussion aims to contribute to the conceptual modelling required as a basis for the development of next generation metadata standards.

Metadata exists in the networked digital environment in ways that demonstrate it is not just an extension of library cataloguing techniques. While it determines a close relationship between certain digital assets (simplistically characterized as 'content' and metadata that describes that content) *all* internet-ready resources can be described as having some kind of 'relationship' to other resources. Moreover, a metadata repository might be understood by many as 'metadata' while for libraries or internet directory services such collections are themselves regarded as 'content'. The enormity of networked relationships (bigger than 'six degrees of separation') point to potentially infinite relationships of digital information 'objects' to each other. The metadata implications, as Shabajee (2002) notes, add further complexity in that 'any object, physical or virtual, could be described and discussed in possibly limitless ways'. Research and development of the Semantic Web over the last few years has been in recognition of this principle and with a view to developing new and smarter ways to coalesce and share knowledge on the internet (Nilsson, Palmér and Naeve, 2002). Critical to this effort is the independent modelling of context from content (Mason, 2003). This may mean some re-working of the information models that form the basis of current metadata standards.

Where *resource discovery* is intended as the main value derived from the classification and cataloguing of resources then well crafted descriptions, controlled vocabularies and keywords become essential tools creating this value. Well crafted metadata in library contexts is typically supported by discovery aids, such as the Dewey Decimal Classification and the Library of Congress Subject Headings. These classification systems also have some value in internet contexts for managing collections but are limited as end-user discovery tools (typically facilitating 'browsing' as opposed to 'searching').

Because of the complexity of possible relationships and data interchange between systems there is much more to solving metadata requirements than standards such as Dublin Core or IEEE LOM. The development in 2002 of the Metadata Encoding Transmission Standard (METS) clearly demonstrates this. METS presents a five-layer schema that includes descriptive, administrative and structural metadata together with two other key layers: 'file groups' (all the sub-files that might comprise a digital object) and 'behaviours' (information concerning behaviours associated with particular content). The METS (2002) documentation argues:

> the metadata necessary for successful management and use of digital objects is both more extensive than and different from the metadata used for managing collections of printed works and other physical materials. While a library may record descriptive metadata regarding a book in its collection, the book will not dissolve into a series of unconnected pages if the library fails to record structural metadata regarding the book's organization. ... The same cannot be said for a digital version of the same book. Without structural metadata, the page image or text files comprising the digital work are of little use.

On a more pervasive level the technical innovations made possible through the development of XML (eXtensible Markup Language) are also important in this discussion. Apart from providing flexibility for web-based publishing XML has become a powerful enabler of e-commerce and transaction-based applications. In the context of this current discussion there are two important features of XML: its capacity to enable the separate management of content from its structure and presentation; and its metadata-rich potential in assigning custom tags, bringing new capabilities to content management. Thus, XML has also become an important technology enabling news syndication technologies such as RSS (Rich Site Summary), which is a minimalist representation of content and metadata. This development shows that even at a minimalist level metadata can be seen as a useful organizing tool – it does not have to be a heavyweight content header or wrapper.

Thus, as web-based infrastructures evolve, both the requirements for and (novel) applications of metadata are demonstrably increasing. As this process continues, the interoperability of applications and services will largely determine value and ongoing viability.

Value creation, content, and next generation metadata

The creation of value from 'raw resources' is an activity that is fundamental to most economies. Given that internet-based applications and knowledge exchange are primary foundations for a knowledge-based economy, then how value is created from what resources becomes a critical consideration for internet-enabled learning, education and training. While metadata is generally understood as a structuring tool enabling interoperability at the data interchange or information-processing level, it can also be seen as a value-creation activity, adding value to data and information. From such a perspective, the assignment of value can be understood as a key organizing principle in the life cycle of information and knowledge creation. However, because of the interactions involved, it is no longer sufficient to assume that all web-based 'resources' are best considered as 'content'.

When considering the metadata requirements of knowledge-based economies, then it is useful to conceptualize the 'raw resources' that sustain knowledge-based interactions. One abstraction is to identify these raw resources as (digital) *data, information* and *knowledge* as these are fundamental in helping us make sense of the world and in negotiating knowledge-based transactions. In learning contexts or educational settings these resources find expression not only as content ('nouns') but over time through 'verbs' that involve interaction, communication and a host of other activities in multiple and changing contexts. Data, information and knowledge are therefore much more than content and a rich source of complex inter-relationships. Knowledge is itself a complex topic. In the context of this discussion one facet of knowledge – explicitly declared knowledge – is what is primarily referred to. Tacit knowledge or applied knowledge is recognized widely as a dynamic flow, a 'verb' rather than a 'noun'.

Such complexity of resource relationships and interactions presents a challenge when developing models and metadata schema that adequately describe internet-enabled learning, education and training. From a perspective shaped by communications theory, Dervin tries to simplify this complexity through a 'sense-making' model – we make sense of the world not just from nouns (such as web-based 'content') but through actions (verbs). As such, she argues, there is 'no [operational] distinction between knowledge and information ... the making and unmaking of sense ... [defines] information/knowledge as product of and fodder for sense making and sense unmaking' (Dervin, 1998, 36). Given that sense-making is also central to learning, then an important corollary is that metadata must be seen as data that describes not only data, but also information and knowledge.

A more traditional way of describing the value-chain relationship between data, information and knowledge is to consider raw data at the bottom of a hierarchy. Thus, it is commonly assumed that data has no value as pure data; it can only be said to acquire value when sense can be determined from it, when comprehended through structures that present and organize it into meaningful chunks – as information. Moving up the value-chain – the rendering of information into knowledge – is not so straightforward and can be described as a complex activity conducted by individuals, communities of practice and organizations. Its complexity derives in part from its dependency upon *context* – with factors such as time, place and requirement always important. And as with the data-to-information relationship, value is generally ascribed in the information-to-knowledge relationship in a hierarchical sense. But that's the traditional view. It may be common sense but it is only part of the story because in the digital domain knowledge can be rendered as data. Moreover, value is created in such a transformation.

Further complexity arises as a result of the malleability and *intrinsic potential malleability* of data, information and knowledge that is made explicit in the digital domain. Everyone knows that *information* on the web is a plentiful resource, and in a state of increasing abundance. This information is supported, enriched and exchanged between *databases* and *knowledge-bases* and is expressed in a multiplicity of ways via web pages, news feeds, web forums and personal 'blogs'. All these resources can intermesh, aggregate or disaggregate depending on the context and application that may be devised. And all resources available for discovery on the web are also available for utilization and transformation in the production of knowledge – this is true even for so-called 'read-only' files.

The rule of complexity on the web becomes, then: 'knowledge for some, data for others'. That is, one person's (or application's) knowledge-base may serve as a data source or information repository for another; one person's metadata may be another's data, as it is for web directories such as Yahoo! or educational resource repositories such as EdNA Online, or even the National Library of Australia. But the richness and complexity doesn't stop there: value-chains also proliferate and operate in multiple directions with knowledge readily being utilized as data, completing a virtuous circle with value flowing forward with it. Thus, when knowledge and information are rendered as data for applications (such as concept builders or dynamic classifier engines) new value is created. This frontier of opportunity is what has driven the emergence of Application Service Providers, and is driving the development of Service Oriented Architectures (Schmelzer, 2003) that are built upon web services technologies and software applications that facilitate knowledge sharing (Norris, Mason and Lefrere, 2003).

Value creation and standardization

The creation of value can also be seen in the standardization life cycle (gathering requirements, consensus building, specification development, implementation, validation, defining standards, revision and update, and so on).

In detailing key features of a product or service a standard encapsulates consensus of a significant constituency as a *finished* reference document. A standard can always be updated and revised but nevertheless represents a stable reference point. And whether we like it or not, the various standards organizations in the world (from Standards Australia to the International Organization for Standardization) impute value on standards that are created (often by committees with voluntary membership) by then selling them in order to sustain their organizational infrastructures.

One of the interesting features about standardization of technologies and protocols that operate over the internet is that standardization in this environment is largely focused on next generation enablers (Synytsya, 2003). Certainly, much of the effort associated with metadata standardization has been focused this way. This contrasts with standardization in most other domains where a standard generally signals a maturity in accepted practice and in marketplace viability. There are likely to be a number of reasons for this. One may be to do with the life cycle of many internet-based technologies and applications – where a new version or order of magnitude capability is always imminent. Other reasons may be to do with a confluence of revolutions under way: revolutions in publishing, knowledge transfer, service delivery, education, organizational management, etc.

Conclusion

The story of metadata standardization on the internet is a story with a script that is played out while it is still being written: it is highly iterative with new requirements being specified as more stakeholders get involved in the discourse and debate. In the case of metadata standardization relevant to learning, education and training two main schema have so far been utilized, extended, abbreviated or customized for local needs. These two schema (now standards) are the Dublin Core Metadata Element Set (ISO 15836) and the IEEE Learning Object Metadata (IEEE

1484.12.1-2002). In both cases many years of consensus building had to proceed before standardization was accomplished. Meanwhile, the pragmatic requirements of many communities have been such that rough approximations to these 'standards' were implemented well before standard status was achieved. This has both informed the standardization efforts while also confusing many natural constituencies as to the value of such effort. There is therefore an ongoing challenge in balancing current pragmatic needs while also contributing to an evolving discourse that will shape the development of next generation metadata standards.

The pragmatic way forward demands that current and next generation metadata standards require simultaneous application and development, with outputs from each informing the other. In order to achieve this, it will likely become a routine necessity to reappraise the scope of the operating environment – in this case, the growth of knowledge-driven economies and the transformation of formal learning, education and training. The consideration of *value* is critical in such reappraisals since it can be seen as a key organizing principle in the life cycle of information and knowledge creation, particularly where learning is concerned. As a consequence, metadata will continue to develop as a structuring tool enabling interoperability of data as well as information and knowledge. In the Australian context the achievements so far of initiatives such as EdNA, AEShareNet, the Le@rning Federation, the Australian Flexible Learning Framework and COLIS are all notable. However, their next challenge is to interoperate where appropriate, where there is a clear value-proposition to do so. Metadata application profiles that are both lightweight and highly specific will likely facilitate this – as will assessments of how best to create value in increasingly complex environments.

References

AICTEC SSC (2000) *Australian ICT (Information and Communications Technology) in Education Committee – Standards Sub-Committee,* http://standards.edna.edu.au/about/committee.html.

Australia. National Office for the Information Economy (1998) *Towards an Australian Strategy for the Information Economy,* Commonwealth of Australia, www.noie.gov.au/projects/framework/reports/july98_report.htm.

Australian Government, (2001) *Backing Australia's Ability: innovation action plan*, Commonwealth of Australia, http://backingaus.innovation.gov.au/.

Beerli, A., Falk, S. and Diemers, D. (eds) (2003) *Knowledge Management and Networked Environments – leveraging intellectual capital in virtual business communities*, New York, Amacom, American Management Association.

Berild, S. (2003) *Metadata – What, When, How, Why?*, The National Agency for Education, Sweden, SC36 (36N0411) Committee document, http://jtc1sc36.org/.

CAVAL (2000) *Mapping Infrastructure for National Networked Information Delivery: a discussion paper*, Coalition for Innovation in Scholarly Communication, www.anu.edu.au/caul/cisc/proj2report-final.doc.

Dalziel, J. (2002) Reflections on the COLIS (Collaborative Online Learning and Information Systems) Demonstrator Project and the 'Learning Object Lifecycle', *Proceedings of the ASCILITE 2002 Conference, Auckland*, www.ascilite.org.au/conferences/auckland02/proceedings/papers/207.pdf.

DCMI (1998) *DC-Education Working Group*, Dublin Core Metadata Initiative, http://dublincore.org/groups/education/.

Dervin, B. (1998) Sense-Making Theory and Practice: an overview of user interests in knowledge seeking and use, *Journal of Knowledge Management*, **2** (2), 36–46.

DETYA (1999) *Australia's Information Future. Proceedings of a workshop held in March 1999 at the Australian National University*, Evaluations and Investigations Programme, www.dest.gov.au/archive/highered/eippubs/eip99-5/eip99_5.pdf.

Duval, E. et al. (2002) Metadata Principles and Practicalities, *D-Lib Magazine*, **8** (4), www.dlib.org/dlib/april02/weibel/04weibel.html.

EdNA (1998) *The EdNA Metadata Standard*, www.edna.edu.au/metadata.

EdNA (2003) *Papers and Presentations about EdNA*, www.edna.edu.au/noticeboards/noticelist.html?id=853.

Friesen, N., Mason, J. and Ward, N. (2002) Building Educational Metadata Application Profiles, In *Proceedings of the International Conference on Dublin Core and Metadata for e-Communities*, Florence, Firenze University Press, 63–9, www.bncf.net/dc2002/program/ft/paper7.pdf.

Houghton, J. (2000) *Economics of Scholarly Communication: a discussion paper*, prepared for the Coalition for Innovation in Scholarly Communication, www.anu.edu.au/caul/cisc/EconomicsScholarlyCommunication.pdf.

Iannella, R. (2002) *COLIS ODRL Metadata Profile*, IPR Systems,
www.iprsystems.com/COLIS/COLIS-ODRL-Profile-06.pdf

IMS Global Learning Consortium (1998) *Specification for Learning Resource Meta-Data*, www.imsglobal.org/metadata/index.cfm.

IMS Global Learning Consortium (2003) *Specification for Digital Repositories Interoperability*, www.imsglobal.org/digitalrepositories/index.cfm.

McLean, N. (1997) *Information Infrastructure for Higher Education in Australia: strategic issues*, UNISON, University of New South Wales,
www.unison.nsw.edu.au/cause.html.

McLean, N. (2003) Towards Global E-learning Standards for Interoperability. In [Proceedings of] *Initiatives 2003: Normes et Standards pour l'Apprentissage en Ligne, 19 March 2003, Versailles, France*, Paris, Agence Universitaire de la Francophonie, www.initiatives.refer.org/Initiatives-2003/_notes/_notes/McLean.htm.

Mason, J. (2003) Context and Metadata for Learning, Education, and Training. In McGreal, R. (ed.) *Online Education Using Learning Objects*, London, Kogan Page.

METS (2002) *Metadata Encoding Transmission Standard*,
www.loc.gov/standards/mets/.

Nilsson, M., Palmér, M. and Naeve, A. (2002) Semantic Web Metadata for e-Learning – some architectural guidelines. In *Proceedings of the 11th International World Wide Web Conference, Honolulu*,
http://kmr.nada.kth.se/papers/SemanticWeb/p744-nilsson.pdf.

Norris, D., Mason, J. and Lefrere, P. (2003) *Transforming E-Knowledge*, Ann Arbor, MI, Society for College and University Planning,
www.transformingeknowledge.info/.

Perriault, J. (2003) Introductory Remarks, In [Proceedings of] *Initiatives 2003: Normes et Standards pour l'Apprentissage en Ligne, 19 March 2003, Versailles, France*, Paris, Agence Universitaire de la Francophonie,
www.initiatives.refer.org/Initiatives-2003/_notes/_notes/cadrageperriault.htm.

Petrides, L. and Nodine, T. (2003) *Knowledge Management in Education: defining the landscape*, Half Moon Bay, CA, The Institute for the Study of Knowledge Management in Education, www.iskme.org/kmeducation.pdf.

Schmelzer, R. (2003) *Content as Services*, Waltham, MA, ZapThink,
www.zapthink.com/flashes/01232003Flash.html.

Shabajee, P. (2002) Primary Multimedia Objects and 'Educational Metadata' – a fundamental dilemma for developers of multimedia archives, *D-Lib Magazine*, **8** (6), www.dlib.org/dlib/june02/shabajee/06shabajee.html.

Synytsya, K. (2003) Learning Objects Metadata: implementations and open issues, guest editorial, *Learning Technology, Newsletter of the IEEE Learning Technology Task Force*, **5** (1), http://lttf.ieee.org/learn_tech/issues/january2003/index.html.

TLF (2003) *The Learning Federation*, www.thelearningfederation.edu.au/.

VPS (2000) *VET Preferred Standards Project*, Australian National Training Authority, http://flexiblelearning.net.au/standards/.

METADATA AND BIBLIOGRAPHIC ORGANIZATION

9

The metadata–bibliographic organization nexus

D. Grant Campbell

Introduction

This chapter explores the juncture between metadata systems, as they have evolved throughout various communities of electronic information, and bibliographic organization systems, as they have evolved within the library community. The two traditions of development exhibit striking similarities, which suggest that libraries have much to give and to receive in collaborating with and participating in digital information projects of many kinds. At the same time, the persistent differences in language, technological infrastructure and approach between these two traditions continue to make collaboration problematic between traditional and non-traditional information organization systems. In this chapter, I will argue that these problems can be significantly illuminated by examining two fundamental tensions that are common to both traditions: the tension between information storage and information transfer, and the tension between human-understandable and machine-understandable data.

Background

'Metadata' is a troubling term in library and information science, because its boundaries are vague and its definitions numerous. Some argue that metadata schemes and architectures are simply cataloguing under a different name, while others argue that metadata systems constitute a fundamental break between information organization in the 20th century and in the 21st. 'Metadata' could refer to markup tags in an electronic document, to the column labels and indexes of a relational database, to a bibliographic record, or to the table of contents of a book. In this chapter, I will be defining metadata as did Sherry Vellucci (1998): as 'data that describe attributes of a resource, characterize its relationships, support its discovery and effective use, and exist in an electronic environment' (192).

To understand how bibliographic control and metadata interact, we can begin by examining the origins of the Dublin Core Metadata Initiative (DCMI). The DCMI began as a hallway conversation at the Second International World Wide Web Conference in 1994 (DCMI, 2003a), and the group that gathered in Dublin, Ohio, in 1995 to define the metadata set represented a range of backgrounds and concerns: 'librarians, archivists, humanities scholars and geographers, as well as standards makers in the Internet, Z39.50 and Standard Generalized Markup Language (SGML) communities' (Weibel, 1995). Librarians, to be sure, were well represented, but they did not initiate the idea of the Dublin Core on their own, nor did they dominate it. As time has passed, librarians have had to share the metadata stage with other communities, each with its own concerns and its own techniques of information management. The communities within the Dublin Core include museums, archives, automation, education, government, product research and publishing (DCMI, 2003b). A cursory glance at the IFLA metadata resource page reveals that separate metadata systems have been created for governments (GILS), archivists (Encoded Archival Description), literary scholars (The Text Encoding Initiative and the TEI Header), and museums (Coded Information for Museum Information), to name a few.

Metadata and traditional resource description

Information resource description is no longer synonymous with bibliographic control, and to understand the effects of this, we should review the assumptions underlying bibliographic control as a professional field. 'Cataloguing' has traditionally possessed the following assets:

1 A well developed and well defined set of bibliographic entities, expressed in national and international standards of description and encoding, including the International Standard Bibliographic Description (ISBD), the Anglo-American Cataloguing Rules (AACR2), and the Machine-Readable Cataloguing standard (MARC).

2 A set of formulated objectives, initially set out by Anthony Panizzi and Charles Cutter and further refined by Seymour Lubetzky, by the Paris Conference of 1961, and by the IFLA Working Group on the Functional Requirements of Bibliographic Records (FRBR). These objectives have most recently been synthesized as the need for location, identification and selection of entities in a database, for obtaining access to these entities and for navigating through a bibliographic database (Svenonius, 2000, 20).

3 A cataloguing community which has been formally trained in a set of consistent and well defined cataloguing procedures.

4 A cataloguing process that is centred at the point of document acquisition and storage, rather than at the point of document creation, or any other point in the history of a document's creation or use.

The introduction of new players has upset this traditional context: metadata is created by different organizations and individuals, with widely varying kinds and levels of expertise, according to objectives defined locally or by a particular community, without any universally accepted descriptive or encoding standards. Furthermore, this metadata could be created by the original authors when the resource is created, by publishers when the resource is made available, or by libraries when the resource is noticed and identified. Metadata can appear within the HTML headers of the document itself, or stored separately.

Despite these differences, the past decade has revealed remarkable continuities between metadata and traditional resource description. Three similarities stand out in particular:

A drive towards international standards. The metadata community has been struggling for some time to create standardized descriptions that can be used by various members of particular communities: the growth of the Dublin Core, GILS, FGDS and the MPEG-7 (the Motion Picture Expert Group) parallel the long and frequently arduous progress towards the ISBD and AACR2. The rationale of the Dublin Core resembles that of the Core Record Standards of the Library of Congress's Program for Cooperative Cataloging, which aims to establish the elements of bibliographic records that are considered minimally necessary for record exchange, as distinct from location-specific descriptive elements that can be added by individual institutions.

Device and system independence. Metadata communities have deliberately adopted international non-proprietary encoding languages such as HTML and XML, just as libraries embraced a MARC standard that is supported by numerous bibliographic systems. Concern for resource sharing and interoperability among different metadata systems has led the metadata community to develop the Open Archives Initiatives Metadata Harvesting Protocol (OAI-PMH) for collecting metadata from different providers, just as bibliographic utilities like OCLC collect MARC records from participating libraries and make them widely available to others.

Name and subject entities. The Semantic Web, as envisioned by Tim Berners-Lee and others at the World Wide Web Consortium (W3C), presents a bibliographic universe in which all entities, whether information resources, people or abstract ideas, have a web presence, identified by a Uniform Resource Identifier (URI). The Resource Description Framework (RDF) will provide an XML-based method of referring within documents to URIs that establish the identity of a name or a concept, thereby enabling intelligent agents to disambiguate between multiple people with the same name, or multiple concepts identified by the same linguistic string. This framework strongly resembles authority control: the establishment of database entities that can be linked to bibliographic records to ensure collocation and distinction, representing bibliographic relationships in a useful and efficient way.

Metadata and librarians

Given the way metadata development parallels the development of bibliographic control in the 20th century, librarians and information professionals can be forgiven for looking and sounding smug. According to Marcia Bates, librarians have a store of expertise that is only now, in the post-Dot-bomb world, being acknowledged:

Everybody understands and takes for granted that there is an expertise needed for the application and use of technology. Unfortunately, many web entrepreneurs fail to recognize that there is a parallel expertise needed about information. ... In the 1970s and 1980s, librarians had ... created multi-million-item online public access library catalogues, when online access was a brand-new concept, and had developed a tremendous amount of expertise about how to handle large, messy databases of textual information. ... Yet it has been almost an article of faith in the Internet culture that librarians have nothing to contribute to this new age.

(2002, 2)

Metadata, we often argue, is old wine in new bottles, to quote one ironic paraphrase (Gradmann, 1999, 88): it is cataloguing without the unpleasant connotations of dusty card files, antiquated systems, rudimentary text-based search interfaces and endless discussions about main entry. Metadata, we assert, is a cool name for a familiar activity, used by ambitious LIS scholars seeking to hook their traditional research activities on to exciting trends and fundable jargon. Metadata is something that we, as librarians, know all about; it's what we do, better, many would argue, than any other professional community anywhere.

Nonetheless, the cordiality between metadata communities and the library cataloguing community has often been reserved, if not strained. As Priscilla Caplan (2000) suggests, the rise of metadata has been a 'mixed blessing for libraries', bringing more work along with greater opportunity:

On the positive side, it has given us new options for describing materials that are poorly served by the AACR2/MARC suite of standards, and it has created a renewed sense of intellectual excitement in resource description. At the same time, these new formats have placed new burdens on the library profession. ... Now suddenly we are confronted by content standards with no syntax and with data structures that we have no systems to support. Suddenly we are charged with supporting any number of schemes, not to mention maintaining registries of them and crosswalks between them. Suddenly there is an expectation we can control and give access to metadata created by organizations outside of our own library community.

The reasons for this strained relationship lie in the fact that the two traditions share common objectives, but emerge from very different cultures. Metadata creation is similar to bibliographic description, but it is not the same as bibliographic description. Digital data objects present unique challenges to the information system, particularly in their 'evanescent nature' and 'the insidious way that data can become corrupted' (Chilvers, 2002, 147). The shift in locale to the universe of remote-access electronic resources has resulted in new technologies, created by new people from new communities. Mapping between the jargon is therefore difficult. An ontology is similar to a controlled vocabulary, but not exactly the same; an RDF description of a person is similar to, but not the same as, an authority record. Different communities require different granularities of description: what satisfies some with the Dublin Core horrifies others trained on MARC and AACR. With the promise of interoperability comes the fear that the highly complex and finely nuanced activities of traditional cataloguing will be inexorably 'dumbed down' to a level of satisfying mediocrity.

A simple realization underlies this fear: the realization that the introduction of new metadata schemes, with new technical systems and new functionalities, has fundamentally altered the entire field of information resource description. While it is true that 'libraries have dealt with metadata for a long time', 'the tools with which metadata is produced and used are multiplying' (Hakala, 1999, 25). No longer the only game in town, traditional bibliographic organization has had to adapt and redefine itself in a new information context: 'catalogues can serve as an effective portal to the Internet so long as we know how to retain its strengths and learn to apply the principles of cataloguing to organize digital resources using cataloguing standards or metadata schemes' (Hsieh-Yee, 2002, 218). In particular, the rise of metadata has exposed two latent distinctions in bibliographic control:

- *Information transfer vs information storage*: the tension between metadata used to transfer a piece of information from one place of storage and use to another, and metadata used to encode a piece of information within a single place of storage and use
- *Human-understandable data vs machine-understandable data*: the tension

between the creation of metadata for humans to read and interpret, and the creation of metadata for machines to interpret in a sophisticated way.

These distinctions have been relatively unimportant up to now, but in the emerging electronic environment they have become crucial. When we examine the effect of metadata systems on the activities of bibliographic organization, we see that these distinctions define the key decisions that libraries will have to make as they redefine themselves in the information environment of the 21st century.

Information transfer versus information storage

Metadata systems have developed along multiple lines, defined by multiple purposes. The Digital Library Federation typically categorizes metadata types: descriptive, administrative and structural metadata (Digital Library Federation, 2000). 'Descriptive metadata' is often defined as 'metadata [that are] used in the discovery, indexing, and identification of a digital resource by semantic means. Examples of descriptive metadata formats are the MARC Cataloguing Records and the Dublin Core' (Bekaert et al., 2002, 364). This grouping, however, fails to do justice to a tension between resource description and resource discovery. In the early days of the Dublin Core, this tension emerged as a conflict between adherents of a structuralist view (emphasizing the need for extensions and qualifiers of the core elements to increase the Core's usefulness in local applications) and a minimalist view (emphasizing the need for simplicity) (Weibel, Iannella and Cathro, 1997).

In the resource description paradigm, electronic metadata schemes, like traditional bibliographic records, are designed for information storage. They describe the resource for purposes of maintaining a useful inventory of a particular information store: as such, the description tends to be highly detailed, geared towards identifying documents, collocating documents according to standard bibliographic relationships, and assisting users in evaluating the potential usefulness of documents.

In the resource discovery view, the metadata schemes are designed to make searchers, whether human or electronic, aware of the existence of potentially useful resources in diverse information repositories established in different knowledge domains. Such metadata schemes are designed for information transfer; resource discovery tends to emphasize interoperability across a set of defined constants. A typical systems paradigm for resource discovery is Weibel's 'View-Filter' model of metadata, which 'involves mapping many description schemas into a common set such as the Dublin Core, giving users a single query model' (1997). In this model, the various metadata schemes are linked by 'a metalevel scheme or terminological ontology which can serve as a 'metadata dictionary' (or 'metadata lingua franca'), and a switching device for assisting end-users searching for metadata-encoded documents or document-like objects in networked knowledge bases' (Howarth, Hannaford and Cronin, 2002, 224).

Most metadata schemes and architectures strive to incorporate both resource discovery and resource description into their design. Ever since the rise of the Warwick Framework, metadata developers have emphasized the concept of distinct metadata modules contained within metadata containers:

> A Dublin Core-based record might be one package, a MARC record another, terms and conditions another, and so on. Such discrete packages might be numerous and varied in content and even source. Users or software agents would need the ability to aggregate these discreet [sic] metadata packages in a conceptual container (a metadata basket of sorts), hence the notion of a container-package architecture.
>
> Dempsey and Weibel, 1996

Such a structure enables systems to 'build up' the metadata for their resources, using a set like the Dublin Core for interoperability and resource discovery, and enhancing that metadata with other, more elaborate elements for resource description. A typical example of this architecture is the Gateway to Educational Materials (GEM), with one level of metadata for resource discovery and another, more complex metadata level for resource description and use (Sutton, 1999, 1185).

Simplifying metadata for information exchange

Similarly, metadata architectures are often designed to 'break down' highly elaborate descriptive schemes into simple metadata for information exchange. The most prominent example of this is the Open Archives Initiative's Metadata Harvesting Protocol: a protocol through which data providers make their metadata accessible, in unqualified Dublin Core, to software agents that harvest 'metadata from multiple repositories and [combine] them into a single system' (Fast and Campbell, 2001, 8).

This distinction between information transfer and information storage exposes an incongruity about conventional cataloguing techniques. Traditional cataloguing in North America uses the MARC record as the basic cataloguing unit: cataloguers create catalogue content according to AACR, using a MARC interface similar to the example in Figure 9.1.

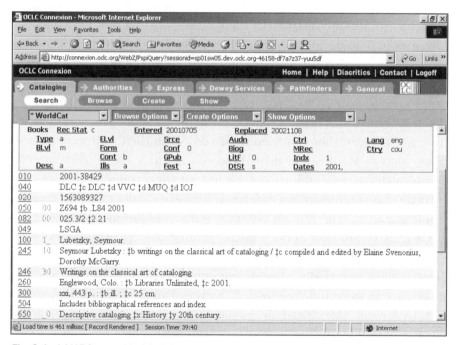

Fig. 9.1 *A MARC record in OCLC Connexion*

AACR is a standard for information storage: the contents of the bibliographic record are assumed to be permanent. MARC format is traditionally viewed as the permanent encoding system for bibliographic data: 'a way of encoding data so that computers can read it' (Danskin, 2002, 1). We must remember, however, that MARC is first and foremost a standard for information transfer rather than for storage. Bibliographic systems need not store records in MARC format; they need only convert records into MARC format when needed for transfer, and to convert MARC records into whatever structure their bibliographic databases use.

Until now, this distinction has been a minor one. Cataloguers create their records in a format for information transfer, partly because it is the most convenient and appropriate format for their task. A record created in MARC format exists as a digital and conceptual unit, ready to be sent either to a bibliographic utility or into a database, whereas a bibliographic record may well be split between multiple relational tables in its home system.

Now, however, the distinction is becoming important, because libraries are deciding the fate of their catalogues in a new environment. Libraries have to decide how to make their catalogue records available in an environment that is becoming more and more populated with digital collections and archives of many different kinds. They also have to decide how to provide access to electronic resources: through the catalogue, or through some other resource guide. In making these decisions, libraries have two choices: they can keep their records in their old encoding systems, such as MARC, and map these systems to a set of metadata elements such as the Dublin Core for information transfer, or they can recreate the complexity needed for traditional cataloguing within electronic metadata sets through library-specific application profiles.

OCLC's Connexion Service (http://connexion.oclc.org) provides an example of using metadata for information transfer. Not only does it generate preliminary MARC records for web resources; it also enables the cataloguer to store fully catalogued items in Dublin Core format, either in HTML or in XML. Similarly, metadata harvesting services such as the UIUC Cultural Heritage Repository (Figure 9.2) enable libraries to store their descriptions in a rich MARC format, and then translate those descriptions into unqualified Dublin Core elements, making it possible for the user of the repository to search the resources of several institutions simultaneously.

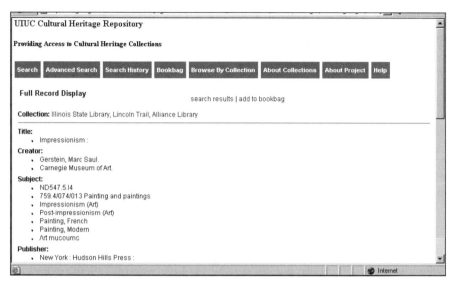

Fig. 9.2 *A bibliographic record from the Illinois State Library, made available through a metadata harvesting service*

Information storage needs

When metadata is used for information storage, on the other hand, the needs change dramatically. A metadata scheme like Dublin Core will typically need to be enhanced to provide the high-level detail considered necessary to meet the full demands of a catalogue. This can be done in two different ways. First, the information organization that is creating and storing the metadata can introduce other metadata elements in addition to those of the Dublin Core, often drawing them from other metadata sets that are used in appropriate domains. The Gateway to Educational Materials (GEM), for instance, posits a continuum between 'simple and terse' metadata and 'complex and rich' metadata. Dublin Core metadata is perfectly adequate to support resource discovery, while resource description is achieved through the addition of 'an eight-element, domain-specific GEM package' (Sutton, 1999, 1185).

Alternatively, the organization can introduce schemes and qualifiers to the core metadata set, to make the elements capable of sustaining complex bibliographic data. In OCLC's Connexion, for example, numerous extensions have been added to elements such as 'Creator' in order to distinguish main from added entries, and to distinguish personal names from corporate and conference names (OCLC, 2002, 1).

Similarly, the digital journal test bed at the University of Illinois, encoded using the Dublin Core Metadata Element Set, made extensive use, not only of standard DC qualifiers, but also local extensions 'in order to retain desired richness of semantics and structure' (Cole, 2002, 79). Typically, an information organization will use some combination of these two methods, clarifying them in an application profile, which enumerates the metadata elements to be used, their sources and the local usage policies, including the allowable schemes and qualifiers.

The most prominent application profile in the library community is the DC-Library Application Profile produced by the Libraries Working Group of the Dublin Core Metadata Initiative (Guenther, 2002). As a declaration of the elements and namespaces to be used in library metadata applications, the profile professes to serve the needs of information transfer: serving as an interchange format, for harvesting, and for exposing MARC data to other communities (Guenther, 2002). However, the DC elements have been elaborated and qualified with refinements and encoding schemes, as well as having either mandatory or optional status. Furthermore, the language and tone of the profile strongly resemble that entrenched code of information description, AACR2. Here, for instance, is the best practice for the DC element, Title:

> Either a Title or an Identifier is mandatory. If no title is available, best practice is to give a constructed title, derive a title from the resource or supply [no title]. If using qualified Dublin Core, an element refinement for titles other than the main title(s) should be included.
>
> Retain initial articles and use local sorting algorithms based on language. A language qualifier may be used to indicate language of title if appropriate. (For example, see: Initial Definite and Indefinite Articles for a list of articles in various languages).   (Guenther, 2002)

This profile is currently being used by various projects. Perhaps the most prominent is DSpace, a digital repository created to 'capture, distribute and preserve the intellectual output of MIT' (MIT Libraries, 2002). Records in DSpace are described using a qualified version of Dublin

Core that employs the DC-Library Application Profile 'as a starting point ... borrowing most of the qualifiers from it and adapting others to fit' (MIT Libraries, 2002). As Figure 9.3 indicates, DSpace adapts the simple Dublin Core elements by adding qualifiers appropriate for the permanent storage of and access to its metadata records; such extensions include multiple interpretations of the date element.

Machine-understandable data versus human-understandable data

In the vision of Tim Berners-Lee and other pioneers of the Semantic Web, the current world wide web suffers from being linked to human-readable information: web pages written in HTML and mounted on current browsers enclose information within tags that emphasize its visual appearance, while making no reference to its semantic content. If the Semantic Web emerges as predicted, web pages of the future will be machine understandable, as well as human understandable. By enclosing

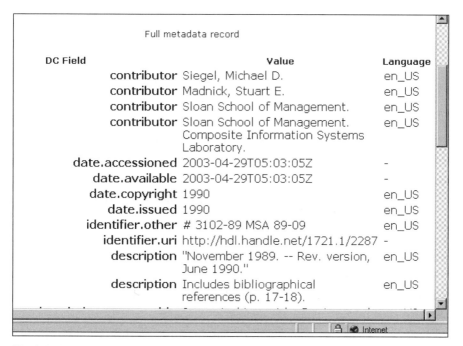

Fig. 9.3 *A record in Dublin Core format from the DSpace collection at MIT*

the information within semantically meaningful tags, and by embedding RDF metadata into their pages, web authors of tomorrow will be able to make their sites searchable with far greater precision than is possible today. Intelligent agents, much more powerful and sophisticated than current search engines, will be able to read these tags and metadata, linked together through namespaces that encourage the re-use of standard tags and ontologies that create links between different namespaces. These agents will retrieve not just documents, but pieces of documents, fitted together to create new resources. They will draw inferences from the data, to produce higher-order reasoning that enables computers to play a collaborative role in human activities:

> The next step is a search engine that can apply logic to deduce whether each of the many responses it gets to an initial search is useful. ... A simple search would have returned an endless list of possible answers that the human would have to wade through. By adding logic, we get back a correct answer.   Berners-Lee and Fischetti, 2000,180

As visions such as this one gather momentum in the electronic authoring community, they highlight an irony that often goes unnoticed in the cataloguing community. The 'MARC record', as the cataloguer typically sees it, is a hybrid display, incorporating elements of machine readability and human readability (see Figure 9.1). The data elements are surrounded by codes that are typically invisible to the end-user of the catalogue: field numbers, subfield codes, indicators and variable control fields. A MARC record in its purely machine-readable form looks very different (see Figure 9.4).

Cataloguers, then, have become accustomed to working at a nexus between human and machine readability: they are, for all intents and purposes, the only participants, human or digital, who see bibliographic records in this format. This may be the optimal position for the cataloguer, but it perpetuates the confusion between human agency and machine agency that has pervaded the history of the computerized encoding of bibliographic records.

Ever since the time of Panizzi, cataloguing methods have typically carried the seeds of their successors within their procedures. Panizzi's

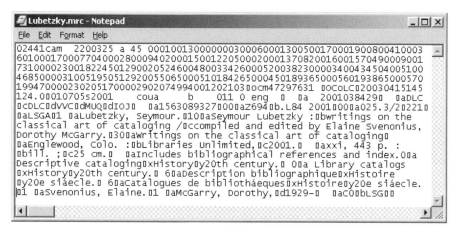

Fig. 9.4 *The MARC record in Fig. 9.1, without the human-readable formatting*

cataloguing code was designed for creating a printed catalogue in book form; his method, however, involved assembling the bibliographic surrogates on slips of paper of uniform size, a method which heralded the card catalogues of the future. Similarly, when MARC coding first emerged in the late 1960s, it was envisioned as a computerized way of transmitting bibliographic records in electronic form so that they could be generated in print format. The end result was a catalogue card that was intrinsically and exclusively human readable.

Even after MARC records were downloaded into electronic catalogues, the designers of these catalogues and their interfaces continued to assume that the intricate structure of these records was exclusively geared towards producing human-readable displays, rather than towards enabling sophisticated and precise searching. To this day, few online catalogues enable the user to do field-specific searches beyond standard numbers and the traditional AACR access points of title, subject and author. Any further searching must be done using a keyword search. All too often, the painstaking coding of cataloguers ensures that the data elements can be positioned strategically for human viewing, either on a card or on a computer screen, but few OPACs fully exploit this coding for search purposes.

As distinctions on the web between human-understandable and machine-understandable metadata gather momentum and urgency, libraries will be faced with a choice: do they wish to retain their allegiance to the human end-user, or do they wish to make their bibliographic records available to intelligent agents? If they choose the former, the OPAC will remain the primary vehicle of catalogue records, and our primary means of networking will be the Z39.50 protocol: a sophisticated and well established but notoriously complex protocol that enables the cross-searching of multiple catalogues using a common interface.

If, on the other hand, libraries choose to make their resources available in the spirit of the Semantic Web, the outlook changes considerably: 'when the information is stored in XML, it is possible to share and combine that data in ways that would not otherwise be possible' (Banerjee, 2002). By transferring bibliographic records into XML, and making them available to robots and agents, libraries could be making their resources available to higher-order forms of computing based on logical inference. The end-user might never see these records; but an agent could use their subject headings, titles, notes, standard numbers, classification numbers, dates and edition statements to assemble a list of resources that fit a user's specified criteria.

The library that chooses this route will want to transfer bibliographic records into XML in a way that preserves the richness of full bibliographic description, while making such descriptions available to XML tools and functionalities. The most direct route is to transfer the MARC records into XML; consequently, the Library of Congress has developed an XML schema for MARC records, which would effectively recreate the MARC record in XML (Library of Congress, 2003). Others, however, have argued that such a practice only preserves an antiquated encoding system, and have instead advocated creating an XML framework on the basis of AACR instead: 'rather than attempting to convert existing MARC tagging into a new syntax based on SGML or XML, a more fruitful possibility is to return to the cataloguing standards and describe their inherent structure' (Fiander, 2001, 17).

Conclusion

In parsing out these two tensions, my aim has not been to reassure cataloguers that there's nothing new to learn; nor has it been to assert that the standoffs that sometimes take place between cataloguers and metadata designers are justified. Rather, I have sought to indicate how decisions can be made which can move both communities forwards. By clarifying the distinction between information storage and information transfer, libraries will be able to distinguish between innovations that break down their highly structured and detailed records, and those that give them new life. By clarifying the distinction between human-understandable and machine-understandable data, libraries could well extend the useful life of bibliographic records beyond the life of the OPAC, thereby reinventing cataloguing and library services for the new century.

References

Banerjee, K. (2002) How Does XML Help Libraries?, *Computers in Libraries*, **22** (8), www.infotoday.com/cilmag/sep02/Banerjee.htm.

Bates, M. (2002) After the Dot-Bomb: getting web information retrieval right this time, *First Monday*, **7** (7), firstmonday.org/issues/issue7_7/bates/index.html.

Bekaert, J. et al. (2002) Metadata-Based Access to Multimedia Architectural and Historical Archive Collections: a review, *Aslib Proceedings*, **54** (6), 362–71.

Berners-Lee, T. and Fischetti, M. (2000) *Weaving the Web: the original design and ultimate destiny of the world wide web*, New York, HarperBusiness.

Caplan, P. (2000) International Metadata Initiatives: lessons in bibliographic control. In *Proceedings of the Bicentennial Conference on Bibliographic Control for the New Millennium: Confronting the Challenges of Networked Resources and the Web. Library of Congress, Nov. 15–17*, Washington DC, Library of Congress, http://lcweb.loc.gov/catdir/bibcontrol/caplan_paper.html.

Chilvers, A. (2002) The Super-Metadata Framework for Managing Long-Term Access to Digital Data Objects: a possible way forward with specific reference to the UK, *Journal of Documentation*, **58** (2), 146–74.

Cole, T. (2002) Qualified Dublin Core Metadata for Online Journal Articles, *OCLC Systems & Services*, **18** (2), 79–87.

Danskin, A. (2002) Today MARC Harmonisation, Tomorrow the World Wide Web: UKMARC, MARC21, XML and ONIX, *Catalogue and Index*, (Spring), 1–3.

Dempsey, L. and Weibel, S. (1996) The Warwick Metadata Workshop: a framework for the deployment of resource description, *D-Lib Magazine*,

(July/August), www.dlib.org/dlib/july96/07weibel.html.

Digital Library Federation (2000) *Structural, Technical and Administrative Metadata Standards: a discussion document*, ww.diglib.org/standards/stamdframe.htm.

Dublin Core Metadata Initiative (2003a) *History of the Dublin Core Metadata Initiative*, www.dublincore.org/about/history/.

Dublin Core Metadata Initiative (2003b) *People Involved in the Dublin Core Metadata Initiative*, www.dublincore.org/about/participants/.

Fast, K. and Campbell, D. (2001) The Ontological Perspectives of the Semantic Web and the Metadata Harvesting Protocol: applications of metadata for improving web search, *Canadian Journal of Information and Library Science*, **26** (4), 5-20.

Fiander, D. (2001) Applying XML to the Bibliographic Description, *Cataloguing & Classification Quarterly*, **33** (2), 17–28.

Gradmann, S. (1999) Cataloguing vs. Metadata: old wine in new bottles?, *International Cataloguing and Bibliographic Control*, **28** (4), 88–90.

Guenther, R. (2002) *DC-Library Application Profile (DC-Lib)*, Dublin Core Metadata Initiative, www.dublincore.org/documents/2002/04/16/library-application-profile/.

Hakala, J. (1999) Internet Metadata and Library Cataloguing, *International Cataloguing and Bibliographic Control*, **28** (1), 21–5.

Howarth, L., Hannaford, J. and Cronin, C. (2002) Designing a Metadata-Enabled Namespace for Accessing Resources Across Domains. In Howarth, C., Cronin, C. and Slawek, A. T. (eds) *Advancing Knowledge: Expanding Horizons for Information Science. Proceedings of the 30th Annual Conference of the Canadian Association for Information Science, 30 May-1 June, 2002*, Toronto, Faculty of Information Studies, 223–32.

Hsieh-Yee, I. (2002) Cataloguing and Metadata Education: asserting a central role in information organization, *Cataloguing & Classification Quarterly*, **34** (1/2), 203–22.

Library of Congress Network Development and MARC Standards Office (2003) *MARC/XML: MARC 21 XML Schema*, www.loc.gov/standards/marcxml/.

MIT Libraries (2002) *DSpace: durable digital depository*, http://dspace.org.

OCLC (2002) *Dublin Core Elements, Qualifiers, and Schemes for Connexion Bibliographic Records*, www2.oclc.org/connexion/documentation/.

Sutton, S. (1999) Conceptual Design and Deployment of a Metadata Framework for Educational Resources on the Internet, *Journal of the American Society for Information Science*, **50** (13), 1182–92.

Svenonius, E. (2000) *The Intellectual Foundation of Information Organization*, Cambridge, MA, MIT Press.

Vellucci, S. (1998) Metadata, *Annual Review of Information Science and Technology (ARIST)*, **33**, 187–222.

Weibel, S. (1995) Metadata: the foundations of resource description, *D-Lib Magazine*, (July), www.dlib.org/dlib/July95/07weibel.html.

Weibel, S. (1997) The Dublin Core: a simple content description model for electronic resources, *Bulletin of the American Society for Information Science*, **24** (1), 9–11.

Weibel, S., Iannella, R. and Cathro, W. (1997) The 4th Dublin Core Metadata Workshop Report, *D-Lib Magazine*, (June), www.dlib.org/dlib/june97/metadata/06weibel.html.

10

Cataloguing and metadata education

Ingrid Hsieh-Yee

Introduction: challenges of the information environment

This chapter looks at how metadata is taught in LIS courses, and which topics are covered. In an increasingly digital environment, metadata has become more prevalent in libraries, so practitioners need to know something about it. After reviewing the literature on metadata education and core competencies, the results from a survey of 52 North American LIS programmes are reported. The recommendations of a joint ALCTS/ALISE task force on the topic are outlined. The current state of metadata education is a work in progress, with room for improvement.

The rapid increase of information on the internet poses challenges for information seekers and underscores the need to organize internet resources. Web crawlers and humans collect or select information from the huge information universe, and keywords, controlled vocabularies, and searching and ranking algorithms are employed to facilitate information exploration on the web. These efforts have resulted in the creation of search engines, subject directories, portals, meta-engines and databases that all attempt to bring order to the information chaos. Unfortunately, all of these tools have their shortcomings. Although search engines are popular tools, their performance is far from perfect (Hsieh-Yee, 1998; Lawrence and Giles, 1998; Su and Chen, 1999). Schwartz (1998) reviewed the development of search engines and was pessimistic about possible significant improvement in general-content search engines. Lawrence and Giles (1998) reported that no single search engine has indexed more than 16% of publicly indexable pages. Lynch (2002) found that search engines continued to have difficulty providing meaningful subject access and separating resources by a person from resources about that person. While subject directory tools, such as Yahoo! and Open Directory, provide some browsing and searching support to users, it can be confusing and frustrating for users to wade through the subject hierarchies. Databases such as BUBL Link (bubl.ac.uk/link/) and INFOMINE (infomine.ucr.edu/) contain carefully selected information resources and are quickly updated, but the size of these databases tends to be small – Rodriguez (2002), for example, reported INFOMINE had over 20,000 items as of June 2000, and BUBL has over 11,000 resources. As more digital collections and digital libraries are added to the web, users have more information tools and more information resources to contend with than before. As a coping strategy some users stick with one search tool such as Google and ignore other tools. While this may be acceptable to some users to some extent, the free exchange and sharing of information and knowledge on the internet is clearly hampered.

The strong interest in digital resources has also added challenges to library information professionals. The need to integrate internet resources into online public access catalogues has added a new format for cataloguers to deal with. Some projects such as INFOMINE adapt cataloguing practices to control internet resources (Rodriguez, 2002). Some libraries ask non-cataloguers to use Dublin Core to create preliminary records, which are later enhanced by cataloguers to MARC (Machine-Readable Cataloguing) records. Many projects use non-library-based metadata standards to organize materials that were usually not catalogued. Bennett and Trofanenko (2002), for example, described how they used Dublin Core to organize digital primary cultural resources and integrated them into primary and secondary curricula and the educational programmes of museums and libraries. In addition to mastering the cataloguing of internet resources, cataloguers of the digital age need to know enough about metadata schemes to apply them intelligently.

Promise of metadata

Metadata seems to hold much promise for information retrieval and access in the digital age. But what is metadata? A few sample definitions may clarify this concept:

- 'Data about data' (Weibel, 1995).
- 'Metadata is data which describes attributes of a resource. Typically, it supports a number of functions: location, discovery, documentation, evaluation, selection and others' (Dempsey and Heery, 1997).
- 'Metadata includes data associated with either an information system or an information object for purposes of description, administration, legal requirements, technical functionality, use and usage, and preservation' (Baca, 2000).
- ' "Metadata" is the Internet-age term for structured data about data' (EU-NSF Working Group on Metadata, 1999).
- 'Metadata is structured information that describes, explains, locates, or otherwise makes it easier to retrieve, use or manage an information resource. Metadata is often called data about data or information about information' (Hodge, 2001).

These definitions confirm 'metadata' is structured data about information-bearing entities. It can represent intrinsic data (data in an information object) and extrinsic data (data about that object) such as its history and system requirements (Borgman, 2000). Depending on the needs of users of an information system, this structured data can serve a number of functions, including description, resource discovery, administration and management of resources, technical specifications, information use management, preservation management, and others (Gilliland-Swetland, 2000). Metadata can be produced manually or by machine. It can be embedded within an information object or stored in a separate system for access and management purposes. Different types of metadata can be provided for information objects by different people at different times (Lynch, 2002). Taking the nature and functions of metadata into account, Borgman (2000) concluded that metadata is 'essential for organizing individual digital libraries, a global digital library, and aggregates of digital libraries at levels in between' (80).

Various communities have developed metadata schemes for different purposes (Hudgins, Agnew, and Brown, 1999). Some are domain specific (e.g. Encoded Archival Description for archival finding aids) while others are intended for cross-domain applications (e.g. Dublin Core). There are many project-specific metadata schemes and several metadata schemes use Dublin Core as the foundation of their data element sets. The GEM (Gateway to Educational Materials) Element Set (www.geminfo.org/Workbench/Metadata/GEM_Element_List.html) and EdNA (Education Network Australia) metadata scheme (www.edna.edu.au/metadata) are two good examples.

There are also library-centred metadata schemes such as AACR2 and MARC that have guided us in the management of resources in many formats, including internet resources. Some metadata schemes such as Dublin Core may include few data elements, while others such as the FGDC (Federal Geographic Data Committee) Content Standard for Digital Geospatial Metadata can be quite elaborate. Many non-library-based metadata schemes focus on resource description and discovery just like AACR2 and MARC. But they also include data elements that are unique and important to their user communities.

The proliferation of metadata schemes may cause concerns about information chaos, but the Warwick Framework presents an infrastructure through which multiple metadata data sets will work together (Lagoze, Lynch and Daniel, 1996). The idea is to enable a metadata scheme to incorporate richer or more detailed metadata sets from other communities to serve the needs of users. RDF (Resource Description Framework) and XML (eXtensible Markup Language) are two enabling technologies that can help us achieve this goal. Miller (1998) explained that RDF provides a model (or structure) for us to identify objects and specify their relations. Because it enables us to have a better understanding of how objects relate to one another, we will be able to analyse information objects creatively and better management systems may be developed. XML, on the other hand, provides a syntax for us to transmit and use the RDF model across applications.

Many researchers and practitioners believe the networked environment will lead to a closer connection between library catalogues and other metadata repositories, and library information professionals will likely be involved in integrating metadata from many sources for users (Lynch, 2002; Mandel, 1998; Miller and Hillmann, 2002; Younger, 2002).

To enable MARC and newer metadata schemes to be interoperable, the Library of Congress's Network Development and MARC Standards Office (www.loc.gov/marc/marcdocz.html) has developed several metadata crosswalks between MARC, GILS (Government Information Locator Service), Dublin Core, FGDC, ONIX (ONline Information eXchange), MODS (Metadata Object Description Schema) (www.loc.gov/standards/mods/) and others. OCLC's Connexion has made use of crosswalks to allow its users to translate a bibliographic record from MARC to Dublin Core and from Dublin Core to MARC (connexion.oclc.org). Washington University has made use of Dublin Core dictionaries in its Digital Initiatives Programme to facilitate searching across collections (www.lib.washington.edu/msd/mig/data-dicts/ default.html). The MARC Standards Office recently released MODS, an XML schema designed to contain MARC 21 records and 'enable the creation of original resource description records'. It will be interesting to see if more efforts will be made to integrate metadata sets from various sources.

Market need and provision of metadata education

The need to organize information in settings other than libraries is strongly felt in many quarters. Individuals, educational institutions, corporations, government agencies and other bodies have all shown interest in creating and managing digital resources. That's part of the reason so many non-library-based metadata schemes have emerged. Libraries, as stated above, are becoming more aware of the need to integrate metadata from traditional sources. Expertise in organizing information is needed in many places and the Library and Information Science (LIS) field and related fields such as information management have an opportunity to meet that need and shape the future of information organization. Ironically, when information organization is being recognized as invaluable, cataloguing education seems to have suffered some neglect in LIS programmes (Hill and Intner, 1999).

Would there be room for metadata education in LIS programmes? If metadata education has been provided, what is the current state of the offerings?

Core competencies and metadata

One way to determine metadata education's place in LIS programmes is to consider how it may be related to competencies expected of LIS graduates. The literature on competencies shows that the Association for Library Collections and Technical Services (ALCTS) issued an Educational Policy Statement (1995) that identifies essential knowledge and skills in the following areas: 1) topics related to users such as information-seeking behaviour and user needs, 2) topics related to the usage of information such as searching, access to information, knowledge of bibliographic record, understanding of the implication of data and record structure for information retrieval, precision and recall, and evaluation of information, and 3) topics in technical areas such as knowledge of cataloguing principles, theory, concepts, tools, knowledge of database design, database management concept and management in general. In 2002, the American Library Association (ALA) Task Force on Core Competencies presented a draft that specifies

> Competence in organizing collections involves thorough knowledge of bibliographic and intellectual control principles and standards, understanding of how to apply these principles and standards in practical, cost-effective operations; and, the ability to collaborate with those who provide systems for managing organizational functions such as library vendors and institutional computer centre staff members.
>
> ALA, 2002

To identify core competencies for their Information Management programme, Gorman and Corbitt (2002) analysed the literature on core competencies in library science education and information systems (IS) education. They found LIS and IS core competencies cover similar areas (see Table 10.1).

Table 10.1 *Core competencies of LIS and IS (presented in hierarchical order)*

Library and Information Science	Information Systems
1) organization of knowledge and knowledge resources[1]	1) technology applications
2) technology utilization	2) information architecture and structure
3) management of people and resources	3) information mastery
4) client needs and services	4) information and knowledge management

[1]Items in bold reflect similar emphasis by LIS and IS.

They concluded that information management graduates need to have competencies in four areas: 1) technology applications and utilization, 2) organization of knowledge and knowledge resources through information architecture, systems and structure, 3) mastering information, and 4) managing information and knowledge for client needs and services.

These lists of competencies show that knowledge and skills in organization of knowledge and knowledge resources is critical for library information professionals, information science professionals and information management professionals alike. The ALA (2002) draft in fact declared 'the ability to organize collections of informational materials in order that desired items can be retrieved quickly and easily is a librarian's unique competency'. Gorman and Corbitt (2002) reported that as the most basic core competency for LIM education, organization of knowledge and knowledge resources focuses on how library information professionals identify, select and acquire, organize, describe and provide access to information in all formats, and cataloguing, indexing, classification and metadata are used to facilitate information use.

Since metadata is essential for organizing and managing information resources, which is a critical competency for various types of information professionals, it would be logical to include metadata in the LIS curriculum. The question is how to cover metadata to ensure certain levels of competency.

Literature review of metadata education

There is a plethora of articles on metadata and some provide good overviews (see, for example, Dempsey and Heery, 1997; Baca, 2000; Hodge, 2001). But the literature on metadata education is very small and limited to North American LIS programmes. Hsieh-Yee (2000) described how she incorporated metadata topics in basic and advanced cataloguing courses and developed a new course on 'Organization of Internet Resources' to help students understand metadata and metadata implementation issues. To explore how electronic resources has been integrated into LIS curricula, Hsieh-Yee organized a programme on 'Teaching the Organization of Electronic Resources' for the Technical Services Special Interest Group of the Association for Library and Information Science Education at the 2000 ALISE conference. Educators from the Catholic University of America, University of North Carolina at Chapel Hill (UNC), University of Pittsburgh and Simmons College presented a range of curricular changes, with some incorporating metadata to a greater extent than others. Saye reported that UNC has devoted a course to 'Metadata Architecture and Applications' and integrated various metadata topics into a large number of courses. His presentation was reported in a paper later (2001).

In a Delphi study on metadata, Hsieh-Yee (2001) solicited metadata experts around the world for their views on metadata education and metadata research. Topics for basic and advanced metadata education were identified. She also surveyed metadata practitioners to obtain their views on these two topics (2002c) and found that metadata experts and practitioners agreed on many of the topics for metadata education. In a volume of *Cataloguing & Classification Quarterly* that was devoted to education for cataloguing and the organization of information, Hsieh-Yee (2002a) described challenges in organizing digital resources, identified curriculum design issues and presented a model programme to illustrate that future cataloguing education could have a broader scope and incorporate metadata. In the same volume, Koh (2002) described how she used cataloguers as online mentors for students in her 'Metadata for Internet Resources' course and discussed the benefit of collaborating with these experts. As part of the effort to respond to an action item on cataloguing and metadata education, which is part of the LC Action Plan for Bibliographic Control of Web Resources, Hsieh-Yee (2002b) surveyed 52 ALA-accredited programmes in the USA and Canada to understand the current state of cataloguing and metadata education. Her findings on metadata education from that study are summarized below. The final report proposes a plan to support cataloguing and metadata education from 2003 to 2005. The final report will be summarized later in this chapter.

Metadata education in North American LIS programmes

Fifty-two Library and Information Science programmes in North America were invited to participate in a survey on the current state of cataloguing and metadata education. Five schools did not respond because of shortage of cataloguing educators or other reasons. With 47 usable responses for analysis the study has a response rate of just over 90%. Significant findings on metadata education are highlighted below.

Educators' views on cataloguing and metadata education

Because many metadata schemes deal with resource description and discovery, which have been the main concerns of cataloguing, each school was invited to designate a few educators to speak for their programme's coverage of cataloguing and metadata. Many educators believed that cataloguing plays an important role in information organization and that cataloguing standards are a good example of metadata. Some of them considered cataloguing metadata and felt little need to do more about metadata. But most educators appreciated the similarities and differences between organizing information through traditional cataloguing practices and using metadata schemes. They recognized metadata is broader in scope than cataloguing, and believed students need metadata education in addition to cataloguing education. Table 10.2 summarizes educators' support for the given statements, using a five-point scale, with '1' meaning 'strongly disagree' and '5' meaning 'strongly agree'. Educators showed a strong preference for not splitting cataloguing and metadata into two separate tracks of study. They also agreed that many

Table 10.2 *Educators' views on cataloguing and metadata education*

Statement	Average score	Mode
We may want to design two tracks of study, one for students interested in cataloguing, and another for those interested in metadata.	2.4	1
While cataloguing and metadata are similar in some ways, there are enough differences for us to devote at least one course to each subject.	3.6	5
The relationship between cataloguing and metadata should be clarified in courses devoted to cataloguing and metadata.	4.1	5
We need to have some coverage of metadata in cataloguing course(s) because both cataloguing and metadata are about information organization.	4.6	5
Students need the knowledge and ability to place metadata in a larger ontology of knowledge management methods, and have an understanding of the role of metadata vis-à-vis cataloguing metadata, classification, subject analysis, authority control, controlled vocabulary and other similar practices.	4.6	5
We need to give them the knowledge and skills to identify areas for metadata development, application, and evaluation.	4.2	5
This topic is equally relevant to aspiring cataloguers and aspiring metadata specialists (Yes? No?)	62% ('Yes')	
We need to help them understand issues of cross-collection, cross-domain searching and various approaches for ensuring interoperability between metadata schemes.	4.2	5
This topic is equally relevant to aspiring cataloguers and aspiring metadata specialists (Yes? No?)	76% ('Yes')	
We need to give them a thorough understanding of a variety of metadata schema and markup languages, their applications, strengths and weaknesses, and impact on library systems.	4	5
This topic is equally relevant to aspiring cataloguers and aspiring metadata specialists (Yes? No?)	64% ('Yes')	
We need to give them experience in implementing a metadata project, including needs assessment, project management, metadata scheme adoption and adaptation, metadata creation, etc.	3.9	5
This topic is more relevant to aspiring metadata specialists (Yes? No?)	49% ('Yes')	
This topic is equally relevant to aspiring metadata specialists and aspiring cataloguers (Yes? No?)	51% ('Yes')	

of the topics are equally relevant to students who aspire to be cataloguers and those aspiring to be metadata specialists.

Metadata topics in introductory courses

Of the 47 participating programmes, only 15 programmes (32%) had a course devoted to metadata, nine programmes (19%) offered advanced metadata courses, and 34 (72%) covered metadata in required introductory courses. A total of 40 introductory courses from these 34 schools were reported. Twenty-nine of these courses focused on organization of information or knowledge and also covered cataloguing topics. Metadata topics covered in the introductory courses varied from school to school. Three topics were covered more often than others: metadata schemes, metadata overview and encoding schemes. Only one educator discussed the relationship between cataloguing and metadata at the introductory course.

Metadata topics in cataloguing courses

Another likely place for metadata topics to be taught is cataloguing courses, so educators were asked to describe metadata topics covered in basic and advanced cataloguing courses. Data show that more than half of the respondents covered metadata issues in their basic cataloguing courses.

Table 10.3 Metadata topics in basic cataloguing courses

Metadata topics	Respondents[1]	
	n	%
Metadata overview	36	71
Relationship between cataloguing and metadata	32	63
Potential of metadata for information organization	27	53

[1]Fifty-one educators from 47 programmes responded.

Table 10.3 reveals that in basic cataloguing courses 71% of educators provided an overview of metadata, slightly over 50% discussed the relationship between cataloguing and metadata and 53% covered the potential of metadata for information organization. Additional metadata topics reported by educators but not covered by them include: CORC, Dublin Core, and crosswalk between Dublin Core and MARC. As for hands-on practice, only 11 (22%) of the educators offered students practice in creating records in non-library-based metadata schemes, and only nine (18%) let students create Dublin Core records in CORC.

Data on the coverage of metadata in advanced cataloguing courses (see Table 10.4) also shows limited coverage of metadata topics. Among the metadata schemes discussed, Dublin Core was the more popular one, covered by 14 (56%) of the educators.

Table 10.4 *Metadata topics covered in advanced cataloguing courses*

	Respondents[1]	
Topic	n	%
Dublin Core	14	56
Metadata types, usage, future	8	32
Metadata schema	6	24
Relationship between cataloguing and metadata	6	24
Crosswalk, interoperability	5	20
CORC	4	16
XML, RDF	2	8
Misc.[2]	7	28

[1] Twenty-five in number.

[2] This category includes topics such as classification schemes, comparison of metadata and MARC in cataloguing web resources, guideline development, metadata tools, management of metadata, search engines and integrated catalogues.

Metadata courses

While it is encouraging that metadata topics have been covered in required introductory courses and some topics are covered in basic and advanced cataloguing courses, no programmes require a metadata course, only 15 of the 47 (32%) programmes devoted a course to metadata and only nine programmes offered advanced metadata courses.

Data from 11 educators of metadata courses shows that several educators did not focus on metadata per se, but considered metadata in a particular context and discussed its applications. For example, one educator examined the use of metadata for the cataloguing of web resources, and another focused on metadata schemes as means for organizing internet resources. Only one educator offered a one-credit workshop that dealt with metadata per se, introducing students to several metadata schemes. Educators reported many topics, with metadata schemes being the most popular one. Topics covered by more than one educator are encoding standards, MARC, metadata history and overview, crosswalks, search engines, technologies for metadata, metadata architecture, management of metadata, metadata and information retrieval, and evaluation of metadata. Students received a range of hands-on practice with metadata in these courses. Experience in metadata record creation was common to 73% of the courses. Table 10.5 lists the types of practice and the number of courses offering them. The list is short but still impressive and suggests some educators are cognizant of critical issues in the metadata world. But the number of educators with such background and knowledge seems small.

Table 10.5 *Hands-on practice with metadata courses*

	Responses[1]	
Hands-on activity	n	%
Creating metadata records	11	73
Concept mapping	8	53
Developing metadata for a project	8	53
Implementing a metadata project	7	47
Evaluating a metadata scheme's effectiveness	7	47
Searching with metadata records	7	47
Creating MARC records	6	40
Other	6	40
CORC	5	33

[1] Fifteen in number.

Five educators of advanced metadata courses reported a large number of topics, with encoding standards and individual schemes covered by at least three educators. Two educators described their advanced courses as essentially hands-on classes. It seems that the coverage of metadata in LIS programmes varies greatly and depends largely on the knowledge and interest of the instructors.

Cataloguing topics in metadata courses

Another issue of interest was how much educators of metadata courses dealt with cataloguing topics. Even though many metadata schemes share with cataloguing the same concern for resource description and discovery, few educators tried to relate the two areas. Table 10.6 shows about half of the educators (53%) covered controlled vocabulary and authority control (47%) but only 40% clarified the relationship between cataloguing and metadata and only 33% covered descriptive cataloguing and purposes and principles of the catalogue. The reasons for the limited coverage of important cataloguing topics will need to be explored later.

Table 10.6 *Cataloguing topics in metadata courses*

Cataloguing topic in metadata course	Responses[1]	
	n	%
Controlled vocabulary	8	53
Authority control	7	47
Classification schemes	6	40
Indexing	6	40
MARC	6	40
Relationship between cataloguing and metadata	6	40
Subject analysis	6	40
Descriptive cataloguing	5	33
Purposes & principles of the catalogue	5	33

[1] Fifteen in number.

Extent of integration of metadata into LIS curricula

A total of 91 courses reported by 28 LIS programmes covered metadata topics, with an average of 3.3 courses covering metadata topics per pro-gramme. This number may be an underestimate because several educa-tors commented that metadata topics were taught in a large number of their courses, and it was impossible to list them all. Nonetheless, this number sheds some light on the extent to which metadata topics have been integrated into LIS curricula.

The significance of this average (3.3) becomes clear as we consider the extent to which cataloguing has been integrated into LIS programmes. A total of 166 courses reported by 43 schools covered cataloguing topics, resulting in an average of 3.9 courses per school. This number may also be an underestimate because one educator mentioned that almost all of their courses have something to do with cataloguing. What is remarkable is that metadata began to receive serious attention around 1995 and in less than a decade it has been integrated to such an extent in North American LIS programmes.

To summarize, most LIS programmes relied on introductory courses to cover metadata topics. Some cataloguing courses included a metadata overview but few educators went beyond that and fewer than 30% of the educators offered practice with non-library-based metadata schemes. The number of cataloguing courses making use of CORC was also very small. In advanced cataloguing courses the coverage of metadata tended to be limited and uneven across programmes.

Few programmes devoted an entire course to metadata topics, and even fewer offered advanced metadata courses. Topics again show a wide range, and two of the five respondents indicated their advanced meta-data courses were basically hands-on practice. There seems to be a small number of educators with a strong background in metadata, and the results suggest that the offering of metadata courses seems to be related to the knowledge of instructors. One way to strengthen the coverage of metadata in LIS programmes is to help faculty members develop exper-tise in this area. Since most of the development and implementation of metadata take place outside LIS programmes, it will be beneficial to involve practitioners in enhancing faculty knowledge in metadata. This will improve the teaching of metadata across the board and provide stu-dents with a more consistent coverage of topics and issues related to metadata. The survey also found that LIS programmes have rapidly incorporated metadata into their curricula. What remain to be analysed are the nature of the integration and the patterns of integration.

Metadata curriculum, metadata experts and practitioners

When a subject is new to a field, there are always debates on what should be taught. The pace of change has increased dramatically in the internet age and LIS educators have quickly incorporated metadata topics into curricula. But there has not been much discussion on whether metadata deserves to be a course on its own and what constitutes a solid education in this area. Since developments and implementations of metadata occur in the field more often than in LIS programmes, a Delphi study was conducted in 2001 to obtain the views of metadata experts around the world on metadata education.

Metadata experts identified metadata concepts, theory and topics that all LIS students need to know:

- A general understanding of AACR2, MARC, Z39.2, name and subject authority, and classification schema, and how these components fit together. The intent is to give students a big picture, instead of preparing them to be cataloguers.
- An overview of metadata, including types of metadata, purposes, communities creating metadata, applications and emerging standards that will impact on metadata projects. An awareness of well known metadata projects such as ROADS (Resource Organization And Discovery in Subject-based services), CORC (Cooperative Online Resource Catalogue) and Nordic Metadata Project is also important.
- A general understanding of some of the following topics: ISBD (International Standard Bibliographic Description), AACR2, TEI (Text Encoding Initiative), Dublin Core, GILS, FGDC, VRA (Visual Resources Association) CDWA (Categories for the Description of Works of Art), EAD, metadata crosswalks, HTML (HyperText Markup Language), XML and SGML (Standard Generalized Markup Language). The top three standards named by metadata experts are Dublin Core, AACR and metadata crosswalks.
- An understanding of interoperability, the role and limitations of meta-

data crosswalks, and knowledge of authority control and how it can be implemented through metadata.
- A knowledge of how library cataloguing schema and practices relate to metadata.

These views were supported by metadata practitioners in a related study. Some of these views were also supported by educators in the 2002 survey described above.

Metadata experts envisaged that LIS graduates would play the following roles in future information organization:

- having substantial involvement in the development, implementation and evaluation of metadata and metadata projects
- being information architects
- being interoperability experts
- conducting research on user needs and the utility of metadata applications.

To prepare students for these challenges, metadata experts recommended LIS programmes treat the following topics in-depth. The topics fall into three categories: schemes and standards, applications, and co-operation and collaboration. The first two categories cover many technical details, while the last category stresses an understanding of the need to co-operate and collaborate with information professionals outside of the library field to manage information resources for access.

Schemes and standards

Students should have:

- A thorough understanding of a variety of metadata schema and markup languages, their applications, strengths and weaknesses, and impact on library systems.
- The knowledge and ability to place metadata in a larger ontology of knowledge management methods and understand the role of metadata vis-à-vis cataloguing metadata, classification, subject analysis,

authority control, thesauri and controlled vocabulary, and other similar practices.

- The knowledge and skills to identify areas for metadata development, application, evaluation and improvement, and the ability to develop metadata standards.
- Experience in implementing a metadata project, including needs assessment, project management, metadata scheme adoption and adaptation.

Application issues

Students should have:

- Knowledge of the applications of metadata sets in various environments by information professionals (e.g. library settings, publishing industry) and understanding of important metadata projects such as CORC.
- An understanding of the issues of cross-domain searching, the role of registries, semantic mappings, controlled vocabulary and thesauri, and approaches to ensure interoperability between schemas.
- Knowledge of automated manipulations of metadata, including creating, harvesting, storing, revising, accessing and transforming for various uses.

Co-operation/collaboration

- We need to help students understand that decisions about how much is 'right' (i.e. right amount and right type of data elements) are the issue rather than only issues like what a standard is and how it is applied. It is also critical for them to understand the role of the user community in developing a domain-specific metadata scheme. This is why collaboration with content specialists is important.
- We need to consider the future of libraries in a networked environment and explore co-operative activities in the metadata area.
- Library services have converged with those of related communities such as museums, archives, government information, etc. More

domain-specific metadata schemes have been developed, so we need to include these communities and their standards to provide a contextual overview of metadata.

These recommendations may give LIS educators a blueprint as they develop courses on metadata.

Actions to support metadata education

To address the challenges of organizing information resources in the 21st century, the Library of Congress hosted a bicentennial conference on 'Bibliographic Control for the New Millennium' in 2000. The conference generated more than 24 action items and two of them deal with education and training. An ALCTS/ALISE Joint Task Force was appointed to address Action Item 5.1 and Ingrid Hsieh-Yee was appointed as the principal investigator and given the charge to prepare a model curriculum that should focus on teaching cataloguing and metadata to new librarians. The Task Force (2003) has recommended changes to current LIS curricula and a series of actions to support cataloguing and metadata education from 2003 to 2005. The proposal has several objectives, all of them closely related to metadata:

- to inform the information community of the effort of LC, ALCTS and ALISE to improve and enrich cataloguing and metadata education
- to promote the integration of metadata topics into cataloguing education
- to identify levels of expertise in cataloguing and metadata and competencies in leadership and management to prepare cataloguing professionals of the 21st century
- to assist educators and anyone who cares about cataloguing and metadata education to prepare for teaching in this area
- to enrich educators' knowledge of cataloguing and metadata by providing opportunities for educators and practitioners to brainstorm best teaching strategies for providing the recommended levels of expertise.

The proposal also includes a description of levels of cataloguing and metadata expertise, a discussion of management and leadership competencies, and an action plan. Instead of offering a model curriculum to the LIS education community, it recommends three levels of expertise in cataloguing and metadata: expertise for all LIS graduates, expertise for metadata cataloguers, and expertise for leaders of cataloguing and metadata projects. The reason for this approach is that individual LIS programmes have their priorities and local constraints and are likely to want to implement any curricula changes in ways that are most suitable for them. For each level specific knowledge and skills are described.

Recommended levels of expertise in metadata

Level I expertise. This level of competency is recommended to all LIS students so that they:

- understand how information is created, evaluated, disseminated, organized and used
- have a solid understanding of the principles and methods of information organization, including cataloguing, classifying, indexing, abstracting, metadata, and database creation and design
- appreciate the role of cataloguing and metadata in information organization and have a good understanding of the relationship between the two
- have the understanding that information is organized for user access and the essence of the LIS profession is 'connecting users with information' (ALA, 2002).

Students are encouraged to learn about the following subjects:

- descriptive cataloguing, access points, authority control, subject analysis, controlled vocabulary (subject headings and classification) and the effects of controlled vocabulary on searching
- cataloguing and metadata (definition, type, function), why and how cataloguing and metadata records are created, how to make use of them, and how to interpret them

- content rules, semantics, representation rules, syntax rules and their applications in cataloguing and metadata
- standards such as AACR and Dublin Core as examples of metadata schema for resource description and discovery; some practice with these standards would be desirable (encoding schema such as MARC format could be used as an example)
- roles of bibliographic utilities and co-operative efforts at bibliographic control
- information-seeking behaviour and information use.

In addition, students are encouraged to obtain:

- exposure to an online catalogue, a database and a well known metadata project
- hands-on practice in searching two information systems, preferably a system based on cataloguing records and another based on metadata records, for students to compare the two systems. Search exercises using controlled vocabulary and natural language would increase their understanding too.

Level II expertise. This level of competency is recommended to metadata cataloguers so that they can:

- perform descriptive cataloguing and subject analysis of print and electronic resources and understand challenges posed by electronic resources
- understand the objectives of the catalogue and how the objectives can be achieved
- have knowledge of national and international standards such as AACR2 and MARC
- use metadata and know how to integrate metadata into cataloguing records
- understand the tradeoffs in organizing information with cataloguing and metadata standards
- have a solid knowledge of a selected metadata scheme, such as Dublin Core, know how to evaluate its effectiveness and how it

compares with traditional cataloguing standards.

Students are strongly encouraged to obtain a solid knowledge of the following topics:

- information cycle, scholarly communication, methods of information organization
- principles of cataloguing and functions of the catalogue
- metadata: types, functions, development of metadata schema, metadata used in library settings (with hands-on practice in Dublin Core), metadata crosswalk, project examples
- relationship between cataloguing and metadata
- descriptive cataloguing concepts such as International Standard Bibliographic Description, Anglo-American Cataloguing Rules, access points and syndetic structure
- process and importance of authority, subject analysis, subject headings (two authority lists), classification systems (two systems)
- working knowledge of bibliographic networks, OPAC and MARC
- arrangement, presentation, and display of records
- treatment of electronic resources using cataloguing standards and metadata.

In addition, students are encouraged to obtain:

- hands-on practice in creating cataloguing and metadata records, using OCLC or RLG to create MARC records, and OCLC's Connexion or other Dublin Core generation tools to create metadata records
- hands-on practice in subject cataloguing.

Level III expertise. This level of competency is recommended to students who would like to be prepared for leadership responsibilities in cataloguing and metadata projects so that they:

- have a strong command of cataloguing standards and practices concerning print, nonprint and digital resources
- know how to utilize a variety of metadata schema such as MARC,

Dublin Core, TEI and EAD
- know the strengths and limitations of using cataloguing and metadata for controlling resources of any format
- understand the history, semantics and structure of at least two metadata schemas and their strengths and limitations
- possess the knowledge of concept mapping, crosswalks and interoperability issues
- know how to identify areas for metadata development and have the ability to develop metadata sets, implement them and evaluate their effects on information access
- know how to facilitate and co-ordinate metadata projects
- understand the process of implementing a metadata project, including needs assessment, metadata scheme adaptation, project management, and working with partners from various sectors
- can develop a framework for organizing a digital collection and understand issues that are critical to making a collection accessible remotely
- understand database design and DTD design
- can assess the application of metadata schema in various environments by information professionals (e.g. library setting, publishing industry).

With this level of expertise students are expected to lead cataloguing and metadata projects, so they need to have a strong background in both areas:

- Cataloguing topics
  - principles of cataloguing and their application to web resources
  - cataloguing of materials of various formats such as sound recordings, videos and electronic files, including descriptive cataloguing and subject analysis
  - knowledge of popular control vocabulary such as LC subject headings and DDC and LC classification systems
  - development of a thesaurus and a classification system
  - various methods for organizing resources
- Metadata topics
  - metadata principles and practicalities

— metadata standard development: principles, process and procedures
— knowledge of interoperability, crosswalk and issues related to integrating diverse collections into an information system
— selection, design, and evaluation of a metadata scheme
— ability to develop guidelines for using a metadata scheme
— metadata project implementation process and issues.

Additional competencies and recommended actions

In addition to technical expertise, leadership and management competencies needed by cataloguing professionals are highlighted for educators and students and teaching suggestions are included. These competencies cover six areas: 1) mission and values, 2) co-operation and collaboration, 3) communication and interpersonal skills, 4) problem solving, 5) managerial skills and 6) growth and change.

Furthermore, the Task Force recommends that an information package, 'Metadata Basics', be assembled for educators, practitioners and students; that a listserv be set up to facilitate discussions of metadata educators and practitioners; that a web clearinghouse be established for pedagogical resources; and a conference for educators and trainers be offered to share expertise and explore teaching strategies. The proposal covers the period from 2003 to 2005. An implementation task force has been appointed with members from ALCTS, ALISE, the Library of Congress and OCLC.

Continuing education

Many professional groups or associations have offered workshops on metadata topics for their target audience or whenever the need arises. The Library of Congress, for instance, offered a 'TEI and XML in Digital Libraries' workshop in 1998.

Three bodies that have offered metadata-related programmes on a more regular basis are highlighted here. The Rare Book School has offered week-long workshops on the Text Encoding Initiative and Encoding Archival Description since the late 1990s. The class size is small and instruction is provided through lectures and hands-on practice.

ALCTS has offered several 'metadata institutes' since 1998 with the ALA annual conference. The institutes cover topics of current interest and usually attract a large number of participants. The first institute was co-sponsored by the Library Information Technology Association (LITA) and focused on metadata and digital libraries. Several metadata experts presented metadata infrastructure and individual metadata schemes and explored their implications for digital libraries (ALCTS, 1998). The 2000 institute focused on metadata for web resources. In addition to cataloguing the web with AACR and MARC21, other approaches and standards were presented and several digital library projects summarized (Jones, Ahronheim and Crawford, 2002). The 2002 institute centred on 'AACR2 2002 and Metadata' (ALCTS, 2002). Topics included FRBR (Functional Requirements for Bibliographic Records) as a new model for bibliographic description, the development of metadata strategies, metadata schemes and controlled vocabulary, and many changes to AACR2.

The OCLC Institute has offered a series of seminars related to metadata applications (www.oclc.org/institute/). 'Knowledge Access Management' is designed for cataloguers. It prepares them to catalogue internet resources with AACR2 and MARC and introduces them to Dublin Core, TEI, EAD and GILS. 'Knowledge Access on the Web' surveys resource description systems on the web and provides detailed instruction on Dublin Core. Students are expected to design a resource description system and evaluate the design and functionality of the system. 'Using Metadata for Knowledge Management' is similar to 'Knowledge Access on the Web' with more hands-on lab experience. OCLC has offered these seminars at conferences and local training programmes.

Conclusion

Rapid development in internet-related technology and strong interest in digital resources have contributed to an explosion of content on the internet. A number of non-library tools such as search engines have been created to provide access to internet resources, many libraries have integrated internet resources, e-books, electronic journals and other digital resources into their online public access catalogues, and many digital projects and libraries have provided access to materials that were formerly unavailable to the public. The organization of information in the 21st century has become more urgent and challenging because of the increase in important resources, emergence of new formats and expanded options for organizing information resources. The field has also become more competitive because more and more information professionals are getting involved in information organization and many of them make use of non-library metadata schemes. To prepare LIS graduates for the challenges and the responsibilities of organizing information in the future, metadata education needs to be part of the LIS training.

Data from recent research shows that metadata education in LIS programmes is a work in progress. While metadata topics have been integrated into many courses, the coverage seems to remain at the introductory level. Only about one-third of the North American LIS programmes surveyed have devoted a course to metadata, and only 19% of the programmes have an advanced metadata course. Courses focusing on metadata cover a range of topics and some of them provide useful hands-on practice. Course contents show that in-depth coverage of metadata issues in North American LIS programmes depends heavily on the interest and knowledge of the faculty, and the number of knowledgeable faculty seems to be small. To learn about trends and best practices of particular metadata schemes, information professionals have a number of training workshops, institutes and seminars to choose from. Some of these programmes provide participants with knowledge and skills in a particular metadata scheme such as TEI or Dublin Core, while others include descriptions of individual digital and cataloguing projects. It is necessary to attend several of these programmes to have a good understanding of metadata. The cost and time commitment could be prohibitive for some.

There are several reasons that metadata education remains a work in progress. First, new metadata schemes continue to emerge and no scheme has been considered *the* standard for organizing resources in all disciplines, although Dublin Core has been more widely adopted than others and has been used as a foundation for several discipline-specific metadata schemes. Rapid development and evolution in the metadata area make it more challenging to offer coherent and comprehensive metadata education. Second, development and implementation of metadata schemes have taken place mainly in the field and few educators are able to keep up with all the new developments. Third, the library and information science field is still struggling to find its niche in the digital environment where many more new players have arrived and the competition has become keener than before. While some programmes have moved to emphasize information and information management, others have chosen to focus on library-related functions and issues, hence the lack of interest in metadata or some resistance to incorporating metadata education into LIS programmes.

The third reason is to be resolved by educators of individual programmes, but as more LIS educators understand the functions of metadata and how it relates to current and future information management and services, more programmes may add metadata to the curriculum. The first and second reasons were addressed by a number of studies. Metadata experts and practitioners identified knowledge and skills in metadata that ought to be included in metadata education (Hsieh-Yee, 2001; 2002c). The process of developing a cataloguing and metadata curriculum was described (Hsieh-Yee, 2002a). Levels of expertise in cataloguing and metadata were explained and specific knowledge and skills for each expertise level specified (ALCTS/ALISE Joint Task Force, 2003). Additional leadership competencies in management, communication, problem solving and collaboration were also identified. Hopefully these studies will assist educators in deciding the scope and content of their courses.

Library and information professionals are well positioned to make significant contributions to information organization and management. First of all, the LIS field is concerned with the needs of users and has insights into user behaviour. Second, the principles of information organization are applicable to new resource formats (Mandel and Wolven, 1996). Third, some cataloguing practices and standards such as controlled vocabularies and authority control can contribute to resource discovery. Fourth, the library community has experience dealing with a variety of resource formats and has demonstrated it can organize resources in new formats. New formats will continue to emerge and we can draw on our experience to manage them. Fifth, librarians have experience in using standards and sharing data and information resources. This experience will be valuable because the networked environment has necessitated cooperation and collaboration between different types of information professionals. Finally, the library community has MARC which provides syntax and structure for bibliographic data and AACR2 which provides semantics for resource description, and both have evolved to accommodate changes in the digital environment. Our experience with the changes in MARC and AACR2 will enable us to make good intelligent use of non-library-based metadata schemes.

Information organization takes place in many settings and library information professionals are increasingly called on to apply cataloguing practices and tools to new resource formats, modify cataloguing practices for digital libraries, use non-library-based metadata schemes, or integrate metadata from several sources into an information system. To remain relevant to information management in the 21st century, the LIS field must actively prepare its students in metadata. As our graduates become involved in the design, testing, implementation and assessment of information tools, information will be organized better and users will be better served.

References

American Library Association (2002) *Task Force on Core Competencies: draft report*, www.ala.org/congress/draft.html.

Association for Library and Information Science Education. Technical Services Special Interest Group (2000) *Teaching the Organization of Electronic Resources, a programme presented at the 2000 Annual Conference of the Association for Library and Information Science Education, San Antonio, Tex,* unpublished.

Association for Library Collections and Technical Services (1995) *ALCTS Educational Policy Statement*, www.ala.org/alcts/publications/educ/edpolicy.html.

Association for Library Collections and Technical Services (1998) *Managing Metadata for the Digital Library: crosswalks or chaos? A metadata institute cosponsored by the Association for Library Collections & Technical Services and the Library and Information Technology Association, Georgetown University Conference*

Centre, Washington, D.C., May 4–5, 1998, www.libraries.psu.edu/iasweb/catsweb/digital/corc/ALCTSMetadataInstitute.htm.

Association for Library Collections and Technical Services (2002) *AACR2 2002 and Metadata*, reported by Sharon Rankin, https://upload.mcgill.ca/libraries-techserv/metadata2002.doc.

Association for Library Collections and Technical Services/Association for Library and Information Science Education Joint Task Force (2003) *Cataloguing and Metadata Education: a proposal for preparing cataloguing professionals of the 21st century*, www.loc.gov/catdir/bibcontrol/CataloguingandMetadataEducation.pdf.

Baca, M. (ed.) (2000) *Introduction to Metadata: pathways to digital information*, Los Angeles, CA, Getty Information Institute, www.getty.edu/research/institute/standards/intrometadata/1_introduction/index.html.

Bennett, N. and Trofanenko, B. (2002) *Digital Primary Source Materials in the Classroom*, www.archimuse.com/mw2002/papers/bennett/bennett.html.

Borgman, C. L. (2000) *From Gutenberg to the Global Information Infrastructure*, Cambridge, MA, MIT Press.

Dempsey, L. and Heery, R. (1997) *A Review of Metadata: a survey of current resource description formats*, www.ukoln.ac.uk/metadata/desire/overview/.

EU-NSF Working Group on Metadata (1999) *Metadata for Digital Libraries: a research agenda*, www.ercim.org/publication/ws-proceedings/EU-NSF/metadata.pdf.

Gilliland-Swetland, A. (2000) Defining Metadata. In Baca, M. (ed.), *Introduction to Metadata: pathways to digital information*, Los Angeles, CA, Getty Information Institute, www.getty.edu/research/institute/standards/intrometadata/2_articles/index.html.

Gorman, G. E. and Corbitt, B. J. (2002) Core Competencies in Information Management Education, *New Library World*, **103** (11/12), 436–45, www.iiu.edu.my/iclise/files/session1/s1p3.pdf.

Hill, J. S. and Intner, S. S. (1999) *Preparing for a Cataloguing Career: from cataloguing to knowledge management*, www.ala.org/congress/hill-intner.html.

Hodge, G. (2001) *Metadata Made Simpler*, Bethesda, MD, NISO Press, www.niso.org/news/Metadata_simpler.pdf.

Hsieh-Yee, I. (1998) The Retrieval Power of Selected Search Engines: how well do they address general reference questions and subject questions?,

Reference Librarian, **60**, 27–47.

Hsieh-Yee, I. (2000) Organizing Internet Resources: teaching cataloguing standards and beyond, *OCLC Systems & Services*, **16** (3), 130–43.

Hsieh-Yee, I. (2001) A Delphi Study on Metadata: curriculum implications and research priorities. In Aversa, E. and Manley, C. (eds) *Information in a Networked World: harnessing the flow. Proceedings of the 64th ASIST Annual Meeting*, Vol. 38, 646, Medford, NJ, Information Today.

Hsieh-Yee, I. (2002a) Cataloguing and Metadata Education: asserting a central role in information organization, *Cataloguing & Classification Quarterly*, **34** (1/2), 203–22.

Hsieh-Yee, I. (2002b) *Cataloguing and Metadata Education in North America LIS Programmes* (manuscript in progress).

Hsieh-Yee, I. (2002c) *Practitioners' Perspective on Metadata Education and Research* (manuscript in progress).

Hudgins, J., Agnew, G. and Brown, E. (1999) *Getting Mileage out of Metadata: applications for the library*, Chicago, American Library Association.

Jones, W., Ahronheim, J. R. and Crawford, J. (eds) (2002) *Cataloguing the Web: metadata, AACR, and MARC 21*, Lanham, MD, Scarecrow Press.

Koh, G. S. (2002) Innovations in Standard Classroom Instruction, *Cataloguing & Classification Quarterly*, **34** (3), 263–87.

Lagoze, C., Lynch, C. and Daniel, R., Jr (1996) *The Warwick Framework: a container architecture for aggregating sets of metadata*, Cornell Computer Science Technical Report TR96-1593, http://cs-tr.cs.cornell.edu:80/Dienst/UI/2.0/Describe/ncstrl.cornell%2fTR96-1593.

Lawrence, S. and Giles, L. (1998) Searching the World Wide Web, *Science*, **280**, 98–100.

Library of Congress (2000) *Bibliographic Control for the New Millennium*, www.loc.gov/catdir/bibcontrol/.

Lynch, C. (2002) Future Developments in Metadata and Their Role in Access to Networked Information. In Jones, W., Ahronheim, J. R. and Crawford, J. (eds), *Cataloguing the Web: metadata, AACR, and MARC 21*, Lanham, MD, Scarecrow Press, 183–7.

Mandel, C. (1998) Manifestations of Cataloguing in the Era of Metadata. Presentation at *Managing Metadata for the Digital Library: crosswalks or chaos? A metadata institute cosponsored by the Association for Library Collections & Technical Services and the Library and Information Technology Association,*

Georgetown University Conference Centre, Washington, D.C., May 4–5, 1998,
www.libraries.psu.edu/iasweb/catsweb/digital/corc/
ALCTSMetadataInstitute.htm.

Mandel, C. A. and Wolven, R. A. (1996) Intellectual Access to Digital
Documents: joining proven principles with new technologies, *Cataloguing &*
Classification Quarterly, **22** (3/4), 25–42.

Miller, E. (1998) An Introduction to the Resources Description Framework, *D-*
Lib Magazine, (May), www.dlib.org/dlib/may98/miller/05miller.html.

Miller, E. and Hillmann, D. (2002) Libraries and the Future of the Semantic
Web: RDF, XML, and alphabet soup. In Jones, W., Ahronheim, J. R. and
Crawford, J. (eds), *Cataloguing the Web: metadata, AACR, and MARC 21,*
Lanham, MD, Scarecrow Press, 57–64.

Rodriguez, J. C. (2002) Anticipating the Deluge: the INFOMINE project and its
approach to metadata. In Jones, W., Ahronheim, J. R. and Crawford, J.
(eds), *Cataloguing the Web: metadata, AACR, and MARC 21,* Lanham, MD,
Scarecrow Press, 87–99.

Saye, J. D. (2001) The Organization of Electronic Resources in the Library and
Information Science Curriculum, *OCLC Systems & Services,* **17** (2), 71–8.

Schwartz, C. (1998) Web Search Engines, *Journal of the American Society for*
Information Science, **49** (11), 973–82.

Su, L. T. and Chen, H. L. (1999) Evaluation of Web Search Engines by
Undergraduate Students. In Woods, L. (ed.), *Proceedings of the 62nd ASIS*
Annual Meeting, Medford NJ, Information Today.

Weibel, S. (1995) Metadata: the foundations of resource description, *D-Lib*
Magazine, (July), www.dlib.org/dlib/July95/07 weibel.html.

Younger, J. A. (2002) Metadata and Libraries: what's it all about? In Jones, W.,
Ahronheim, J. R. and Crawford, J. (eds), *Cataloguing the Web: metadata,*
AACR, and MARC 21, Lanham, MD, Scarecrow Press, 3–11.

11

Developments in cataloguing and metadata

Shirley Hyatt

Introduction

People not involved with cataloguing have never really understood or sympathized with the difficulties involved in creating and maintaining a library catalogue. In 1674 in his preface to the *Catalogue for the Bodleian Library*, Sir Thomas Hyde wrote:

> 'What can be more easy (those lacking in understanding say), having looked at the title-pages than to write down the titles?' But these inexperienced people, who think making an index of their own few private books a pleasant task of a week or two, have no conception of the difficulties that rise or realize how carefully each book must be examined when library numbers myriads of volumes. In the colossal labour, which exhausts both body and soul, of making into an alphabetical catalogue, a multitude of books gathered from every corner of the earth there are many intricate and difficult problems that torture the mind.
>
> (Svenonius, 2000)

Three centuries later, this hasn't changed. The labour is colossal and the empathy scant. This chapter examines a few issues that continue to bedevil us. It examines some of the transformations occurring in the metadata environment that are impacting libraries, collection managers and online information providers. After a brief synopsis of some legacy issues, I discuss a few of the trends that are near-future givens. These include growth in the shared networked space and proliferation and movement of communities using that space; an emphasis on simplification; a renewed interest in and ability for collocation; and an increase in modularity and recombination of metadata. I close with a high-level overview of research that OCLC is presently exploring related to these trends.

Where we've been: a matter of principles

In 1841, Antonio Panizzi, assistant librarian with the British Museum's Department of Printed Books, published his descriptive cataloguing scheme entitled *Ninety-One Rules*. These rules caused an uproar among staff and users of the Reading Room. At the heart of the debate was the British Museum's practice of publishing the catalogue as an alphabetized inventory list, ordered by author, and Panizzi's *Rules* of collecting all manifestations of a particular work through a single main entry.

> The former cataloguing practice viewed books in a library's collection as discrete entities, unrelated to any other book, and so represented in the catalogue as unrelated to other catalogue entries. Panizzi's view was that a book is a particular edition of a work, a part of a complex web of editions and translations, and that catalogue users should be able to see these relationships even as they search for a particular book.
>
> Wilson, 2001

Between 1852 and 1876, Charles C. Jewett, Charles Ammi Cutter and Melvil Dewey all published their own seminal works in the USA – Jewett the first US cataloguing code, *On the Construction of Catalogues of Libraries and of the General Catalogue, and Their Publication by Means of Separate Stereotype Titles: with rules and examples*; Cutter, *Rules for a Dictionary Catalogue*, and Dewey, *DDC1*. All were strongly influenced by Panizzi. Panizzi and his *Rules* prevailed at the time at the British Museum, but the classic dispute has returned several times since.

In the mid-19th century, the industrial revolution ushered in a manufacturing revolution in printing, binding, and book production. 'Before 1800, book printing still closely resembled the processes that Gutenberg had used 300 years earlier. By the end of the 19th century, practically all book and newspaper printing had become mechanized, and it was possible to print thousands of pages per hour' (Wilson, 2001). Librarians were unable to catalogue the huge amount of new material being produced, much of which they viewed as ephemeral and of questionable quality. Faster, simpler and less expensive methods of cataloguing were preferred. In this context, Panizzi's *Rules* were viewed as time-consuming and costly. Over the rest of the 19th century, cataloguing and its rules moved away from collocation toward something closer to the older concept of describing the item in hand, unrelated to other items. The catalogue became, and to a large extent remains, a tool for managing a physical collection rather than a way of presenting knowledge about the collections and the relationships among the items.

In 1908, the American Library Association and the Library Association in the UK published *Catalog(u)e Rules: author and title entries* – in two editions, one for each country, because they could not come to agreement. Marking the beginning of 'codification by committee', it was primarily concerned with the construction of author/title catalogues, case-law style. The principles on which it was based were in fact the everyday practices in American and British cataloguing. As a work of practising libraries, rather than librarian-scholars, it lacked a set of unifying principles. As a result, the rules were complex and difficult to apply – problems that are still with us today.

Seymour Lubetsky, in his critique of the 1949 *ALA Cataloguing Rules for Author and Title Entries* made famous the question, 'Is this rule necessary?' He contended that the proliferation of rules, with their complexity and specificity, were obscuring the principles and reasons for cataloguing.

> Lubetsky advocated two main objectives for the catalogue: to allow the user to determine if the library has the desired item; and to reveal to the user what other works the library has by a given author, including other editions, manifestations and translations. It is this second principle which links Lubetsky to Panizzi and Cutter. He distinguished between 'books', which are specific manifestations and

'works', which are abstractions of the manifestations. In Lubetsky's catalogue, a user entering the title *Harry Potter and the Sorcerer's Stone* would retrieve a record that had in it information about all the versions/manifestations of that title – the paperback, the second edition, the spoken word version. The focus is on the content and its description, rather than on a specific physical item.

(Wilson, 2001)

Lubetsky had sufficient influence to induce dialogue and change, but not to overturn the gravitation toward complex, practice-based cataloguing aimed at describing specific physical items. The ensuing 1967 *Anglo-American Cataloguing Rules* did not yield collocation of manifestations under works, especially in its US version, and subsequent editions have, by and large, followed suit.

Metadata has always been driven by the technologies available. Technologies supporting cataloguing were slow to come about in the 19th and 20th centuries. The typewriter notwithstanding, three innovations are key: in 1901, the Library of Congress introduced its programme of distributing printed catalogue cards to purchasing libraries. No longer did libraries have to bear the total burden and costs of producing their cataloguing. This distribution method introduced the concept of cataloguing as a commodity for commonly held quality books ('copy cataloguing'), and freed librarians to work on more complex tasks of creating handcrafted cataloguing unique to the local library, for those items not catalogued by Library of Congress. Nevertheless, it was not without its detractors: some fretted that it would spell the demise of high-quality, handcrafted, handwritten catalogue cards.

Second, the MARC format was released in 1968 under the tutelage of Henriette Avram at the Library of Congress. It was intended to facilitate the electronic distribution of the Library of Congress's cataloguing data for use in computer installations. This standard, which enabled communication of bibliographic data between machines, was pivotal. That it is still in active use 35 years after it became a standard is testament to its robustness and flexibility.

Third, in 1967, Frederick G. Kilgour and Ralph H. Parker were inspired to propose a computerized, shared cataloguing system, and an online catalogue, and Kilgour was commissioned to implement one by the Ohio College Association.

> For those of us for whom WorldCat has been a fixture of our work-
> ing lives, it is hard to grasp the enormous audacity of this recom-
> mendation. In 1965, Parker and Kilgour did not have such a system.
> In fact, no hardware or software existed that could do what was pro-
> posed. ... There weren't even agreed-upon means of communicating
> bibliographic data between computers because the [MARC] standard
> had yet to be developed.
>
> (Wilson, 2001)

Overcoming these challenges, the OCLC service went live in 1971, and
has since been leveraged for interlibrary loan, resource discovery by end-
users, full-text access, registry services, and many other activities.

Today, WorldCat has more than 52 million bibliographic records representing nearly 888 million library locations. It is an amazing feat of social
engineering: the OCLC system serves as a switching centre around which
librarians coalesce for distributed input and shared output and is in that
sense uncannily 'napster-like'. That 43,000 libraries in 86 countries would
collectively share costs, labour, intellectual equity and resources to build and
maintain this service reflects a degree of co-operation, collaboration and
community that may be unparalleled among professions and industries.

Nevertheless, cataloguing (including its embodiment as WorldCat) has
continued to be chiefly a description of the physical item in hand, and
cataloguing rules remain complex. Most cataloguing processes, too, have
remained basically unchanged since the 19th century. It has taken innovations outside of the library world – introduction of the internet and
hypertext-based web – to change those processes. With the web comes
the opportunity to transform the catalogue record from a surrogate of
something to an essential part of the thing itself. With the web also
comes the opportunity for sharing a network space with many other
libraries, many other communities and many other approaches to metadata creation and structure.

Where we are: a shared network space

Lorcan Dempsey (2003), Vice President of OCLC Research, has devel-

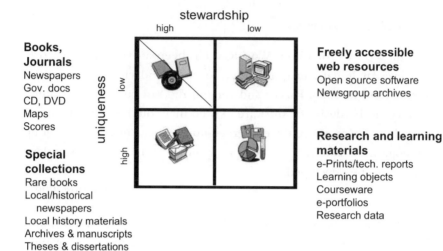

Books, Journals
Newspapers
Gov. docs
CD, DVD
Maps
Scores

Special collections
Rare books
Local/historical newspapers
Local history materials
Archives & manuscripts
Theses & dissertations

Freely accessible web resources
Open source software
Newsgroup archives

Research and learning materials
e-Prints/tech. reports
Learning objects
Courseware
e-portfolios
Research data

Fig. 11.1 *Changes in the information landscape*

oped a schematic to illustrate some changes taking place in the information landscape today. (See Figure 11.1.)

In this schematic, the *horizontal axis* represents the degree of custodial care that is given by libraries to informational things. Commodity goods and special collections alike are catalogued and indexed, provided climate-controlled storage conditions, repaired as needed and made publicly accessible though a variety of costly methods and systems. Both are found on the left side of the grid. The right side of the grid, in contrast, represents items that are not conventionally given that special 'librarian's touch': freely accessible web pages, e-prints and preprints, learning objects, and so forth.

The *vertical axis* represents the degree of uniqueness or 'published-ness' that informational things have. In this schematic, the upper half contains books – the quintessential published item held by libraries – and other information commodities, and also all that openly accessible information distributed worldwide via the web. The lower half of the grid represents those items that are unique and not generally publicly available.

The upper left quadrant – published and highly curated goods – includes such items as books, published CDs, DVDs, albums, scores, videos, journals and magazines, and maps. The lower left quadrant – unique and highly curated items – includes rare books, archives and manuscripts, local newspapers, local theses and dissertations. The upper right quadrant – widely published but uncurated items – contains freely accessible web pages, open source software, and newsgroup archives. The lower right quadrant – unpublished and undercurated items – contains items such as researchers' data and lab notebooks, teachers' curricular materials, e-prints and technical reports, courseware, e-portfolios, and so forth.

It is informative to map the sea changes in the information and metadata landscape, against this grid.

Above the line. The upper left quadrant is a mature quadrant. Library technical processes – cataloguing, authority control, material handling – have been oriented toward these sorts of commodity materials. Here libraries are in their element; traditional library metadata technologies like MARC and AACR2 are well honed. Because these are commodities (identical items owned by many libraries), shared-copy cataloguing systems offer efficiencies and bibliographic utilities such as OCLC and RLG reign supreme. Google, on the other hand, with its automatic extraction of metadata from the text itself, rules the upper right square at present. Search engines have many problems, but nevertheless provide access that, for some queries, is superior to the traditional library approach. Google may be viewed as trying to push the gridlines down and leftward as they 'push the envelope' of their text-search technologies to provide more and better access to today's hidden web information. This – and costs, and public perception – puts pressure on the upper left quadrant structures.

Below the line. The lower sector is less mature, and is also where the vast majority of digital library activity is occurring. There are a plethora of metadata standards and a diversity of metadata creation practices and approaches (see Figure 11.2).

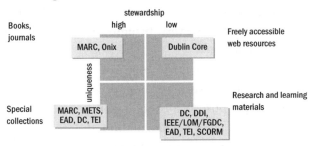

Fig. 11.2 *Metadata standards and creation practices and approaches*

There is growing appreciation among libraries that unique or rare materials are valuable research and learning resources that are underutilized. When resources are not digitally accessible, the chances of their use rapidly decline. Interest in digitizing cultural heritage materials is growing, therefore; doing so offers opportunities for releasing their value in new ways, and promotes, for posterity's sake, a community's identity. At the same time, research and teaching communities (whose output is on the right side) are increasingly entering the network space. Institutions and faculty have an interest in surfacing research, scholarship and learning materials as part of their enterprise. There are the beginnings of recognition that these communities have reciprocal interests with libraries: library resources need to be available at the appropriate stage within the learning and research environments; web-accessible research and learning items present major management and curatorial issues.

There are many movements to and fro on this grid. Growth within the upper left quadrant, mature though the quadrant may be, continues apace. Endless streams of new formats are entering this quadrant every day, and for those items that are digital, new material is being added seamlessly as if they were loose-leaf services or serial publications. There is pressure on material in all sectors to become recombinant. Libraries have finite resources. Increasingly attentive to special collections, they are shifting resources and staff from the upper left quadrant to the 'below the line' activities. Resources for training, attention to new standards activities, and equipment, are being reallocated from the upper left quadrant to the lower quadrants. Universities and other publicly funded organizations, eager to leverage their investment in scholarship and education, are investing in 'institutional repositories' which gather resources from across the organization into a single 'knowledge bank'. Digital and hybrid library projects are likewise bringing together discipline-related resources from all quadrants.

Some convergence among quadrants will take place, but these are, after all, different kinds of stuff representing an assortment of human and domain-specific purposes. Convergence is hampered by the the special needs of the various types of information, different intellectual property constraints, contrasting needs of communities, differing community cultures, and so forth.

Who needs metadata?

In paper-based systems the need for summaries of a library's collection was obvious – there were few other ways to make physical material available, and the only way to make physical resources available to remote users (Jordan and Hickey, 2001). It is sometimes presumed that with the web and its marvellous Google-style free-text searching, structured, formal metadata created by metadata experts based on rules and principles is outmoded. Who can afford it? Who needs it? Can't we just get everything digitized and let Google take care of our retrieval? ('What could be more easy...?')

As Amazon has proved, and proved to both publishers and libraries: in a shared networked environment, we actually have to know a good deal of 'metastuff' to retrieve information. We need metadata about what sort of stuff it is, what format it is in, what it looks like, its technical properties, rules for using it, e-commerce information, marketing data, etc. We cannot not have metadata. People need and want metadata. Furthermore, users want to supply metadata. Here, Amazon has again proven the value of pictures and excerpts, of peer reviews, user-supplied content and commerce ratings. In the online environment, a data representation of the object *is* the object, and the community of users who supply metadata are your *best* customers, your heaviest users.

Metadata is most useful when:

- there is nothing explicit in the document that can give the information
- when you actually need additional information, e.g. type of document, structural information
- people have to manage their collection inventories
- and, of course, when the information is itself physical. Physical things must have metadata to serve as a bridge to, a surrogate on behalf of, the information seeker.

There has been a traditional tension between quality of metadata and the cost of producing it. As the quantity of information to be analysed and described goes up, so does the overall cost of metadata creation and maintenance. Efficiencies have to be found to contain costs, which means compromises have to be made about quality. While information stewards tend to insist that bibliographic descriptions must be accurate or they are no good, clearly metadata has to be cheap and *good enough*.

Where we're going: making data work

In the midst of this change, several trends are emerging, and OCLC is conducting research in these areas in conjunction with other information science organizations. This is a brief synopsis of selected trends and research.

Simplicity

Traditional library cataloguing has always been relatively expensive to create and to maintain. It involves providing a detailed description of the item in hand, determining the people and organizations involved and checking these against authority files, and identifying the relationships that the item has with other items. As 'below the line' information joins the shared network space, it requires new forms of metadata. This fuels the need to reduce costs while concurrently providing opportunities for cost reduction.

> When the materials described in a library's catalogue are directly accessible to a user from his/her computer terminal, the need for elaborate description is obviously less than that needed for physical materials which may take hours, days, or even weeks to obtain. In other words, as the cost to view items declines, less descriptive information is needed for users to make an informed decision before attempting to view it. For much material in digital form the cost is often simply that of clicking on a URL and waiting a few seconds for a display. When this level of access is obtained, even bibliographic information such as the item's relationship with other items (e.g. what series or larger work it is part of) becomes less important because the item itself can often answer such questions.   (Jordan and Hickey, 2001)

In this environment Dublin Core is significant. Dublin Core is the outcome of a workshop held in 1995 by OCLC and the National Center for Supercomputing Applications (NCSA) at which the participants explored simpler ways of describing the wide variety of resources held by various organizations including libraries, museums, archives, governments and publishers. Participants proposed a core set of metadata elements for describing web-based resources for easier search and retrieval. The resulting Dublin Core is a 15-element set intended to emphasize retrieval, as described above, rather than description. It facilitates discovery of electronic resources and enables interoperability between metadata repositories. To this day, OCLC is a key supporter of the Dublin Core Metadata Initiative and remains the host of the DCMI directorate (www.dublincore.org/).

Another response to the need for simplification is OCLC's Faceted Application of Subject Terminology project, based on the Library of Congress Subject Headings schema (LCSH). LCSH is by far the most commonly used and widely accepted subject vocabulary for general application. It is the de facto universal controlled vocabulary and has been a model for developing subject heading systems for many countries. However, LCSH's complex syntax and rules for constructing headings restrict its application by requiring highly skilled personnel and limit the effectiveness of automated authority control. To make bibliographic control systems easier to use, understand and apply, OCLC has modified LCSH with a simpler syntax. FAST retains the very rich vocabulary of LCSH while making the schema easier to understand, control, apply and use. The schema maintains upward compatibility with LCSH, and any valid set of LC subject headings can be converted to FAST headings (OCLC, 2003).

Both Dublin Core and FAST are presumably usable by non-metadata professionals (non-cataloguers) and even by authors, as opposed to third-party information professionals.

A return to emphasis on collocation

In 1998, the International Federation of Library Associations and Institutions (IFLA) studied the information-seeking needs of users to develop a new framework for bibliographic catalogues. The outcome of this study is the Functional Requirements of Bibliographic Records (FRBR) model, a set of recommendations to restructure catalogues to reflect the conceptual structure of information resources.

The FRBR model specifies that intellectual or artistic products include the following types of entities:

- *the work*, a distinct intellectual or artistic creation
- *the expression*, the intellectual or artistic realization of a work
- *the manifestation*, the physical embodiment of an expression of a work
- *the item*, a single exemplar of a manifestation.

A *work* is realized through one or more *expressions*, each of which is embodied in one or more *manifestations*, each of which is exemplified by one or more *items*. In traditional cataloguing, bibliographic units are described out of context. With the FRBR model, the items must be described in context sufficient to relate the item to the other items comprising the work (IFLA Study Group, 1998).

Having resources brought together under the 'works' umbrella will help users sift through the myriad information resources available digitally. It will help them acquire the work, or content, that they are looking for, irrespective of the specific 'container' the content is carried in.

Widespread adoption of FRBR will require major changes to bibliographic databases, including WorldCat. OCLC's research group has been investigating the feasibility and cost of automatically converting large databases to the FRBR model. The techniques and approaches developed by OCLC researchers should facilitate the conversion of WorldCat, and possibly other bibliographic databases, to FRBR standards. OCLC has undertaken a series of experiments with algorithms to group existing bibliographic records into works and expressions. Working with both subsets of records and the whole WorldCat database, the algorithm OCLC developed achieved reasonable success identifying all manifestations of a work. Experience from the projects has resulted in recommendations about how FRBR should be evaluated and implemented in large databases.

If successful – and we believe it will be – this allows the library community to implement Panizzi's original principles, at least to the manifestation level.

Growth in the shared networked space

As described above, there is much proliferation and movement among communities using the web.

As a result, there has been a call to fuse metadata from one repository with that of other repositories. The Open Archives Initiative Protocol for Metadata Harvesting (OAI-PMH, aka OAI, www.openarchives.org/) is a standard to allow locally created metadata in a variety of formats to be shared. It is a low-barrier interoperability specification for recurrent exchange of metadata between systems. Institutions that want to share metadata make their metadata available for harvesting by placing it in an OAI server which can respond to requests to send all or part of the file. The metadata can either be sent in its native format or in Dublin Core. (The Dublin Core version makes it easier for harvesters of the metadata to consolidate it into federated databases.) The data provider may register its availability on OpenArchives.org so that OAI harvesters know it's there. The important point here, though, is that OAI-PMH 'includes a mechanism to indicate that the metadata on this server has changed, allowing harvester programs to keep the federated site up-to-date. This gives the creator of the metadata a great deal of control over the metadata' (Jordan and Hickey, 2001).

OAI is being used by preprint and e-print archives, digital libraries, institutional repositories and intranets. Anyone requiring integration of information stored in diverse locations can use OAI to collocate the metadata. There is growing interest by search engines in using OAI to make hidden web resources available.

The OCLC Office of Research has developed three OAI components, which are available as open source software:

- *An OAI harvester* (software that anyone can use, by installing it in front of their service, to harvest data from other organizations' OAI repositories).
- *An OAI server* (software that anyone can use, by installing it in front of their legacy repository, to make their data available to harvesters). OCLC's server software is called OAICat. MIT and Hewlett-Packard Lab's DSpace product incorporates OCLC's OAICat package as its

OAI server.

* *Databases.* Using OAI, OCLC has built the world's largest collection of metadata for theses and dissertations. This repository contains over 4.3 million records and is one of the largest OAI repositories in existence. It is itself available for harvest by other organizations. The database is called XTCat (Experimental Thesis Catalogue). Several other OAI databases are also available.

OCLC has also been exploring the application of standardized vocabularies – authority control and Dewey Decimal Classification numbers – to harvested records in the ePrints UK project, and has been actively engaged in digital learning and teaching initiatives.

Machine-to-machine web services

As more participants enter the metadata arena, libraries are creating more metadata for more types of material. They are using different formats, and often different systems. There is also an interest in harvesting metadata and in fusing it with metadata from other repositories into a 'union catalogue'. Such metadata may not have been created within a framework of consistent practice. Metadata will be required to 'work harder', serve multiple masters, and serve multiple purposes.

OCLC is exploring the use of 'web services' to provide functionality in support of these metadata needs. Web services are modular web-based machine-to-machine applications that use the HTTP protocol, return XML and can be combined in various ways. 'These services can be woven into people's workflow and diverse systems. ... They are deliberately discrete and the intention is that they may work together in various ways' (Dempsey, 2002).

Some of the functionality OCLC is exploring includes building services that take a record from one format (Dublin Core, perhaps) and return it in another format (MARC); that take a document and return a classification number or authority record; that take a name and return candidate-matching authorized headings; that enrich a record with data from other records for the same item, and so forth.

Key elements to this approach are the notions that these services are intended for machine-to-machine interfacing, that they are modular (OCLC is learning to decompose services that users can build back up within their own environments and workflows), and that they are small but versatile (a function may be equally useful in two quite different environments).

Conclusion

In the juggernaut advance of automation, the issues of the burgeoning growth in and sharing of the network space, collocation, simplification, and metadata re-use will doubtless be appeased, but not eradicated. Though the problems remain intricate and difficult, hopefully every iteration of these issues lessens the burdens of cataloguing and reduces their 'colossal labour'. And, while cataloguing may never be fully understood, perhaps it will be more fully appreciated by those who consult the emerging knowledge maps that are being created by the cartographers and techniques of the digital age.

References

Dempsey, L. (2002) Libraries Change Lives, and Research Changes Libraries, *OCLC Newsletter*, **258** (October), 12–15, www.oclc.org/news/newsletter/oclcnewsletter258.pdf.

Dempsey, L. (2003) Place and Space: collections and access in light of changing patterns of research and learning. In *A Community Commons: libraries in the new century. Association of Research Libraries Proceedings of the 142nd Annual Meeting, Lexingron, Kentucky, May 14–17, 2003*, www.oclc.org/research/presentations/dempsey/arlkentucky_20030515.ppt. Note: the grid and its concepts are the work of Mr Dempsey and Eric Childress.

IFLA Study Group on the Functional Requirements for Bibliographical Records (1998) *Functional Requirements for Bibliographical Records: final report*, www.ifla.org/VII/s13/frbr/frbr.pdf.

Jordan, J. and Hickey, T. B. (2001) Metadata Trends. In Chen, C. (ed.) *Global Digital Library Development in the New Millennium: fertile ground for distributed cross-disciplinary collaboration*, Beijing, Tsinghua University Press, 115–20.

OCLC Research (2003) *FAST: Faceted Application of Subject Terminology*, www.oclc.org/research/projects/fast.

Svenonius, E. (2000) *The Intellectual Foundations of Information Organization*, Cambridge, MA, MIT Press.

Wilson, A. (2001) 2001: a bibliographical odyssey, *OCLC Newsletter*, **251** (May/June), 35–9, http://www2.oclc.org/oclc/pdf/news251.pdf.

Part 6

METADATA AND OTHER APPLICATIONS

12

Preservation metadata

Michael Day

Introduction

Ensuring the long-term preservation of information in digital form will be one of the greatest challenges for the information professions in the 21st century. While there has been an awareness of digital preservation problems for some time, their importance has recently been magnified because of the increasing dependence of the world on computers and networks. For example, the recent rapid growth in the use of the internet in the past decade has demonstrated how much it has become, in the words of Manuel Castells, 'the fabric of our lives' (Castells, 2001, 1). Chen (2001, 24) has described the digital preservation problem as the 'critical, cumulative weakness in our information infrastructure'.

In response, things are now beginning to happen. For example, in 2001 the Digital Preservation Coalition was set up in the UK to form the basis of co-operation and already (April 2003) has ten full institutional members and 13 associates. Also, in February 2003, the US Congress approved the Library of Congress's plan for a National Digital Information Infrastructure and Preservation Program (NDIIPP).

The other chapters in this volume demonstrate the wide range of roles that metadata can serve. Since the mid-1990s, however, there has been a growing awareness of the part that metadata can play in supporting the long-term preservation of digital objects (e.g. Day, 2001). Preservation is integral to some definitions of metadata. For example, Cunningham

(2000, 9) defines it as 'structured information that describes and/or allows us to find, manage, control, understand or preserve other information over time'. This chapter will introduce some proposed digital preservation strategies, noting how metadata comprises a key component of them all. This will be followed by short introductions to the influential Open Archival Information System (OAIS) reference model and a number of other selected initiatives, based on projects originating from national and research libraries, digitization projects and the archives community. The final sections will highlight some issues and look at what needs to be done in the future.

Preservation strategies and metadata

Digital preservation is both a technical and organizational challenge. The technical problems of relatively short media lifetimes and hardware and software obsolescence coincide with a realization that the essential malleability of digital information, though useful in many ways, means that it can be difficult to have trust in its authenticity. Digital preservation, however, means much more than just providing solutions to these problems, but refers to the whole 'series of actions that individuals and institutions take to ensure that a given resource will be accessible for use at some unknown time' (Smith, 2003, 2).

In practical terms, the successful preservation of digital information is dependent upon organizations identifying and implementing suitable preservation strategies. To date, there have been a number of attempts to characterize these. For example, Lee et al. (2002) have identified four distinct strategies, based on preserving technology, emulation, migration and encapsulation.

- *Preserving technology*: a strategy based on collections of obsolete hardware and operating systems being maintained so that data could be read in its original hardware and software environment. It is difficult, however, to *see* this as being more than a short-term solution.
- *Emulation*: the development of emulator programs that can mimic the behaviour of obsolete hardware and operating systems. There is currently a great deal of interest in this strategy, and Rothenberg (2000)

has experimented with an implementation based on an evolving sequence of virtual emulation machines that would enable the technical context of preserved objects to be run on new platforms.

- *Migration*: the periodic transfer of information from one generation of computer technology to a subsequent one. This is currently the most tried-and-tested preservation strategy and is often combined with some kind of format standardization. Migration strategies can also take other forms. For example, researchers at the University of Leeds have recently proposed a form of 'migration on demand' whereby the object's original bit-stream is preserved – helping to maintain its authenticity – and migrating it only at the point of delivery (Mellor, Wheatley and Sergeant, 2002). In this context, the focus of migration moves on to the migration tools themselves, rather than the preserved objects.

- *Encapsulation*: based on the idea that preserved objects should – to some extent – be self-describing. The content is encapsulated with all of the information required for it to be deciphered and understood. This is one of the basic concepts of the OAIS reference model, and has also underpinned the development of the Universal Preservation Format (Shepard, 1998) and the Victorian Electronic Records Strategy (Waugh et al., 2000, 175). Encapsulation can also be used in concert with other strategies, e.g. emulation or migration on demand.

With the possible exception of technology preservation, all of these strategies will depend upon the capture, creation and maintenance of metadata, e.g. emulation strategies will depend upon metadata that links the preserved object with an emulator specification. Migration strategies will depend on metadata that records the intellectual and technological contexts of an object's creation and its migration history. Encapsulation techniques presuppose the linking of data object and metadata.

Preservation metadata is all of the various types of data that will allow the re-creation and interpretation of the structure and content of digital data over time (Ludäsher, Marciano and Moore, 2001). Defined in this way, it is clear that such metadata needs to support a number of distinct, but related, functions. Lynch (1999), for example, has written that within a digital repository, 'metadata accompanies and makes reference to each

digital object and provides associated descriptive, structural, administrative, rights management, and other kinds of information'. The wide range
of functions that preservation metadata is supposed to fulfil means that
defining metadata standards is not a simple task and that most of the currently published schemas are either extremely complex or only attempt to
define a basic framework. The situation is complicated further by the perception that different kinds of metadata will be required to support different digital preservation strategies or digital information types.

The OAIS reference model

The *Reference Model for an Open Archival Information System (OAIS)* is an
attempt to provide a high-level framework for the development and comparison of digital archives. Its development was co-ordinated by the
Consultative Committee on Space Data Systems (CCSDS) as part of an
ISO (International Organization for Standardization) initiative to
develop standards that would support of the long-term preservation of
satellite data, but it has been developed as a generic model, applicable in
any preservation context.

The model aims to provide a common framework that can be used to
help understand archival challenges, especially those that relate to digital information. This is the model's real value, providing a high-level
common language that can facilitate discussion across the different
communities interested in digital preservation. The standard defines a
high-level reference model for an OAIS, defined as an organization of
people and systems that have 'accepted the responsibility to preserve
information and make it available for a Designated Community'
(CCSDS, 2002, 1–11).

The OAIS model has a much wider scope than metadata. It defines
both a functional model and an information model. The functional
model outlines the range of functions that would need to be undertaken
by a repository, and defines in more detail those functions described
within the OAIS specification as access, administration, archival storage,
data management, ingest and preservation planning (Figure 12.1). The
information model defines the broad types of information (or metadata)
that would be required in order to preserve and access the information

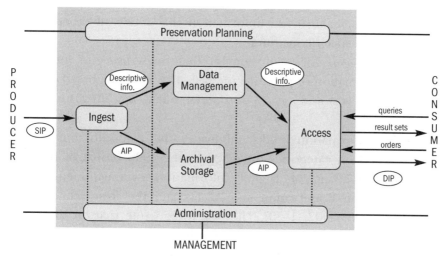

Fig. 12.1 *OAIS functional entities (source: CCSDS, 2002, Fig. 4-1)*

stored in a repository. However, it is important to realize that the OAIS standard is a reference model, not a blueprint for an implementation. All of the many different communities interested in digital preservation will have to apply the model (including the information model) in their own particular contexts, both organizational and technical.

The OAIS information model

The OAIS information model defines a number of different Information Objects that cover the various types of information required for long-term preservation. A basic assumption of the model is that all Information Objects are composed of a Data Object – which would typically be a sequence of bits for digital data – and the Representation Information that would permit the full interpretation of this data into meaningful information (CCSDS, 2002, 4–19). The OAIS model then defines four distinct Information Objects.

- *Content Information*: the information that requires preservation.
- *Preservation Description Information (PDI)*: any information that will allow the understanding of the Content Information over an indefinite period of time.

- *Packaging Information*: the information that binds all other components into a specific medium.
- *Descriptive Information*: information that helps users to locate and access information of potential interest. This could be based on information that is stored as part of the PDI, but is logically distinct.

The OAIS information model subdivides the PDI into four distinct groups based on categories discussed in the 1996 report of the Task Force on Archiving of Digital Information commissioned by the Commission on Preservation and Access and the Research Libraries Group (CCSDS, 2002, 4–28). The task force wrote that 'in the digital environment, the features that determine information integrity and deserve special attention for archival purposes include the following: content, fixity, reference, provenance and context' (Garrett and Waters, 1996). Having already defined Content Information, the OAIS information model divided PDI into the four remaining categories. These are defined as follows:

- *Reference Information*: any information that helps to identify and describe the Content Information. This would specifically include the unique identifiers used to identify the Content Information within the repository and, where appropriate, basic descriptive-type information that could be extracted to form part or all of the Descriptive Information.
- *Context Information*: defined as information that 'documents the relationships of the Content Information to its environment ... why the Content Information was created, and how it relates to other Content Information objects existing elsewhere' (CCSDS, 2002, 4–28). The CPA/RLG report suggested that 'context' should include information on the technical context of a digital object (Garrett and Waters, 1996), but some of this information is assigned in the OAIS model to the Packaging Information (CCSDS, 2002, B-1).
- *Provenance Information*: information that documents the history of the Content Information. This might include information on its source or origin, any changes that may have taken place (e.g. migrations), and a record of the chain of custody. The CPA/RLG report says that the

'assumption underlying the principle of provenance is that the integrity of an information object is partly embodied in tracing from where it came' (Garrett and Waters, 1996).

- *Fixity Information*: refers to any information that documents the particular authentication mechanisms in use within a particular repository. The CPA/RLG report comments that if the content of an object is 'subject to change or withdrawal without notice, then its integrity may be compromised and its value as a cultural record would be severely diminished' (Garrett and Waters, 1996). Changes can either be deliberate or unintentional, but either type would adversely affect the integrity of Content Information.

The OAIS model also defines a conceptual structure for information packages. This is viewed as a container that logically encapsulates Content Information and its associated PDI within a single Data Object. Information packages are defined for submission (SIP), archival storage (AIP) and dissemination (DIP). Of these, the Archival Information Package (AIP) is the most important for digital preservation, as it contains, in principle, 'all the qualities needed for permanent, or indefinite, Long Term Preservation of a designated Information Object' (CCSDS, 2002, 4–33). The OAIS information model has influenced the development of a number of preservation metadata element sets and has informed the development of others. In the next section we will introduce some of these initiatives.

Selected initiatives

To date, the majority of preservation metadata initiatives have originated from three contexts, namely to deal with the preservation concerns of national and research libraries, digitization initiatives and archives (recordkeeping metadata). This section will look at each of these in turn and introduce some of the most prominent initiatives. At this point, however, it should be emphasized that many other metadata standards will contain things that have relevance to digital preservation. For example, the MPEG-7 standard (ISO/IEC 15938) is intended to support the management of audiovisual content, and its description schemes can store information about compression methods, data size, access conditions, etc. (Chang, Sikora and Puri, 2001, 690). The IEEE Learning Object Metadata (LOM) standard (IEEE 1484.12.1-2002) includes elements that describe technical requirements and remarks on installation. It clear that one of the most important challenges of preservation metadata initiatives will be to make best use of all the relevant metadata that exists in other forms.

National and research libraries

National libraries and some research libraries have had a traditional interest in preservation. In particular, national libraries are motivated by their statutory obligation to collect and retain copies of certain types of publication in perpetuity. Many have already adapted legal deposit legislation to enable the collection of digital materials. This has led to a growing awareness of the digital preservation problem, including the need for preservation metadata.

One of the first to address these issues was the National Library of Australia (NLA), who from the 1990s onwards developed a practical response to the collection and preservation of Australia's published digital content. Chief among these has been the creation of its PANDORA (Preserving and Accessing Networked Documentary Resources of Australia) Archive of online publications. In 1999, the NLA issued an exposure draft of its *Preservation Metadata for Digital Collections*. This defined 25 high-level elements (some with sub-elements) that a digital storage system would need to generate in order to facilitate the preservation management of digital information (Phillips et al., 1999). The main focus of the NLA element set was pragmatic, based on the Library's experiences with PANDORA and other initiatives. While its development had been informed by the OAIS model, Webb (2000, 182) commented that the Library's 'focus on building and managing an existing archive, rather than developing an universal model for archiving ... produced some differences in language as well as approach.'

Shortly afterwards, another draft element set was published by the UK Cedars (CURL Exemplars in Digital Archives) project (Russell et al., 2000). Unlike the practical focus of the NLA element set, the Cedars specification was developed to support the development of the project's demonstrator services and as a contribution to the international standardization of preservation metadata. The element set was described as an 'outline specification' because it only defined the highest levels of the metadata that would be required for a full implementation. Unlike the NLA element set, it arranged elements explicitly using the OAIS information model as a framework. It also attempted not to make too many assumptions about the actual form of the digital objects being preserved or about the 'granularity' of specific objects. It was hoped that the specification would be applicable at any level of granularity, but the authors recognized that the specifics of implementation would need to be the responsibility of individual repositories. The specification also made no assumptions about which particular preservation strategy would be used, although it was understood that this would have an impact on which particular elements would be required. The project team were aware that the proposed metadata element set would not necessarily support all of the wider roles identified in the OAIS functional model, e.g. the administration or data management functions. However, it was recognized that some of the information would be able to be used elsewhere within a preservation system, e.g. parts of the Provenance Information could help support administrative functions like rights management. In fact, the Provenance Information defined in the Cedars outline specification contained a number of elements specific to rights management that went well beyond the assumption of the OAIS model that provenance is primarily concerned with supporting the integrity of a given Data Object. This reflected the difficulty of defining metadata schemas where the same information can be used by functionally different parts of a system.

The NEDLIB (Networked European Deposit Library) project developed a deposit system for electronic libraries (DSEP) based on the OAIS model and as part of this tried to define the minimum metadata that would be necessary for preservation management (Lupovici and Masanès, 2000). Like the Cedars specification, the NEDLIB element set explicitly adopted the terminology and structure of the OAIS information model. The element set was much smaller than that proposed by Cedars (18 elements with 38 sub-elements), partly because it was focused only on the identification of mandatory elements, but also because it was only concerned with defining the metadata that would address the problem of technological obsolescence, not with data that would be used for descriptive, administrative or legal purposes.

By 2000, there was a need to find a way of bringing these three schemas together into a single framework. In response to this challenge, OCLC Online Computer Library Center and the Research Libraries Group (RLG) convened an international working group to consider the further development of preservation metadata. The group first produced a state-of-the-art report. This described the OAIS reference model in some detail – noting its importance as a conceptual framework – and provided a comparison and mapping between the NLA, Cedars and NEDLIB element sets (Working Group on Preservation Metadata, 2001). The Working Group next set to work on producing a fresh metadata framework. This resulted in two proposals for Content Information and Preservation Description Information (PDI) that were collected together and published in June 2002 as: *A Metadata Framework to Support the Preservation of Digital Objects* (Working Group on Preservation Metadata, 2002).

The framework produced by the Working Group effectively supersedes the element sets developed by the older initiatives, and represents a good starting point for future practical implementations of preservation metadata. Like the Cedars and NEDLIB element sets, the OCLC/RLG metadata specification explicitly uses the OAIS information model as its framework. The recommendation for Content Information includes the Content Data Object (bit streams) and as Representation Information, both elements that relate to the object itself (e.g. file descriptions, significant properties) or its hardware and software environment (e.g. operating systems). The PDI recommendation defines elements according to the OAIS headings of reference, context, provenance and fixity. The Provenance Information is organized on an event-based model, defining generic elements associated with processes that might be carried out on the Content Digital Object, e.g. transformations undertaken at ingest, format migrations, etc. It was not envisaged that the whole metadata framework would be utilized for each and every object within a preservation system, but that metadata would be implemented at varying levels of specificity. The Working Group noted that the elements were not necessarily atomic and that it was 'easy to imagine cases where the needs and characteristics of particular digital archiving systems ... [would] require deconstruction of these elements into still more precise components.' In 2003, a new group called PREMIS (Preservation Metadata: Implementation Strategies) was formed by the same sponsoring organizations to look at the metadata framework and investigate in more detail the practical aspects of implementing preservation metadata in digital preservation systems.

A step in the same direction has also been taken by the National Library of New Zealand (NLNZ), which published its own preservation metadata specification in November 2002. The metadata is intended to accompany preservation masters kept by the library and to refer to four entities, the objects themselves, the processes undertaken on them, individual files and administrative metadata (National Library of New Zealand, 2002). The framework specification also includes a mapping of the NLNZ element set to the OCLC/RLG framework, the OAIS information model and the draft NISO metadata standard for digital still images.

Digitization projects

Some of the first projects and initiatives to consider the need for preservation metadata were those involved in digitization. A heavy financial investment in digitization meant that there was a need to consider the long-term management of digitized materials. As part of this, there was an awareness that some important information could only be captured at the time of digitization (e.g. Kenney and Rieger, 2000). In response, the RLG constituted a Working Group on the Preservation Issues of Metadata in 1997 to help identify the kinds of information that would be required to manage a digital image master file over time. The final report of the Working Group defined 16 metadata elements (RLG, 1998). A more complex metadata scheme was developed by the Making of America II (MOA2) testbed project (Hurley et al., 1999), the general framework of which has recently been taken up by the METS initiative.

METS, the Metadata Encoding and Transmission Standard

(www.loc.gov/standards/mets/), is an attempt to provide an XML-based document format for encoding metadata to aid the management and exchange of digital library objects. The initiative has adapted the XML Document Type Definition developed by the MOA2 project to create an XML schema. This schema separates metadata into four sections. These are 'descriptive metadata', 'administrative metadata', 'file groups' and 'structural maps', the last two of which are intended to group together all of the files that make up a particular digital object and to link content and metadata to a particular structure. The administrative metadata section is intended to store technical information about the file, as well as information about intellectual property rights held in the resource, the source material, and provenance metadata that records relationships between files and migrations. Broadly speaking, the METS schema provides an XML-based container that could be used to store much of the metadata defined in preservation metadata specifications like that published by the Cedars project. Also, a document fully encoded in METS could easily be viewed as a conceptual Information Package, as defined by the OAIS model.

As part of a separate initiative, a specification of *Technical Metadata for Digital Still Images* is currently under review as a NISO (National Information Standards Organization) draft standard for trial use (NISO Z39.87-2002 AIIM 20-2002). The development of this standard first grew out of an 'Image Metadata Workshop' held in 1999, sponsored by NISO, the Council for Library and Information Resources (CLIR) and the RLG. The draft standard is not intended to duplicate work on descriptive metadata schemas, but to help define a standardized way of recording the technical attributes of digital images and the production techniques associated with them. The data dictionary includes elements that will record detailed information about images themselves (e.g. formats, compression, etc.), the image creation process, some quality metrics and any change history (e.g. migrations). No particular encoding of the elements is recommended, although the Network Development and MARC Standards Office of the Library of Congress maintains an XML schema implementation of it called MIX (www.loc.gov/standards/mix/). Development of the standard is particularly based on the experiences of digitization centres. If and when it is adopted as a standard, it will be of particular use for helping to support the long-term preservation of the products of digital imaging projects.

Recordkeeping metadata

The archives and records professions have also been investigating what metadata might be required to support the long-term preservation of digital objects. As might be expected, their primary focus is on records, defined by ISO 15489 as 'information created, received, and maintained as evidence and information by an organisation or person, in pursuance of legal obligations or in the transaction of business' (Healy, 2001, 138). Recordkeeping metadata specifications, therefore, tend to have a strong emphasis on the development of systems that ensure the authenticity and integrity of electronic records.

There have been a number of initiatives that have attempted to identify and define the basic requirements for recordkeeping metadata. One of the first was based on the Business Acceptable Communications (BAC) model developed by the Functional Requirements for Evidence in Recordkeeping project (the Pittsburgh Project). This proposed a metadata structure that would contain a 'handle layer' for basic discovery data while other layers would store information on terms and conditions of use, data structures, provenance, content and the use of the record since its creation (Bearman and Sochats, 1996). It was envisaged that much of this information would be automatically generated at the time of creation, would be directly linked to each record, and would be able to describe the content and context of the record as well as enabling its decoding for future use (Bearman and Duff, 1996). Duff (2001, 292) has since commented that a large proportion (44%) of the elements defined in the BAC model related to structural information, e.g. the technical information that a computer would use to render a file.

The Pittsburgh Project inspired the development of a whole new series of recordkeeping metadata initiatives, especially in Australia. For example, in 1999 the National Archives of Australia (NAA) published a *Recordkeeping Metadata Standard* that defined the metadata that the NAA recommended should be captured by the recordkeeping systems used by Australian government agencies (NAA, 1999). Another significant development was the development of the Victorian Electronic Records Strategy (VERS). This defined a self-documenting exchange format (the VERS Encapsulated Object) that permitted the transfer of record content (and metadata) over time (Public Record Office Victoria, 2000). Waugh et al. (2000, 179) describe the function of encapsulation in VERS as wrapping the information that needs preservation with the metadata that describes aspects of this information. At the current time, the VERS Encapsulated Object is implemented as an XML object, chosen because this can be read using basic text-editing tools.

All of these developments have been informed by the development of a framework known as the Australian Recordkeeping Metadata Schema (RKMS) by a research project that was led by Monash University. The project, among other things, attempted to specify and standardize the whole range of recordkeeping metadata that would be required to manage records in digital environments (McKemmish et al., 1999). The RKMS was also concerned with supporting interoperability with more generic metadata standards like the Dublin Core and relevant resource discovery schemas like the AGLS Metadata Standard. The RKMS defined a highly structured set of metadata elements conforming to a data model based on that developed for the Resource Description Framework (RDF). The schema was designed to be extensible and to be able to inherit metadata elements from other schemas.

The emphasis of the RKMS on interoperability reminds us that there is a need for recordkeeping metadata standards (as with all preservation metadata) to be able to interoperate with a wide variety of other schemas. Hedstrom (2001, 247) reminds us that metadata is expensive to create, capture and manage, noting that there may be a need to identify which aspects of existing metadata standards could (possibly with adaptation) be used to support recordkeeping requirements.

Issues

Compared with other areas of metadata deployment, preservation metadata standards are still very much in the early stages of their development. The first generation of library-based element sets were published less than five years ago and there is still not enough feedback from practical experience to *see* whether they can solve the problems that they claim to address. The metadata framework published by the OCLC/RLG Working Group represents a good attempt at consensus, but needs considerable work before a version could be implemented for particular formats or repositories. It will be interesting to *see* how the PREMIS working group will address the implementation issue. Some recent criticism of the OCLC/RLG metadata framework suggests that there may be a need to revisit first principles. For example, Hofman (2002, 16) notes that the metadata framework, as with the OAIS information model, omits information on preservation strategies, policies and methods. There may be, therefore, a need to link the elements defined in the framework with the preservation processes that they intend to support.

Interoperability

The multiplicity of initiatives and specifications available makes for a good deal of confusion. There will be an ongoing need to analyse how new standards like the National Library of New Zealand standards framework, METS, NISO Z39.87 or the XML DTD for e-journals proposed by Harvard University Library (Inera, 2001) fit into the rapidly evolving 'landscape' of preservation metadata.

One key concern will be interoperability, e.g. standards that will permit the easy exchange of preservation metadata (or information packages) between repositories. At the present time, it *seems* unlikely that it would be possible to develop a single preservation metadata schema, but some kind of agreement on a baseline exchange format would be useful, possibly based on a schema like METS.

In addition, there will be a need for some kind of interoperability with the range of metadata formats developed for other purposes, but which would provide useful information in a preservation system, e.g. descriptive data from MARC21 or Dublin Core databases, rights metadata, etc. It is interesting that both the Cedars specification and the OCLC/RLG framework defined an 'existing metadata' element, indicating the importance of capturing what metadata already exists, wherever this is possible.

Costs

The complexity and highly technical nature of preservation metadata suggest that it will be expensive, especially where interventions in the creation and maintenance processes are required. There may be ways, however, of reducing some of these costs. One way, for example, would be to learn from the experiences of library cataloguing and to try to minimize the duplication of effort through co-operation.

In a digital preservation context, minimizing duplication will in the first place depend upon timely information being available about which resources digital repositories have attempted to preserve. Second, a repository might also be able to reduce costs by partially automating the creation of metadata, wherever this is possible. So, for example, it would be useful if the systems that will need to be developed to facilitate the ingest or migration of digital objects can automatically output metadata about the processes being carried out, and the people and organizations that have authorized them. Third, some thought should also be given to how best digital repositories should deal with any metadata that already exists. In the longer term, it may be useful to open a dialogue with the creators and distributors of digital objects concerning the nature of the metadata they create. If they were able to adopt metadata strategies conforming to the best practice for preservation metadata, there would be potential cost-savings for repositories. It is also worth noting that any significant time delay between the creation of a digital object and its ingest into a repository may have adverse cost implications, as there is a possibility that some significant information will be lost.

Generating and maintaining preservation metadata is likely to be expensive but is, however, a prerequisite of ensuring successful digital preservation. The difficulty of preserving digital objects without metadata may mean that to create it is ultimately a cheaper and more effective option than the alternative. Chen (2001, 26–7) has written, 'although more semantics in metadata will increase costs, it will minimise human intervention in accessing data; seamless support, transition of stewardship and lifetime maintenance will improve.'

Looking to the future

Future work on preservation metadata will need to focus on several key issues. First, as suggested earlier, there is an urgent need for more practical experience of undertaking digital preservation strategies. Until now, many preservation metadata initiatives have largely been based on theoretical considerations or high-level models like the OAIS. This is not in itself a bad thing, but it is now time to begin to build metadata into the design of working systems that can test the viability of digital preservation strategies in a variety of contexts. This process has already begun in initiatives like VERS and the 'self-validating knowledge-based archives' researched by the San Diego Supercomputer Center (Ludäscher, Marciano and Moore, 2001). Hopefully, the work of the new PREMIS working group will also help move the OCLC/RLG metadata framework towards implementation.

A second need is for increased co-operation between the many metadata initiatives that have an interest in digital preservation. This may include the further comparison and harmonization of various metadata specifications, where this is possible. The OCLC/RLG working group is an example of how this has been taken forward within a particular domain. There is a need for additional co-operation with recordkeeping metadata specialists, computing scientists and others in the metadata research community.

Third, there is a need for more detailed research into how metadata will interact with different formats, preservation strategies and communities of users. This may include some analysis of what metadata could be automatically captured as part of the ingest process, an investigation of the role of content creators in metadata provision, and the production of user requirements.

Conclusion

This chapter outlined some proposed digital preservation strategies, all of which have metadata as a key component. Short introductions were given to the Open Archival Information System reference model and a number of other initiatives, based on projects originating from national and research libraries, digitization projects and the archives community. The issues of interoperability and costs were discussed. Finally, there were suggestions for the work that needs to be done in the future.

References

Bearman, D. and Duff, W. (1996) Grounding Archival Description in the Functional Requirements for Evidence, *Archivaria*, **41** (Spring), 275–303.

Bearman, D. and Sochats, K. (1996) *Metadata Requirements for Evidence*, www.archimuse.com/papers/nhprc/BACartic.html.

Castells, M. (2001) *The Internet Galaxy: reflections on the internet, business and society*, Oxford, Oxford University Press.

Chang, S.-F., Sikora, T. and Puri, A. (2001) Overview of the MPEG-7 Standard, *IEEE Transactions on Circuits and Systems for Video Technology*, **11** (6), 688–95.

Chen, S. S. (2001) The Paradox of Digital Preservation, *Computer*, **34** (3), 24–8.

Consultative Committee on Space Data Systems (2002) Reference model for an Open Archival Information System (OAIS), CCSDS 650.0-B-1 Blue Book, wwwclassic.ccsds.org/documents/pdf/CCSDS-650.0-B-1.pdf.

Cunningham, A. (2000) Dynamic Descriptions: recent developments in standards for archival description and metadata, *Canadian Journal of Information and Library Science*, **25** (4), 3–17.

Day, M. (2001) Metadata for Digital Preservation: a review of recent developments. In Constantopoulos, P. and Sølvberg, I. T. (eds), *Research and Advanced Technology for Digital Libraries: 5th European Conference, ECDL 2001, Darmstadt, Germany, September 4–9, 2001*, Lecture Notes in Computer Science, 2163, Berlin: Springer, 161–72.

Duff, W. (2001) Evaluating Metadata on a Metalevel, *Archival Science*, **1** (3), 285–94.

Garrett, J. and Waters, D., (eds) (1996) *Preserving Digital Information: report of the Task Force on Archiving of Digital Information*, Washington, DC, Commission on Preservation and Access, www.rlg.org/ArchTF/.

Healy, S. (2001) ISO 15489 Records Management – its development and significance, *Records Management Journal*, **11** (3), 133–42.

Hedstrom, M. (2001) Recordkeeping Metadata: presenting the results of a working meeting, *Archival Science*, **1** (3), 243–51.

Hofman, H. (2002) Some Comments on Preservation Metadata and the OAIS

Model, *DigiCULT.info Newsletter*, 2 (October), 15–20, www.digicult.info/downloads/digicult_info2.pdf.

Hurley, B. J. et al. (1999) *The Making of America II Testbed Project: a digital library service model*, Washington, DC, Council on Library and Information Resources, www.clir.org/pubs/abstract/pub87abst.html.

IEEE 1484.12.1-2002 *IEEE Standard for Learning Object Metadata*, Piscataway, NJ, Institute of Electrical and Electronics Engineers.

Inera Incorporated (2001) *E-journal Archive DTD Feasibility Study*, Cambridge, MA, Harvard University E-Journal Archiving Project, www.diglib.org/preserve/hadtdfs.pdf.

ISO 15489:2002 *Information and Documentation – records management*, Geneva, International Organization for Standardization.

ISO/IEC 15938:2002 *Information Technology – multimedia content description interface*, Geneva, International Organization for Standardization.

Kenney, A. R. and Rieger, O. Y. (eds) (2000) *Moving Theory into Practice: digital imaging for libraries and archives*, Mountain View, CA, Research Libraries Group.

Lee, K. H. et al. (2002) The State of the Art and Practice in Digital Preservation, *Journal of Research of the National Institute of Standards and Technology*, **107** (1), 93–106.

Ludäscher, B., Marciano, R. and Moore, R. (2001) Preservation of Digital Data with Self-Validating, Self-Instantiating Knowledge-Based Archives, *SIGMOD Record*, **30** (3), 54–63.

Lupovici, C. and Masanès, J. (2000) *Metadata for the Long Term Preservation of Electronic Publications*, The Hague, Koninklijke Bibliotheek, www.kb.nl/coop/nedlib/results/NEDLIBmetadata.pdf.

Lynch, C. (1999) Canonicalisation: a fundamental tool to facilitate preservation and management of digital information, *D-Lib Magazine*, **5** (9), www.dlib.org/dlib/september99/09lynch.html.

McKemmish, S. et al. (1999) Describing Records in Context in the Continuum: the Australian Recordkeeping Metadata Schema, *Archivaria*, **48** (Fall), 3–43, http://rcgr.dstc.edu.au/publications/archiv01.htm.

Mellor, P., Wheatley, P. and Sergeant, D. (2002) Migration on Request: a practical technique for preservation. In Agosti, M. and Thanos, C. (eds), *Research and Advanced Technology for Digital Libraries: 6th European Conference, ECDL 2002, Rome, Italy, September 16–18, 2002*, Lecture Notes in Computer

Science, 2458, Berlin, Springer, 516–26.

National Archives of Australia (1999) *Recordkeeping Metadata Standard for Commonwealth Agencies*, v. 1.0, Canberra, National Archives of Australia, www.naa.gov.au/recordkeeping/control/rkms/summary.htm.

National Library of New Zealand (2002) *Metadata Standards Framework – preservation metadata*, Wellington, National Library of New Zealand, www.natlib.govt.nz/files/4initiatives_metaschema.pdf.

NISO Z39.87-2002 *AIIM 20-2002 Data Dictionary – technical metadata for digital still images*, Bethesda, MD, National Information Standards Organisation, www.niso.org/standards/resources/Z39_87_trial_use.pdf.

Phillips, M. et al. (1999) *Preservation Metadata for Digital Collections: exposure draft*, Canberra, National Library of Australia, www.nla.gov.au/preserve/pmeta.html.

Public Record Office Victoria (2000) *PROS 99/007 Standard for the Management of Electronic Records*, v. 1.2, Melbourne, Public Record Office Victoria, www.prov.vic.gov.au/vers/standards/pros9907.htm.

Research Libraries Group (1998) *RLG Working Group on Preservation Issues of Metadata: final report*, Mountain View, CA, Research Libraries Group, www.rlg.org/preserv/presmeta.html.

Rothenberg, J. (2000) *An Experiment in Using Emulation to Preserve Digital Publications*, The Hague, Koninklijke Bibliotheek, www.kb.nl/coop/nedlib/results/NEDLIBemulation.pdf.

Russell, K. et al. (2000) *Metadata for Digital Preservation: the Cedars project outline specification*, www.leeds.ac.uk/cedars/metadata.html.

Shepard, T. (1998) Universal Preservation Format (UPF): conceptual framework, *RLG DigiNews*, **2** (6), www.rlg.org/preserv/diginews/diginews2-6.html.

Smith, A. (2003) *New-Model Scholarship: how will it survive?*, Washington, DC, Council on Library and Information Resources, www.clir.org/pubs/abstract/pub114abst.html.

Waugh, A. et al. (2000) Preserving Digital Information Forever. In *ACM 2000 Digital Libraries: proceedings of the fifth ACM Conference on Digital Libraries, June 2-7, 2000, San Antonio, Texas*, New York, Association for Computing Machinery, 175–84.

Webb, C. (2000) Towards a Preserved National Collection of Selected Australian Digital Publications, *New Review of Academic Librarianship*, **6**, 179–91.

Working Group on Preservation Metadata (2001) *Preservation Metadata for Digital Objects: a review of the state of the art*, www.oclc.org/research/pmwg/presmeta_wp.pdf.

Working Group on Preservation Metadata (2002) *A Metadata Framework to Support the Preservation of Digital Objects*, www.oclc.org/research/pmwg/pm_framework.pdf.

13

Metadata and spatial data

Patrick McGlamery

Introduction

This chapter will explore the history and nature of digital geospatial data, GIS and metadata, and it will describe current best practices and point toward the emerging use of metadata in the field.

For centuries, geospatial data has been documented in field manuals, records and maps. More recently this data has become digital. Digital geospatial data is processed in a Geographic Information System or GIS. GIS data, which is stored in a database management system, can be rendered as maps, graphs, tables and reports of various formats. The data is generally Cartesian in structure, representing latitude and longitude as X/Y point sets, with higher resolution data manifesting more point sets, and lower resolution fewer. These large numeric datasets, representing, for example, the banks of a particularly serpentine river, can be very large indeed and typically lack narrative details. Metadata has emerged as the procedure for describing the data, its co-ordinate type, projection and provenance.

Maps

There are a variety of types of maps: topographic and special purpose or thematic. Cartography is the science of map-making. In cartography, data is rendered graphically. On a topographic map rivers and water bodies are

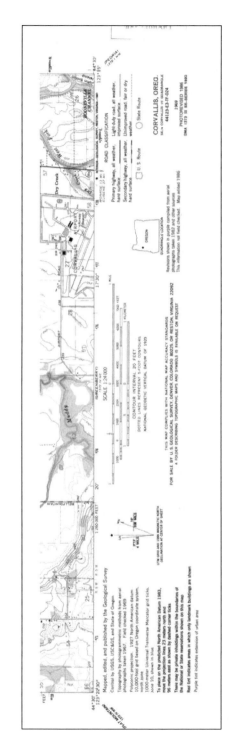

Fig. 13.1 Bottom margin of standard USGS 7.5 minute topographic quadrangle

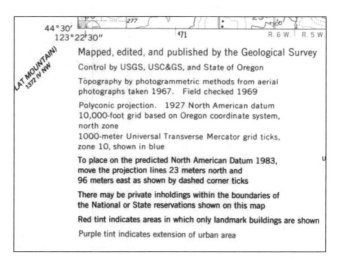

Fig. 13.2 Citation information

shown as blue lines and polygons; on a thematic map, the lines may be coloured to indicate what sort of hydrography they represent, such as palastrine or lacustrine. The cartographer has developed standardized symbology to render complex data into a map. The first step for a cartographer is data compilation. After pulling all the information together, the cartographer then synthesizes the information. The final map communicates hard scientific data as a digestible, cartographic information object.

Much the same way monographs contain a title page, bibliography and index, maps contain citations of compiled data as marginalia. A US

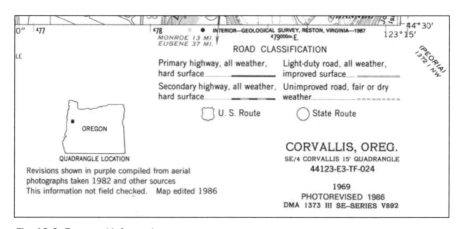

Fig. 13.3 Temporal information

Geological Survey 7.5 Minute Topographic Survey map sheet's bottom margin is typical of most national mapping series topographic maps. The example shown in Figure 13.1 from the Corvallis, Oregon Quadrangle shows five areas: citation, true north, scale and contour, location and print information.

The citation information, as shown in Figure 13.2, documents the source of the information. Topography was taken by photogrammetry from aerial photography in 1967, field checked in 1969. There are three Cartesian systems represented on this map: Latitude/Longitude, Universal Transverse Mercator (a national 1000-metre grid) and Oregon co-ordinate system (a state 10,000-foot grid). This map uses the North American Datum 1927 for the neatline, or extent of the map, but pre-dicts the North American Datum 1983 by indicating with a cross-hair or 'dashed corner tick' where 44°30´ is located. A narrative directs the user, 'To ... move the projection lines 23 metres north and 96 metres east' to conform to our current understanding of geodesy.

The centre portions of information report that the scale of the map is 1:24,000 and that the contour intervals are five feet.

The temporal information is on the bottom right of the map as shown in Figure 13.3. The base map information is 1969 as noted in the citation, but this map was 'photorevised' in 1986 from aerial photography taken in 1982. These revisions are shown in purple on the map. The map was printed in 1987 providing a temporal continuity and record of change.

These various data elements transform the graphic map into a carto-graphic information object. The lines take on scientific precision and accuracy. Topographic maps are rarely created whole. More often, they are copied from previous surveys and revised, either in a remote sensing lab, or in the field. For the serious user, understanding the provenance of the features as they are rendered on the map is extremely important. Maps are, after all, secondary information objects. Highly edited and concise, they hint at reality. For a more primary record, aerial photogra-phy or other remotely sensed imagery is required.

Aerial photography is simply a picture. However, installed in the right equipment the picture becomes scientific data for the precise measure of the Earth's surface. In order to calibrate the photogrammetric instru-ment, elements of the photograph are needed: the scale, the lens used, the day of the year and the time of the day. These are not normally written in the margin and care must be taken to supply the information, if the aerial photography was not catalogued or described.

Cataloguing maps and aerial photography and other remotely sensed imagery, like satellite imagery, has been done in MARC format since the 1960s. Map cataloguing requires fields distinct from the book format, like the 034 Mathematical Data and 255 Scale, Co-ordinates and Projection. Map cataloguers have typically been diligent in assuring that these elements are captured and noted. This has benefited the user by providing them with the capability at the catalogue of determining the best selection of map for a particular project, especially as digital data and analogue material begin to merge.

In 1987 the International Cartographic Union debated the changing nature of 'the map' and cartography. Visvalingam (1989) suggested, 'if cartography is concerned with the making and use of maps, then it is not just concerned with visual products: it is equally concerned with the processes of mapping, from data collection, transformation and simplification through to symbolism and with map reading, analysis and interpretation. These intellectual processes are expressed in terms of prevailing technologies and computer-based Information Technology is fast becoming the dominant technology of the day.' Her observation marked the transition of the map from a static, printed document to a dynamic, structured dataset that can be accessed and queried through a Geographic Information System.

Geographic Information Systems (GIS)

GIS has emerged as a response to the burgeoning of spatial information since World War 2. Aerial photography, expanding cities and suburbs, highway building and resource exploitation all combined to drive the mapping sciences and explode the amount of geographic data. GIS database management systems process the vast amounts of data available to today's decision makers. In the 1960s, the Canadian government built the first GIS. The Canada Geographic Information System was designed to analyse data collected by the Canada Land Inventory. The system tracked land and resources classification. Heavily dependent on mainframe computing, GIS systems were not widely used until the late 1970s, when the PC was introduced, and technological improvements at lower costs made computers widely available. GIS sales boomed during the 1980s, as governments and businesses found more uses for the systems.

An early adapter of GIS and geospatial data for enumeration and analysis in the USA was the Bureau of the Census. While hardly one of the powerhouse mapping agencies in the government, the Bureau has, for the past three decades, been keenly attuned to the needs of its users. Beginning with the DIME (Dual Incidence Matrix Encoding, later Dual Independent Map Encoding) files in 1967 and then fulfilling the vision with the 1990 TIGER files (Topologically Integrated Geographic Encoding and Referencing) the Bureau pushed the limits of computer mapping. DIME and TIGER were used to address-match mailed census responses and geocode them to census geographies like census tracts (Cooke, 1998). TIGER implementation coincided with the advent of PC computing and CD-ROM technologies. With the advent of the personal computer and the CD-ROM the tyranny of the mainframe and 9-track tape mount and their attendant coding requirements was broken. In the US, this meant the distribution of geospatial data to some 1400 libraries in the US Federal Depository programme. It also drove low-cost digital mapping. For a brief time DeLorme's Street Atlas was one of the hottest selling products in the PC market. Now Microsoft's Streets & Trips is distributed as part of their Works Suite, making it part of most PCs sold in the USA. Digital mapping has become an everyday part of many people's lives, through MapQuest (where you can enter an address and get the relevant map), but also through routing of delivery services, market analysis and placement and the ubiquitous polling. All are directly linked to the Bureau of the Census' vision of automating encoding for the 1970 US decennial census.

Institutional sharing of spatial geo-data

Coming from the Bureau's social science data background, data dictionaries and documentation were strong with both DIME and TIGER. However, the concept, structure and format of metadata would have to wait until 1992 when a Specialist's Meeting of the National Center for Geographic Information and Analysis (NCGIA) was held. 'Institutions Sharing Geographic Information' recommended five areas of research issues and activities. The area 'Metadata Issues and Sharing Geographic Data' recommended:

> Effective sharing of geographic data on a widespread basis requires that individuals and organizations must be able to determine whether data already acquired by others is appropriate for their use. For the following questions, geographic or spatial 'metadata' is defined as digital information that allows potential users of digital geographic data to understand that data's fitness for use.
>
> Onsrud and Rushton, 1995

A meeting was held at the US Geological Survey during the summer of 1992 and the Federal Geographic Data Committee (FGDC) was charged with developing spatial metadata standards. Essentially users recognized that the very large numeric datasets that comprise geospatial data is ill equipped to provide the sort of citation, true north, scale and contour, location and print information that a basic topographic map provides. This lack of fundamental information begged the question of whether the data was 'fit to use'. Goodchild (1995) sums it up:

> No one should be willing to make use of data they do not trust, or whose accuracy they do not understand. But since the effective description of quality is a function of use, the task of describing quality against all possible uses is formidable . . . traditionally mapmakers have provided data-quality reports that satisfy the largest possible number of users while requiring only a reasonable level of effort . . . it is essential that quality be handled and transmitted as metadata, fully integrated with the data themselves . . . With better forms of metadata and better methods of tracking data quality through GIS operations, we have the opportunity to study the impact of such information on the decision-making process itself.

Directed spatial information policy

The US Office of Management and Budget (OMB) issued a directive

(Circular A-16) in October 1990 that established the Federal Geographic Data Committee. The FGDC was charged with fostering co-ordination among US federal agencies and also among the non-federal sectors that have an interest in spatial data. A major objective of A-Circular 16 is creating a 'national digital spatial information resource'. This came to be called the National Spatial Data Infrastructure (NSDI).

The concept of a national spatial data infrastructure was first advanced by the Mapping Science Committee (MSC) in its 1993 report, *Toward a Coordinated Spatial Data Infrastructure for the Nation*. Subsequent MSC reports have addressed specific components of the NSDI, including partnerships (*Promoting the National Spatial Data Infrastructure through Partnerships*, 1994), basic data types (*A Data Foundation for the National Spatial Data Infrastructure*, 1995), future trends (*The Future of Spatial Data and Society*, 1997), conceptual infrastructure (*Distributed GeoLibraries*, 1998) and licensing of geodata (a current study, 2003).

The Mapping Science Committee serves as a focus for external advice to federal agencies on scientific and technical matters related to spatial data handling and analysis. The purpose of the committee is to provide advice on the development of a robust national spatial data infrastructure for making informed decisions at all levels of government and throughout society in general.

Developing standards

Executive Order 12906, 'Coordinating Geographic Data Acquisition and Access: The National Spatial Data Infrastructure' signed on 11 April 1994 by President Clinton, mandated that all federal agencies would document their spatial data one year from the Order date. On 8 June 1994, the FGDC issued the Content Standards for Digital Geospatial Materials. In 1997 the European Committee for Standardization (CEN), Technical Committee (TC) 287 published a draft of a European Standard for Geographic metadata (Smits, 1996). In April 1997, the FGDC formed an FGDC/ISO Metadata Task Force, which was disbanded when the ISO Metadata Standard 15046-15 was approved by ISO Technical Committee 211 Geographic information/Geomatics (TC211) as a Committee Draft. The International Metadata Standard ISO/DIS 19115 was approved in the northern autumn of 2002. As of April 2003, it was still 'under publication'. Until ISO/DIS 19115 various metadata standards for describing spatial geodata have been in use around the world. As ISO 19115 is approved, these national standards will be mapped to the ISO standard. The process, as long term as it has been, has provided for the harmonization of the various national standards into an international standard. The voting members are Australia, Austria, Belgium, Canada, China, Czech Republic, Denmark, Finland, Germany, Hungary, Iran, Italy, Jamaica, Japan, Republic of Korea, Malaysia, Morocco, Netherlands, New Zealand, Norway, Portugal, Russia, Saudi Arabia, South Africa, Spain, Sweden, Switzerland, Tanzania, Thailand, UK, USA, and Yugoslavia.

Content standards for spatial metadata

ISO/DIS 19115 provides a schema for describing digital geospatial data using a comprehensive set of mandatory and optional metadata elements. These elements support four major uses:

1 *Discovery of data* – Metadata elements have been selected that enable users to locate geospatial data and also allow producers to advertise the availability of their data.
2 *Determining data fitness for use* – Users can determine if a dataset meets their needs by understanding the quality, accuracy, spatial and temporal extents and the spatial reference system used. Metadata elements have been selected accordingly.
3 *Data access* – After locating and determining if a dataset will meet their needs, users may require metadata elements that describe how to access a dataset and transfer it to their site. Metadata elements have been selected to provide the location of a dataset (e.g. through a URL) in addition to its size, format, price and restrictions on use.
4 *Use of data* – Metadata elements have been selected so that users know how to process, apply, merge and overlay a particular dataset with others, as well as understanding the properties and limitations of the data.

The ISO standard uses the hierarchical structure utilized by most of the national standards. In the ISO standard, metadata is presented in the

UML (Unified Modelling) packages listed below. Each package contains one or more entities (UML class attribute), and within each entity there are mandatory and optional metadata elements.

- Metadata entity set information
- Identification information (includes data and service identification)
  - Browse graphic information
  - Keyword information
  - Representative fraction information
  - Resolutions information
  - Usage information
- Constraint information (includes legal and security)
- Data quality information
  - Lineage information
  - Process step information
  - Source information
  - Data quality element information
  - Result information
  - Scope information
- Maintenance information
  - Scope description information
- Spatial representation information (includes grid and vector representation)
  - Dimension information
  - Geometric information
- Reference system information (includes temporal, co-ordinate and geographic identifiers)
  - Ellipsoidal parameter information
  - Identifier information
  - Oblique line azimuth information
  - Oblique line point information
  - Projections parameter information
- Content information (includes Feature catalogue and Coverage descriptions)
  - Range dimension information (includes Band information)
- Portrayal Catalogue information

- Distribution information
  - Digital transfer options information
  - Distributor information
  - Format information
  - Medium information
  - Standard order process information
- Metadata extension information
  - Extended element information
- Application Schema information
  - Feature type list information
  - Spatial attribute supplement information
- Extent information
  - Geographic extent information
  - Temporal extent information
  - Vertical extent information
- Citation and responsible party information
  - Address information
  - Contact information
  - Date information
  - OnLine resource information
  - Series information
  - Telephone information
- Metadata Application information.

These elements and structure are only different in format from the older FGDC. Until ISO 19115 is the accepted standard, and we can reasonably expect that decision to be made this year, FGDC provides the best model of how a metadata standard and format provide for the user. In existence for a decade, the FGDC Content Standard for Digital Geospatial Metadata has provided the building blocks for a dynamic and effective information-sharing network.

FGDC content standards as a working model

The elements used in FGDC metadata is not radically different from those that will be used in IOS 19115. Both standards are strictly hierarchical and both cover the basics (and maybe a bit more) of describing geospatial data. There are seven sections: 1) Identification, 2) Data Quality, 3) Spatial Data Organization, 4) Spatial Reference, 5) Entity and Attribute, 6) Distribution and 7) Metadata Reference information, and three supplemental sections: 8) Citation, 9) Time Period and 10) Contact information.

When the content standards were devised by the FGDC Working Group, they had the good fortune of having an excellent map cataloguer working with them. Elizabeth Mangan (retired from the Geography and Map Division of the Library of Congress), one of the authors of the MARC Maps Format, provided strong guidance in the underlying concepts of the standards. The concepts of Required, Mandatory and Optional are clearly stated in the documentation. They make what could be a complex and difficult format reasonably articulate at least to the cataloguing librarian.

(The example of TIGER metadata shown below is illustrative and not a comprehensive example of the format. It is included to show the scope of the format and its hierarchical nature.)

Identification information

The Identification information is the first section. Large numeric data files typically lack descriptive information, as even when headers are included the information is highly structured and idiosyncratic. The section provides basic information on the dataset title, the area covered, keywords, the purpose and an abstract, and access and use restrictions. This key section includes the Citation and Time Period supplemental sections. While these sections are repeated this is the first and primary use.

Citation information is, again, fairly straightforward for the librarian. A particular consideration for spatial information is the Geospatial_Data_Presentation_Form (element 8.6 in the CSDGM [Content Standard for Digital Geospatial Metadata] Manual). This 'mandatory if applicable' element provides the opportunity to cite, whether the data came from an atlas, audio file, diagram, document, globe, map, tabular digital data, etc. The documentation states, 'the listed domain is partially from pp 88–91 in Anglo-American Committee on Cataloguing Cartographic Materials, 1982, *Cartographic materials: A manual of interpretation for AACR2*' (FGDC, 1998).

```
Citation:
    Citation_Information:
        Originator: U.S. Department of Commerce, U.S. Census
Bureau, Geography Division
        Publication_Date: 2001
        Title: TIGER 2000 streets
        Edition: Census 2000
        Geo-spatial_Data_Presentation_Form: vector digital data
        Series_Information:
            Series_Name: TIGER/Line Files
        Publication_Information:
            Publication_Place: Washington, DC
            Publisher:
                U.S. Department of Commerce
                U.S. Census Bureau
                Geography Division
        Online_Linkage:
\\bunko\magic\data\vector\37800\tran\s24\ctdep\Transportation.mdb
```

The Identification information section's purpose is to provide a narrative describing the dataset's 'fitness for use'. Spatial data is complex in many ways. The data represents a scale or granularity of information. Spatial data is often re-used for a variety of purposes. For the data producer, as much as the data user, there is an anxiety that the data will be used irresponsibly. For example that TIGER street centreline data (represented at 1:100,000 scale, or 1 cm equals 100,000 cm, or 1 inch equals 100,000 inches) can be used to site a storm drain (typically requiring an engineering scale 1 inch equals 1000 feet or 1:12,000). The Abstract and Purpose provide a place to put down in plain language why the dataset was created and what it is meant to do. The particular spatial component of the Identification information section is the Spatial_Domain. This bounding box describes a 'footprint' of the data, and in a clearinghouse can enable spatial location of information. If looking for information about Hartford, Connecticut, whose centre point is N41° 45' 49"/W72° 41' 08", code can determine that the point is within the bounding box for Connecticut.

Description:

Abstract: *TIGER, TIGER/Line, and Census TIGER are registered trademarks of the U.S. Census Bureau. ZCTA is a trademark of the U.S. Census Bureau. The Census 2000 TIGER/Line files are an extract of selected geographic and cartographic information from the Census TIGER data base. The geographic coverage for a single TIGER/Line file is a county or statistical equivalent entity, with the coverage area based on January 1, 2000 legal boundaries.*

Purpose: *In order for others to use the information in the Census TIGER data base in a geographic information system (GIS) or for other geographic applications, the Census Bureau releases to the public extracts of the data base in the form of TIGER/Line files.*

Supplemental_Information: *To find out more about TIGER/Line files and other Census TIGER data base derived datasets visit http://www.census.gov/geo/www/tiger.*

Time_Period_of_Content:

Time_Period_Information:

Single_Date/Time:

Calendar_Date: *2000*

Currentness_Reference: *2000*

Status:

Progress: *Complete*

Maintenance_and_Update_Frequency: *TIGER/Line files are extracted from the Census TIGER data base when needed for geographic programs required to support the census and survey programs of the U.S. Census Bureau. No changes or updates will be made to the Census 2000 TIGER/Line files. Future releases of TIGER/Line files will reflect updates made to the Census TIGER data base and will be released under a version numbering system based on the month and year the data is extracted.*

Spatial_Domain:

Bounding_Coordinates:

West_Bounding_Coordinate: *-73.73333*

```
      East_Bounding_Coordinate:  -71.78333
      North_Bounding_Coordinate: +42.06667
      South_Bounding_Coordinate: +40.96667
  Keywords:
    Theme:
      Theme_Keyword_Thesaurus: None
      Theme_Keyword: Line Feature
      Theme_Keyword: Feature Identifier
      Theme_Keyword: Boundary
    Place:
      Place_Keyword_Thesaurus: FIPS Publication 6-4 FIPS Publication 55
      Place_Keyword: Connecticut
  Access_Constraints: None
```

Use_Constraints: *None. Acknowledgment of the U.S. Census Bureau would be appreciated for products derived from these files. TIGER, TIGER/Line, and Census TIGER are registered trademarks of the U.S. Census Bureau. ZCTA is a trademark of the U.S. Census Bureau.*

Native_Data_Set_Environment: *Microsoft Windows 2000 Version 5.0 (Build 2195) Service Pack 3; ESRI ArcCatalog 8.2.0.700*

Data Quality information

The Data Quality information section documents horizontal and vertical accuracy assessment, dataset completeness and lineage. Lineage is perhaps the most important element of the metadata record, and perhaps the least applied. Data is, by its nature, processed and re-processed. Each time a process step is performed, it should be noted in the lineage. The Process_Step element can, and should, be repeated as needed. This element probably goes the farthest in assuring peace of mind for the user determining the fitness for use of the dataset for their needs.

```
Data_Quality_Information:
  Attribute_Accuracy:
    Attribute_Accuracy_Report: Accurate against Federal
information Processing Standards (FIPS), FIPS Publication 6-
```

4, and FIPS-55 at the 100% level for the codes and base names. The remaining attribute information has been examined but has not been fully tested for accuracy.

Logical_Consistency_Report: The feature network of lines (as represented by Record Types 1 and 2) is complete for census purposes. Spatial objects in TIGER/Line belong to the 'Geometry and Topology' (GT) class of objects in the 'Spatial Data Transfer Standard' (SDTS) FIPS Publication 173 and are topologically valid. Node/geometry and topology (GT)- polygon/chain relationships are collected or generated to satisfy topological edit requirements.

These requirements include:

    * Complete chains must begin and end at nodes.

    * Complete chains must connect to each other at nodes.

    * Complete chains do not extend through nodes.

    * Left and right GT-polygons are defined for each complete chain element and are consistent throughout the extract process.

    * The chains representing the limits of the files are free of gaps.

The Census Bureau performed automated tests to ensure logical consistency and limits of files. All polygons are tested for closure.

Completeness_Report: Data completeness of the TIGER/Line files reflects the contents of the Census TIGER data base at the time the TIGER/Line files (Census 2000 version) were created.

Positional_Accuracy:

  Horizontal_Positional_Accuracy:

    Horizontal_Positional_Accuracy_Report: The information present in these files is provided for the purposes of statistical analysis and census operations only. Coordinates in the TIGER/Line files have six implied decimal places, but the positional accuracy of these coordinates is not as great as the six decimal places suggest. The positional accuracy varies with the source materials used, but generally the

*information is no better than the established national map
Accuracy standards for 1:100,000-scale maps from the U.S.
Geological Survey (USGS); thus it is NOT suitable for high-
precision measurement applications such as engineering
problems, property transfers, or other uses that might
require highly accurate measurements of the earth's surface.*
  Lineage:
    Source_Information:
      Source_Citation:
        Citation_Information:
          Originator: *U.S. Department of Commerce, U.S.
Census Bureau, Geography Division*
          Publication_Date: *Unpublished material*
          Title: *Census TIGER data base*
          Edition: *Census 2000*
      Type_of_Source_Media: *On line*
      Source_Time_Period_of_Content:
        Time_Period_Information:
          Single_Date/Time:
            Calendar_Date: *2000*
        Source_Currentness_Reference: *Date the file was made
available to create TIGER/Line File extracts.*
        Source_Citation_Abbreviation: TIGER
        Source_Contribution: *Selected geographic and cartographic
information (line segments) from the Census TIGER data base.*
    Process_Step:
      Process_Description: *In order for others to use the
information in the Census TIGER data base in a GIS or for
other geographic applications, the Census Bureau releases
periodic extracts of selected information from the Census
TIGER data base, organized as topologically consistent
networks.*
        Source_Used_Citation_Abbreviation: *Census TIGER data base*
        Process_Date: 2000

Spatial Data Organization information

This section relates how the data is organized, with raster, vector, or an indirect (e.g. address) link to location. Spatial data is organized in a variety of ways, some more appropriate for certain types of analysis than others. A raster dataset provides continuous data, but can be difficult to interpret. Vector data can *see*m easier to interpret, though it may reflect aggregated data that by its nature is more imprecise. The user often must choose one over the other, and determine the spatial authenticity of the choice. The information in this section is essentially software supplied and is primarily mathematical data.

```
Spatial_Data_Organization_Information:
  Indirect_Spatial_Reference:
    Federal Information Processing Standards (FIPS) and
    feature names and addresses.
  Direct_Spatial_Reference_Method: Vector
  Point_and_Vector_Object_Information:
    SDTS_Terms_Description:
      SDTS_Point_and_Vector_Object_Type: String
      Point_and_Vector_Object_Count: 199730
    SDTS_Terms_Description:
     SDTS_Point_and_Vector_Object_Type: Entity point
    SDTS_Terms_Description:
      SDTS_Point_and_Vector_Object_Type: Complete chain
      Point_and_Vector_Object_Count: 790 to 83,000
    SDTS_Terms_Description:
      SDTS_Point_and_Vector_Object_Type: GT-polygon composed
      of chains
      Point_and_Vector_Object_Count: 290 to 33,000
```

Spatial Reference information

The Spatial Reference information section contains latitude–longitude or other co-ordinate system information and/or the map projection. In a spatial dataset, a very large numeric dataset, the numbers require context. The Spatial Reference information is critical to determining what the number means. Without this critical set of information the GIS displays the numbers where they lie. The map layers may not line up, unless or until the co-ordinate systems and projections are resolved. This information is often supplied by software systems as well.

```
Spatial_Reference_Information:
  Horizontal_Coordinate_System_Definition:
    Planar:
      Grid_Coordinate_System:
        Grid_Coordinate_System_Name: State Plane Coordinate
System 1983
        State_Plane_Coordinate_System:
          SPCS_Zone_Identifier: 600
          Lambert_Conformal_Conic:
            Standard_Parallel: 41.200000
            Standard_Parallel: 41.866667
            Longitude_of_Central_Meridian: -72.750000
            Latitude_of_Projection_Origin: 40.833333
            False_Easting: 999999.999996
            False_Northing: 499999.999998
      Planar_Coordinate_Information:
        Planar_Coordinate_Encoding_Method: coordinate pair
        Coordinate_Representation:
          Abscissa_Resolution: 0.001024
          Ordinate_Resolution: 0.001024
        Planar_Distance_Units: survey feet
    Geodetic_Model:
      Horizontal_Datum_Name: North American Datum of 1983
      Ellipsoid_Name: Geodetic Reference System 80
      Semi-major_Axis: 6378137.000000
      Denominator_of_Flattening_Ratio: 298.257222
  Vertical_Coordinate_System_Definition:
      Altitude_System_Definition:
      Altitude_Resolution: 0.000010
      Altitude_Encoding_Method: Explicit elevation coordinate
included with horizontal coordinates
```

Entity and Attribute information

The Entity and Attribute information section is perhaps the least developed of the sections. FGDC metadata was devised to describe spatial data, specifically cartographic data. Ten years later, which means ten years' worth of demographic data from various censuses, datasets mapping demographics have become common. This section is where the particulars of social science tabular data could be described. FGDC pre-dates the social science data librarian's DDI or Data Documentation Initiative, a sophisticated and complete metadata format for statistical data. The DDI is as thin on spatial data description as FGDC is for statistical data. Hopefully the two disciplines will share standards development more effectively in the future, especially as the technologies of the two communities merge. The shortcoming is accentuated with demographic spatial datasets when the users look to the metadata to serve as a data dictionary in highly encoded statistical data. As it now stands, there are two levels of description in the Entity and Attribute information section: the Detailed and Overview Descriptions. The Detailed Description deals with attributes or variables while the Overview provides the opportunity to give a narrative description. There can be hundreds of attributes; in this TIGER set there are 59, abbreviated here to three. Moreover, in an attribute there can be hundreds of codes. The CFCC, Class Feature Category Code, is the variable in TIGER which describes the type of street; for example 'Primary road with limited access or interstate highway, unseparated, in tunnel'. In this example this code is best given in the Overview Description as a narrative, though it might be handled better in the DDI.

```
Entity_and_Attribute_Information:
  Detailed_Description:
    Entity_Type:
      Entity_Type_Label: street
    Attribute:
      Attribute_Label: OBJECTID
      Attribute_Definition: Internal feature number.
      Attribute_Definition_Source: ESRI
      Attribute_Domain_Values:
```

Unrepresentable_Domain: *Sequential unique whole numbers that are automatically generated.*
Attribute:
Attribute_Label: *Shape*
Attribute_Definition: *Feature geometry.*
Attribute_Definition_Source: *ESRI*
Attribute_Domain_Values:
Unrepresentable_Domain: *Coordinates defining the features.*
Attribute:
Attribute_Label: *CFCC*
Overview_Description:
Entity_and_Attribute_Overview: The line features and polygon information form the majority of data in the TIGER/Line files. Some of the data/attributes describing the lines include coordinates, feature identifiers (names), CFCCs (used to identify the most noticeable characteristic of a feature), address ranges, and geographic entity codes.
Feature Class A, Road:
The U.S. Census Bureau uses the term divided to refer to a road with opposing traffic lanes separated by any size median, and separated to refer to lanes that are represented in the Census TIGER® data base as two distinct complete chains. The term, rail line in centre, indicates that a rail line shares the road right-of-way. The rail line may follow the centre of the road or be directly next to the road; representation is dependent upon the available source used during the update. The rail line can represent a railroad, a streetcar line, or other carline.
Primary Highway With Limited Access:
Interstate highways and some toll highways are in this category (A1) and are distinguished by the presence of interchanges. These highways are accessed by way of ramps and have multiple lanes of traffic. The opposing traffic lanes are divided by a median strip. The TIGER/Line® files may depict these opposing traffic lanes as two distinct lines in

which case, the road is called separated.
    CFCC Description
            A11 Primary road with limited access or
interstate highway, unseparated
            A12 Primary road with limited access or
interstate highway, unseparated, in tunnel
            A13 Primary road with limited access or
interstate highway, unseparated, underpassing
            A14 Primary road with limited access or
interstate highway, unseparated, with rail line in centre
            A15 Primary road with limited access or
interstate highway, separated
            A16 Primary road with limited access or
interstate highway, separated, in tunnel
            A17 Primary road with limited access or
interstate highway, separated, underpassing
            A18 Primary road with limited access or
interstate highway, separated, with rail line in centre.
    Entity_and_Attribute_Detail_Citation: U.S. Census Bureau,
TIGER/Line files, Census 2000 Technical Documentation. The
TIGER/Line documentation defines the terms and definitions
used within the files.

Distribution information

The Distribution information section provides the distributor, file format
of data, offline media types, online link to data, and fees, if any.

```
Distribution_Information:
  Distributor:
    Contact_Information:
      Contact_Organization_Primary:
        Contact_Organization:
          U.S. Department of Commerce
          U.S. Census Bureau
          Geography Division
```

```
        Products and Services Staff
    Contact_Address:
      Address_Type: Physical address
      Address: 8903 Presidential Parkway, Room 303 WP I
      City: Upper Marlboro
      State_or_Province: Maryland
      Postal_Code: 20772
    Contact_Address:
      Address_Type: Mailing address
      Address: 4700 Silver Hill Road, Stop 7400
      City: Washington
      State_or_Province: District of Columbia
      Postal_Code: 20233-7400
    Contact_Voice_Telephone: (301) 457-1128
    Contact_Voice_Telephone: (301) 457-1128
    Contact_Facsimile_Telephone:
      (301) 457-4710
      Contact_Electronic_Mail_Address: tiger@census.gov
  Resource_Description: Census 2000 TIGER/Line Files
  Distribution_Liability: No warranty, expressed or implied
is made and no liability is assumed by the U.S. Government in
general or the U.S. Census Bureau in specific as to the
positional or attribute accuracy of the data. The act of
distribution shall not constitute any such warranty and no
responsibility is assumed by the U.S. Government in the use
of these files.
  Standard_Order_Process:
    Digital_Form:
      Digital_Transfer_Information:
        Format_Name: TGRLN (compressed)
        Format_Version_Number: Census 2000
        File_Decompression_Technique: PK-ZIP, version 1.93A
or higher
      Digital_Transfer_Option:
        Online_Option:
          Computer_Contact_Information:
```

Network_Address:
        Network_Resource_Name:
www.census.gov/geo/www/tiger
    Fees: *The online copy of the TIGER/Line files may be*
accessed without charge. See www.census.gov/geo/www/tiger for
information on availability on CD-ROM/DVD and associated
costs for these products.
    Ordering_Instructions: *To obtain more information about*
ordering TIGER/Line files visit www.census.gov/geo/www/tiger.
    Technical_Prequisites: *The Census 2000 TIGER/Line files*
contain geographic data only and do not include display or
mapping software or statistical data. For information on how
to use the TIGER/Line data with a specific software package
users should contact the company that produced the software.
A list of vendors who have developed software capable of
processing TIGER/Line files can be found by visiting
www.census.gov/geo/www/tiger. The TIGER/Line files are
provided in ASCII text format only. Users are responsible for
converting or translating the files into a format used by
their specific software package.

Metadata Reference information

Finally the Metadata Reference information section relates who created
the metadata and when.

Metadata_Reference_Information:
  Metadata_Date: *20030408*
  Metadata_Contact:
    Contact_Information:
      Contact_Organization_Primary:
        Contact_Organization:
          U.S. Department of Commerce
          U.S. Census Bureau
          Geography Division
          Products and Services Staff

```
       Contact_Person: John Doe
    Contact_Address:
       Address_Type: Physical Address
       Address: 8903 Presidential Parkway, Room 303 WP I
       City: Upper Marlboro
       State_or_Province: Maryland
       Postal_Code: 20772
    Contact_Voice_Telephone: (301) 457-1128
    Contact_Electronic_Mail_Address: tiger@census.gov
  Metadata_Standard_Name: FGDC Content Standards for Digital
Geo-spatial Metadata
  Metadata_Standard_Version: FGDC-STD-001-1998
  Metadata_Time_Convention: local time
  Metadata_Extensions:
    Online_Linkage: www.esri.com/metadata/esriprof80.html
    Profile_Name: ESRI Metadata Profile
```

Trends in spatial metadata

As we have *see*n, the spatial metadata format is a mature, hierarchically structured format designed to describe complex spatial data to enable the discovery of data, the determination of data fitness, data access and use. As the spatial data community awaits the acceptance of the international standard ISO 19115, some trends can be observed. These trend lines are stimulated by five driving forces: the user's workstation, the critical mass of metadata, software, the role of the librarian and evolving computer language.

The user's workstation

Fifteen years ago GIS was done on Unix workstations. The out-of-the-box PC was simply not up to the chore of processing hundreds of thousands of vectors, to say nothing of multiple 40 Megabyte raster files. The PC as it has evolved (primarily for the home gamer market) is now capable of not only processing vectors and raster files but with accelerated graphics cards viewing those processes in a reasonable amount of time, and storing large files as well (though there is never enough space). The standard home computer in the USA ships with Microsoft Works Suite 2000, which includes Streets and Trip 2002, the TIGER-derived street data for the entire country. Today's standard office computer is capable of handling most geospatial data.

The critical mass of metadata

In 2003 the US National Spatial Data Infrastructure links over 260 spatial data servers. This was achieved by a decade of building the programme through metadata building, training and directed co-operation. Spatial data servers at the local, county, state and national levels utilize thousands of metadata records. The quality of the metadata varies, as does the quality of the data, but clearly there is now enough data to provide a viable discovery opportunity to today's growing spatial data user community. Expectations for metadata quality grow as the user community becomes more sophisticated.

The role of the librarian

Quality metadata is identified with librarians. From the beginning of spatial metadata creation, the library community has been *seen* as a leader. Among information professionals librarians are *seen* as the experts in description, controlled language and searching. Positions are being created in large research libraries for spatial metadata and GIS librarians.

Software as a driver

GIS software has come of age with the growth in the power of personal computers and of computer networks. Combined with the explosion in the amount and size of spatial datasets, and evolutions in database design, GIS software companies have reworked their software over the past decade. ESRI, a world leader in GIS software, is a case study in adaptive change. In the past 20 years, ESRI's data structure has moved from a simple though proprietary 'coverage' format that managed the topological issues of spatial data to a more open 'shapefile' format. In 2000

ESRI, with its latest release of ArcGIS 8.0, settled on a geodatabase structure. Relying on spatial tools and functions developed for Relational Database Management Systems (RDMS) like Ingress and Oracle, ESRI is focusing on moving spatial data into and out of these RDMS for spatial data producers and users. With a highly networked ArcGIS, the first step a data producer takes in creating a data layer is in ArcCatalog. ArcCatalog begins a metadata record that lives with the data, documents Identification, Data Quality, Spatial Data Organization, Spatial Reference, Entity and Attribute, Distribution and Metadata Reference information. As process steps occur, they are documented. As attributes are added, the data producer is prompted to document them. ArcGIS *sees* metadata as integral to the spatial data. For a cataloguer who has created spatial metadata using notepad.exe, an ASCII editor, in the very early days, ArcCatalog is a wonderful tool, crafted for the metadata cataloguer – with active feedback from the cataloguing community. It includes templates, rule interpretations and context help.

ArcIMS, the ESRI internet Map Server, utilizes a number of server types. The latest is the Metadata Server which will enable users to discover data, determine if the data is fit for the user's needs, whether the user has access and, if they do have access, whether they can they use the data. ESRI has integrated metadata into its spatial data structure at the most fundamental level.

Evolving computer language; XML

FGDC's mp.exe, a utility which checks hierarchically indented text metadata against the CSDGM (Content Standard for Digital Geospatial Metadata), produces a hierarchically indented (two-space indent) text output, a standard presentation HTML output with a 'table of contents', an HTML presentation of the metadata in the form of questions and answers (FAQ style), an SGML output, an XML output and a DIF (Directory Interchange Format) output. Mp.exe was created when XML was a twinkle in the eye of metadata administrators. Extensible Markup Language has since become a basic tool for networked data on the world wide web. XML-formatted spatial metadata is currently utilized in two ways: simply as a more robust, dynamic database and as a tagged data transfer format.

ESRI's use of XML is sophisticated and extensive. The ARC products are structured to be shared on a network in a client–server environment. Metadata, cartographic presentation and ArcIMS all use XML, each in their own way and for their own purposes.

Endeavor's EnCompass for Digital Collections uses XML as well. At this point, early in its generation, EnCompass only uses XML as a transfer format, plugging the tagged fields into a mapped database in order to aggregate various metadata formats into a cohesive, integrated library system. It is a short-sighted solution that overlooks the dynamic nature of the XML metadata record. It assumes that a metadata record is a static object, which for spatial metadata cannot be farther from the truth. Spatial metadata describes a dataset that documents a changing world. In a geodatabase, the metadata records change as the geodatabase grows. The strength of EnCompass comes from mapping disaggregate metadata records in Dublin Core, qualified Dublin Core, EAD, TEI, etc. This mapping has the ability to join various digital data with spatial attributes, extending the discovery process for the user.

Conclusion

One of the problems of format-specific data, like spatial geodata, is that the data often lives in a proscribed universe. Breaking free of that universe and working with other forms of data is the challenge of metadata – and of the librarians who create and manage them.

Geo-spatial information is essentially cartographic, or at least graphical, in format and therefore requires extensive descriptive metadata to provide basic levels of information. Spatial metadata is a mature technology that is undergoing a developmental shift as it evolves to meet international standards. The GIS industry is eagerly anticipating the ISO 19115 standard for Geographic information/Geomatics.

As we have *seen* there are five forces driving the development of geo-spatial metadata: the user's workstation, which is providing ever-increasing processing power for moderate resources; the critical mass of metadata, which is growing exponentially as national, state, provincial and local governments create geo-data; software, which is incorporating metadata concepts in order to control the burgeoning amount of data; the role of the librarian, which is changing to meet the challenges of an information age; and evolving computer languages, which are becoming less platform and application dependent.

We should expect to *see* geo-spatial metadata become ubiquitous in the next five years as data producers' software generates metadata in order to make data more available and viable in a global networked environment.

References

Cooke, D. (1998) Topology and TIGER: the Census Bureau's contribution. In Foresman, T. W., (ed.), *The History of Geographic Information Systems: perspectives from the pioneers*, Upper Saddle River, NJ, Prentice Hall, 47–57.

Federal Geographic Data Committee, Metadata Ad Hoc Working Group (1998) *Content Standard for Digital Geospatial Metadata*, www.fgdc.gov/metadata/contstan.html.

Goodchild, M. (1995) Sharing Imperfect Data. In Onsrud, H. J. and Rushton, G. (eds), *Sharing Geographic Information*, New Brunswick, NJ, Rutgers University Center for Urban Policy Research, 413–25.

Onsrud, H. J. and Rushton, G. (1995) Fundamental Questions and Issues. In Onsrud, H. J. and Rushton, G. (eds), *Sharing Geographic Information*, New Brunswick, NJ, Rutgers University Center for Urban Policy Research, 494–500.

Smits, J. (1996) Digital Metadata, Standards for Communication and Preservation, *The LIBER Quarterly, the Journal of European Research Libraries*, **6** (4), www.kb.nl/infolev/liber/articles/metamalta.htm.

Visvalingam, M. (1989) Cartography, GIS and Maps in Perspective, *The Cartographic Journal*, **26** (1), 26–32.

14

International initiatives in the implementation of metadata standards

Priscilla Caplan

Introduction

This paper gives an update on activities within selected metadata initiatives in the last few years, and finds some common trends. These include efforts to develop content standards and application profiles, a clear preference for XML as a transport syntax, a trend towards developing non-descriptive metadata schemes (particularly preservation metadata, structural metadata, and content packaging), and a renewed focus on presentation issues. A future trend is likely to be an increasing focus on tools for facilitating metadata creation, use and exchange.

By now the usefulness of metadata schemes to supplement traditional library cataloguing (AACR2/MARC) *see*ms to be well accepted within the library community. For example, a recent Delphi study conducted by Ingrid Hsieh-Yee (Hsieh-Yee, 2002) included among topics that all students of library and information science should know, 'An overview of metadata, including types of metadata, purposes, communities creating metadata, applications, and emerging standards that will impact on metadata projects.' The same researcher found a strong consensus among educators that cataloguing and metadata is not mutually exclusive but can be used together to organize resources effectively. There are several signs of this in practice. ALCTS, for example, delivered a regional workshop series in 2002 and 2003 that unapologetically combined topics in metadata with topics in AACR2. The Library of Congress Action Plan for Bibliographic Control of Web Resources (n.d.) focuses equally on traditional library cataloguing and other metadata standards.

Current status of some metadata initiatives
Dublin Core

The original Dublin Core Metadata Element Set of 15 elements was approved as ANSI/NISO Standard Z39.85 in 2001, and as ISO standard 15836 in early 2003. However, the up-to-date specification is a dynamic list of terms maintained by the Dublin Core Metadata Initiative (DCMI) Usage Board (n.d.). That document records elements, element refinement qualifiers and registered encoding schemes along with the status assigned to them by the Usage Board. Elements and element refinements can have the statuses 'Recommended', 'Conforming', or 'Obsolete'. Recommended terms are those considered to have demonstrated usefulness for cross-domain resource discovery. Terms that don't meet that standard but don't violate Dublin Core grammatical and semantic principles are designated as 'conforming'. As of February 2003, the list contained several new qualifiers and one additional Recommended element, Audience, defined as 'a class of entity for whom the resource is intended or useful'.

The Usage Board was established in 2001 to provide more formal maintenance of the element set. There are other signs of the organizational maturing of the DCMI. In 2001 a managing director was hired to provide project management of the various working group activities. The following year a Board of Trustees was established to provide strategic leadership and to help improve financial support to the organization. In 2003 an international 'affiliate' programme was launched, establishing geographically based Dublin Core authorities throughout the world. The Dublin Core metadata workshops have evolved into annual international conferences with preconferences and multiple tracks, and a virtual reference-based 'Ask DCMI' feature has been added to the DCMI website.

At the same time, the DCMI has been criticized for an apparent inability to produce timely decisions and documentation to support practitioners in their use of the Dublin Core. Guidelines for implementing qualified Dublin Core in XML were not approved as a DCMI Recommendation until April 2003, although this has been a pressing need for years. There are still no guidelines for representing citation information, although a qualifier of the Identifier element for bibliographic citations was approved as 'conforming' in 2002. The library community has been frustrated by the lack of an approved method for recording role information in Creator and Contributor elements, and the development of a library application profile has been hindered awaiting this and other decisions from the Usage Board.

Despite these perceived problems, use of Dublin Core has probably increased in practice, owing primarily to its incorporation into other systems and specifications. The Open Archives Initiative Protocol for Metadata Harvesting (OAI-PMH) requires participating repositories to support the contribution of metadata records in an XML representation of simple Dublin Core. The METS (Metadata Encoding and Transmission Standard) specification, which has been heavily promoted in the digital library community, includes simple Dublin Core as one way of recording descriptive metadata. Library systems vendors have included out-of-the-box support for Dublin Core metadata elements, if not in their main cataloguing modules, in their digital library products such as Endeavor's Encompass and Ex Libris's DigiTool Library. The OCLC CORC service, which helped mainstream Dublin Core into cataloguing departments, has been terminated as a separate system, but its functionality is being integrated into OCLC Connexion, the planned successor to Passport as the primary cataloguing client.

VRA Core

The VRA Core Version 3 has remained stable since its introduction in June 2000. The Visual Resources Association's Data Standards Committee has directed its attention to the development of content standards suitable for use with both the VRA Core and the Categories for the Description of Works of Art (CDWA). The resulting document, which will be called *Cataloguing Cultural Objects: a guide to describing cultural objects and their images*, is expected to be released in 2003. The guide will include selected categories from both standards, and will give for each category both general rules for formatting content, such as capitalization and punctuation, and specific rules related to describing particular types of objects.

The VRA is also working on XML bindings for VRA Core 3.0, with the ultimate goal of providing access to several alternative schemas for different needs.

ONIX

ONIX International was born of the union of the Association of American Publishers' *Guidelines for Online Information Exchange* (ONIX) and EDItEUR's EPICS Data Dictionary, two independently developed metadata specifications for exchanging product information for the book trade. Since its introduction in 2000, it has been heavily promoted and slowly but steadily adopted by publishers and booksellers. ONIX 2.0, a major revision of the ONIX Product Information Standards, was released in 2001 and contained new data elements to support e-books. ONIX for Serials, a second family of specifications describing serial titles, items and subscription packages, was released in draft form and piloted in 2002.

The ONIX product record is an XML representation of bibliographic, trade and marketing information. Although ONIX can be mapped to MARC, the format has few associated content rules and does not support AACR cataloguing. Nonetheless, libraries and library systems vendors have been active in exploring uses for ONIX in their bibliographic systems. ONIX data can be used in cataloguing systems to create provisional or acquisitions-level records subject to upgrade or replacement. A use inspiring even more interest is as a source of 'enriched' data such as tables of contents, descriptions and cover art. Several library systems vendors have developed the ability to incorporate ONIX data into their own catalogue and portal products. The Library of Congress, through its Bibliographic Enrichment Advisory Team (BEAT) initiative, has been particularly active in exploring uses of ONIX content. One project uses

ONIX data to create HTML tables of contents (TOCs). The web TOCs are linked to LC's catalogue records and vice versa. This not only provides the catalogue user with TOC information, but also, since the HTML TOCs get indexed by internet search engines, they provide a means of drawing internet searchers into the library's catalogue. Other projects use ONIX data to create links from catalogue records to descriptions of books, sample texts provided by publishers, and reading group guides.

The ONIX product information specifications were drafted by publishers for the book trade with little input from the library community. In contrast, developers of ONIX for Serials have had library applications in mind from the beginning, and have involved libraries, library systems vendors and subscription agents as well as primary and secondary publishers. Projected uses of ONIX for Serials include the communication of rich publisher catalogue information, automated library check-in for e-journals, and content alerting services. It might also be used to transmit library holdings and supplier information needed to configure reference linking systems. *The Exchange of Serials Subscription Information*, a NISO White Paper by Ed Jones (2002), documented numerous types of exchanges between libraries, content aggregators, publishers, subscription agents and third-party service providers, and concluded that ONIX for Serials could provide a standard format for most of these communications. A NISO/EDItEUR joint working party will pilot the use of ONIX for some of these transactions in 2003.

Encoded Archival Description (EAD)

The second production release of the Encoded Archival Description (EAD) was issued in late 2002. Along with the new DTD there is a new tag library, and new application guidelines are under way.

Version 2002 supersedes Version 1.0 published in August 1998. Most changes arose from one of three reasons: the experience of early implementers, the desire to maintain compatibility with the 2000 edition of the General International Standard Archival Description (ISAD(G)), and the need to accommodate international archival practice. For example, the preface to the new version notes that most semi-closed lists of attribute values have been eliminated, as these were found to be Anglocentric, inhibiting international use.

One of the most interesting applications of the EAD was made by the MOAC (Museums and the Online Archive of California) project funded by the Institute of Museum and Library Services from 1999 to 2002. One of the goals of MOAC was to determine whether the EAD could be effectively applied to museum collection guides as well as to archival finding aids. MOAC participants created collection descriptions in EAD format and contributed these to the Online Archive of California, which already aggregated finding aids from archives across the state. Descriptive practice in museums varies substantially from that in archives, particularly in the amount of attention given to item-level description. Nonetheless, the project found that best practice guidelines written for use by museums and archives overlapped by more than 80%. It also found significant benefits to users in integrating access to museum and archival collections (Rinehart, 2003).

Learning objects

Since the late 1990s there have been a number of intensive and well funded efforts to develop metadata specifications for learning objects, bits of educational content designed to be shareable and re-usable. The Learning Object Metadata (LOM) specification, developed by the Learning Technology Standards Committee (LSTC) of the Institute of Electrical and Electronics Engineers (IEEE), became an approved IEEE standard in June 2002. The IMS Global Learning Consortium, Inc. developed its IMS Metadata Specification in concert with IEEE LOM development and is largely congruent with the LOM specification. At the same time the Advanced Distributed Learning (ADL) initiative of the Office of the US Secretary of Defense has been developing the Sharable Content Object Reference Model (SCORM). SCORM provides a framework for interoperable, re-usable web-based learning content, and includes a metadata implementation that is nearly identical to IMS. Finally, the international standards committee ISO/IEC JTC1/SC36 is charged to develop standards in information technology in the areas of learning, education and training. Concerned about the possibility of the development of conflicting or multiple standards, the LTSC recently invited members of ISO/IEC JTC1/SC36 to participate in the maintenance of the LOM.

It is to the credit of the educational community that they have largely avoided the 'not invented here' syndrome and have co-ordinated their metadata efforts to the extent that they have. With the growing maturity of the metadata specifications, attention has turned first to developing bindings in XML, and second to implementations within content management frameworks. Although libraries do not *seem* to have adopted learning object metadata into their own workflow and digital library projects to the extent they have adopted Dublin Core, the VRA Core and the EAD, this situation is bound to change as library portals and course management systems become more closely integrated. Meanwhile the IMS initiative has been reaching out to the digital library community. The recently released Digital Repositories Interoperability (DRI) specification is intended to be applicable to libraries and museum collections as well as to learning object repositories, and incorporates Z39.50 as well as XQuery and other XML technologies (IMS, n.d.). IMS and the Coalition for Networked Information (CNI) announced a working alliance in March to explore common models, joint specifications and improved interoperability in the areas of digital libraries and learning object repositories.

Commonalities and trends

Looking broadly across these and other metadata initiatives, there appear to be some common trends.

Developing content standards

If there is any single lesson to take from the history of international metadata initiatives, it is that metadata schemes without content rules are of limited usefulness. Agreement upon a common set of metadata elements and their definitions is really only the first step in the development of an effective metadata specification. To support consistent search and retrieval, there must be some consistency in how data values are supplied. This means that for most metadata elements, there must be content rules describing the legitimate use of the element and specifying how data values are obtained (as from an authority list) or formulated.

The last few years have *seen* considerable activity towards the development of content standards. As noted above, the Visual Resources Association has launched a major effort to develop content standards suitable for use in describing works of art and their surrogates. There has also been progress in the development of standards related to the EAD and the Dublin Core.

The development of the EAD exposed widely differing practice in the construction of finding aids and provided incentive for archivists to work towards the continued development of content standards. Archivists have never had a content standard specifically for finding aids, but have used three existing content standards for different purposes: *Archives, Personal Papers and Manuscripts* (APPM), the Canadian Rules for Archival Description (RAD) and the General International Standard Archival Description (ISAD(G)). An NEH-funded project known as the Canadian–US Task Force on Archival Description (CUSTARD) has been working to reconcile these three documents into a single descriptive standard. The product, tentatively titled *Describing Archives: a content standard*, may be released in 2003 and is expected to be the foundation of a truly international content standard. It will have a strong theoretical basis and will include specific instructions for describing archives of all media.

The lack of content guidelines for use with Dublin Core has been a continuing problem for implementers, to the extent that most projects attempting to use Dublin Core for resource description have had to develop their own local guidelines for use. With funding from the Institute of Museum and Library Services, the University of Denver and the Colorado Digitization Project developed the *Western States Dublin Core Metadata Best Practices* (Western States Digital Standards Group, 2003). This guide, intended to be generally suitable for use by diverse cultural heritage institutions such as libraries, museums, historical societies and archives, was warmly welcomed by the library community at its release in 2003. It gives detailed and explicit instructions for 13 Dublin Core elements and three elements locally defined by the Western States Digital Standards Group.

An application profile is not a content standard per se, but is related in that it documents rules that a particular group of practitioners agree to follow in their metadata implementation. An application profile can clarify or narrow the usage of a metadata element, make optional elements required, stipulate the use of particular authority lists, and in general restrict implementation options so that metadata created in conformance with the profile will be more interoperable. In the DCMI, application profiles are under development for several communities including libraries, government and education. Publishers and retailers have also been active in establishing application profiles for various uses of ONIX.

The dominance of XML

XML is undisputedly the transport syntax of choice for descriptive metadata. Metadata schemes originally defined as SGML have been reworked to support XML implementations. The EAD developers were early implementers of XML, revising the SGML beta version of the EAD DTD (Document Type Definition) to be XML compliant in Production Version 1.0. The TEI DTD, which defines the TEI Header, can now be configured as either an SGML or an XML DTD and *TEI P4: Guidelines for Electronic Text Encoding and Interchange*, incorporating XML support, was released in 2002. The popular Chapter 2 of TEI P3, 'A Gentle Introduction to SGML', has been rewritten in TEI P4 as 'A Gentle Introduction to XML' (Sperberg-McQueen and Burnard, 2002).

XML bindings are also being provided for syntax-independent schemes. The VRA Data Standards Committee aims to provide one, and possibly more, XML schema for the VRA Core Version 3. The DCMI has published XML schema for representing simple and qualified Dublin Core. The IMS has published XML bindings of its Meta-data and Content Packaging specifications.

The Open Archives Initiative, which promotes a Protocol for Metadata Harvesting (PMH) allowing aggregated collections of metadata to be built from diverse sources, has provided a big incentive for communities to develop XML DTDs or schema for their metadata schemes. The OAI-PMH requires data providers to support metadata export in an XML representation of simple Dublin Core, and allows export of data in other schemes so long as they are encoded in XML. The Library of Congress developed MARCXML, a schema for lossless conversion of MARC to XML, to support the exchange of MARC data in an XML environment. LC is also developing the Metadata Object Description Schema (MODS), a bibliographic element set, expressed as an XML schema, compatible with MARC semantics.

A sub-trend within the trend towards XML is an emerging preference for XML schema. XML schema language provides an alternative to the XML DTD for defining document types. Schema are more powerful and flexible than DTDs, with support for namespaces and sophisticated constraints on element content. However, because the XML schema specification was only approved in 2001 and is a bit of a moving target, there have been until recently relatively few software tools supporting schema use. As more and better tools become available, metadata implementers will increasingly utilize XML schema for defining their metadata representations.

Focus on non-descriptive metadata

Metadata is commonly characterized as descriptive, administrative or structural. Stated rather broadly, descriptive metadata supports resource discovery and identification, administrative metadata supports management functions such as access control and preservation, and structural metadata describes the internal organization of complex objects. The many metadata schemes developed in the 1990s were primarily descriptive schemes, focused on describing particular types of materials for particular user communities. Metadata element sets were defined for many different types of resources, including but not limited to art objects, visual resources, encoded texts, publishers' trade lists, archival finding aids, government information, geospatial information, educational resources, learning objects, social science datasets, environmental resources and biological specimens.

Although these specifications continue to be revised and updated, it appears that the focus of metadata development has now switched to schemes that can more properly be called administrative or structural. Preservation metadata, or metadata to support long-term archiving and preservation processing of digital objects, has been a particularly active area.

Preservation metadata

The National Library of Australia (NLA) issued an 'exposure draft' of their preservation metadata element set in late 1999 based upon their experience with the PANDORA (Preserving and Accessing Networked Documentary Resources of Australia) Archive. In early 2000 the Cedars project in the UK, which was established to explore practical issues in digital archiving and to develop a distributed archive prototype, issued their own metadata framework and element set. About the same time the Networked European Deposit Library (NEDLIB) (2000) project issued its own framework and element set *Metadata for Long Term Preservation*. Later that year the National Library of New Zealand (2002) published the metadata element set that it will use as the basis for the design of its own preservation management systems. The New Zealand scheme attempts to balance OAIS principles with practical implementation issues, while trying to maintain compatibility with other international initiatives.

In 2001–2, OCLC and RLG jointly convened the OCLC/RLG Preservation Metadata Working Group, a committee with wide international representation, to consider fundamental issues associated with the use of metadata to support digital preservation. The group's first white paper compared the NLA, Cedars and NEDLIB element sets and placed them overtly in the context of the OAIS reference model (OCLC/RLG Working Group on Preservation Metadata, 2001). A second report further articulated the OAIS model and recommended a consolidated set of preservation metadata elements mapped to that structure (OCLC/RLG Working Group on Preservation Metadata, 2002). Following that report, the original group was discharged and a successor group formed to review and revise the recommended metadata element set in light of the practical aspects of implementing preservation metadata in digital preservation systems. The second group, called PREMIS (PREservation Metadata: Implementation Strategies), is charged to develop a core set of implementable preservation metadata elements and to evaluate alternative strategies for the actual encoding, storage and management of preservation metadata within a digital preservation system. Their report is expected by mid-2004.

Details about the creation and physical characteristics of files, called technical metadata, are an important component of preservation metadata. Different media types, such as images, text, audio and video, require different metadata schemes. At this time, technical metadata for images is closest to reaching true standardization. *Data Dictionary – Technical Metadata for Digital Still Images* (NISO Z39.87-2002 AIIM 20-2002) is a proposed NISO standard released as a draft standard for trial use until December 2003. Elements from this data dictionary have been incorporated into several schemes for preservation metadata, and an XML schema representing the full data dictionary (Metadata for Images in XML, or MIX) has been developed by the Library of Congress. The LC has also done extensive work on technical metadata for digital audio and video through its Digital Audio-Visual Preservation Prototyping Project. Schemes for other digital media are under development, often in co-ordination with the METS initiative.

The development of schemes for preservation metadata is complicated by the need to manage digital objects as both logical entities and as sets of physical files. A book, for example, is a logical object with a title and an author, but it may be manifested digitally as a collection of PDF files and structural metadata. A PDF file in turn might be normalized to a set of XML-encoded text and image files. Implementable preservation metadata schemes must allow multiple levels of management and support complex relationships between physical files. Another complication is the great variation in models for preservation implementations. A project designed to crawl the web, identifying and archiving all sites on a particular topic, has substantially different metadata needs than a repository that archives submissions from a particular community on a fee-for-service basis. It is possible that if multiple preservation metadata schemes emerge, they will be differentiated by the model of preservation implementation they support.

Structural metadata

There has also been progress in the standardization of structural metadata. In the library community, one of the most significant new developments is METS, the Metadata Encoding and Transmission Standard developed by the Digital Library Federation. METS, which is represented as an XML schema, is subdivided into five main sections: descriptive metadata, administrative metadata, a file inventory, structural metadata and behaviours. However, only the structural metadata section is fully defined within the schema, causing METS to be considered primarily a structural metadata scheme. Descriptive and administrative metadata elements are not defined within METS but can be supplied using 'extension schema' externally defined and maintained XML schema. For example, the Dublin Core can be used within METS as an extension schema for descriptive metadata.

The structural metadata section of METS, called the structural map, defines a hierarchical structure which can be used by presentation applications to allow users to display and navigate their way through digital objects of any format. For texts, logical hierarchies such as pages within chapters within parts can be represented, while for audio files, the structural map might define beginning and end times for different segments.

Widespread use of METS would enable the development of shareable presentation utilities which could interpret and present digital objects regardless of the repository in which they were stored. METS also enables the standardized exchange of digital objects between repositories. However, the use of METS which is attracting the most attention is as a format for use in an OAIS-compliant digital archive. The Reference Model for an Open Archival Information System (OAIS) defines 'packages' for submission of data to an archive, storage of data within an archive, and dissemination of data from an archive (Consultative Committee on Space Data Systems, 2002). METS has been used experimentally as a format for each of these functions.

The beta version of the METS schema was released in mid-2001 and the first production version, METS Schema 1.1, in mid-2002. The Library of Congress serves as maintenance agency, and an editorial board oversees changes to the METS schema and encourages registration of new extension schema.

Content packaging

While METS is commonly thought of as a scheme for structural meta-data describing the internal structure of a complex object, it can also be *seen* as a mechanism for content packaging. Content packaging is a term used primarily in the educational arena to indicate the bundling of content into self-descriptive packages for exchange between applications. Content packages could be used to transfer content from one learning management system to another, for example, or to import educational content into a course development tool for re-use.

The IMS developed a content packaging information model and specification in 2001 which has been adopted by SCORM and is likely to become an IEEE standard. In this model, every package must contain an XML document called a manifest which describes itself, the other content files included in the package, and one or more ways of organizing the content. Appropriate metadata from the IMS Metadata Specification can be embedded at any level. Applications such as Blackboard, Microsoft LRN Toolkit and EC-PAC, can, in theory at least, interoperably import and export packages created according to the content packaging specification.

The term content packaging is not widely used in the library community but this may change as cross fertilization occurs through the IMS/CNI collaboration and other alliances. The concept, however, has been implemented using METS, particularly in the context of archival ingest and dissemination.

Making sense in presentation

The integration of metadata from multiple schemes, and the design of display and navigation systems that make heterogeneous descriptions understandable to the user, are problems attracting considerable attention from both researchers and practitioners. Some of the impetus for this comes from the popularity of portal and broadcast search facilities that aggregate results returned from multiple systems. The development of services based on OAI metadata harvesting has also contributed to a focus on presentation.

The Research Libraries Group's Cultural Materials project is an ambitious effort to aggregate digital materials in a wide variety of formats from libraries, museums and archives. As of May 2003 the service contained 180,020 works from 73 different collections using a variety of different metadata schemes and thesauri. Because of a heavy emphasis on visual materials such as photographs, maps and artwork, the search interface is designed to return thumbnail images when possible. However, searches may also retrieve textual documents, collection-level descriptions and materials in other formats for which thumbnails are inappropriate. The development of presentation services that help the user make sense of such heterogeneous results is an important effort that makes the ongoing evolution of Cultural Materials worth watching.

A number of research projects focus on improving searching and presentation of heterogeneous materials. For example, Project Perseus, a digital library of humanities resources, has focused on building and linking collections, and on developing tools to improve access to materials and interpretation of results. An ongoing project of the University of Illinois in Urbana-Champaign is building a repository of item-level metadata from all digital collections that have received funding from the Institute of Museum and Library Services (IMLS). This project will research best practices not only for sharing metadata from diverse collections, but also for supporting the interests of diverse user communities.

The library cataloguing community has been focused on presentation in the context of the IFLA Functional Requirements for Bibliographic Records (FRBR). The FRBR model relates four entities: the work (an abstract intellectual creation), the expression (a realization of a work, such as a performance of a symphony), the manifestation (a physical embodiment of an expression, such as a CD recording of a performance), and the item (a single exemplar of an expression, such as your own copy of a CD). Although AACR2 cataloguing rules focus on describing the manifestation, in the FRBR model the relationship between manifestations, expressions and works must be described and coherently presented. While the Joint Steering Committee for Revision of Anglo-American Cataloguing Rules has been trying to nudge AACR2 into closer harmony with FRBR, the Library of Congress, OCLC and others have been investigating methods for displaying structured result sets to the user within the FRBR framework. The library systems vendor VTLS has already introduced some 'FRBRization' in its Virtua online catalogue.

Future directions

As noted above, descriptive metadata schemes developed in the 1990s have now been through several revisions and are becoming more widely implemented. Basic tools for use, such as XML bindings and content standards, are being put into place. It *see*ms reasonable to expect that as time goes on, less attention will be paid to the continued development of particular specifications, and more attention will focus on the development of tools and mechanisms to facilitate metadata creation, use and exchange.

Metadata registries

Several different concepts fall under the broad heading of metadata registries. In the narrowest sense, a registry could record all of the terms used or proposed for use in a particular metadata scheme, along with each term's definition, history and status. The Dublin Core Metadata Registry does this, allowing terms to be searched and information retrieved in 23 languages. Such a basic registry could be expanded to register known application profiles as well, and to include in term documentation its usage in various application profiles. More broadly, a metadata registry could register multiple metadata schemes, and could document relationships between terms in different schemes as defined by formal crosswalks. The registry could then serve as a mechanism for translating from one scheme to another, with obvious uses in cross-domain retrieval. Though there are few operational metadata registries at this time, this is an area attracting attention in the research community, and we can expect to *see* an increasing number of registry initiatives in the future.

Collection registries

The proliferation of digital collections of content, small and large, makes it difficult for searchers to locate digital materials in which they might have an interest. One response to this has been to aggregate metadata from multiple collections into large central databases along the OAI model. Another has been an increased interest in searchable registries of digital collections. Interestingly, there is no standard scheme for collection-level description (excepting the EAD, which describes archival collections, a related but not identical concept). The most mature specification at this time is the Research Support Libraries Programme (RSLP) collection description schema, coming out of the RSLP Collection Description Project. A DCMI Collection Description Working Group was dormant in 2002 and may or may not resume activity in 2003.

Collection-level description offers several challenges, not least of which is the lack of a clear definition of collection. Regardless, the practical need for registries of digital collections in a number of contexts should guarantee that the development of collection registries, and the continued development of metadata element sets appropriate for collection-level description, will attract increasing attention over the next few years.

RDF and the Semantic Web

No discussion of metadata should end without a mention of the Resource Description Framework (RDF) and the Semantic Web. It does not appear that RDF has achieved widespread adoption, at least in the library community. Published or in-process bindings for the EAD, the VRA Core and ONIX are XML schema that do not utilize RDF, nor do the implementations of Dublin Core recommended for use with OAI and METS. It may be that the added overhead and complexity of RDF is not warranted for simple use and exchange of metadata, and that the development of more applications exploiting RDF will be a prerequisite for its wider implementation.

The 'killer application' for RDF is, of course, the Semantic Web, a network of information that can be processed by automated agents as well as by human beings. RDF is a tool for making statements that are machine-processable in such a way that applications can be written that appear to 'understand' them, using logic and drawing conclusions. The

Semantic Web Activity of the World Wide Web Consortium (W3C) has been working on an RDF Core and a Web Ontology Language (OWL) to support the development of the Semantic Web, as has the Darpa Agent Markup Language project (DAML).

While this is something to watch, it is probably fair to say that at this point most library-related metadata initiatives would be happy to create consistent, high-quality, interoperable metadata, using well developed content standards as a guide and XML as a transport syntax.

Conclusion

This paper began by looking at the current status of the following metadata initiatives: Dublin Core, VRA Core, ONIX, EAD and learning objects. The common trends among these examples include the development of content standards and the dominance of XML. Another trend discussed was the development of non-descriptive metadata, comprising preservation and structural metadata and content packaging. There is also a focus on improving searching and presentation of heterogeneous materials. Finally, future directions were outlined: metadata and collections registries, and the Semantic Web.

References

Cedars (2000) *Metadata for Digital Preservation: The Cedars Project Online Specification,* www.leeds.ac.uk/cedars/MD-STR~5.pdf.

Consultative Committee on Space Data Systems (2002) *Reference Model for an Open Archival Information System (OAIS),* CCSDS 650.0-B-1 Blue Book, http://www.classic.ccsds.org/documents/pdf/CCSDS-650.0-B-1.pdf.

DCMI Usage Board (n.d.) *DCMI Metadata Terms,* www.dublincore.org/documents/dcmi-terms/.

Hsieh-Yee, I. (2002) *Cataloguing and Metadata Education: a proposal for preparing cataloguing professionals of the 21st century,* unpublished.

IMS Global Learning Consortium (n.d.) *Digital Repositories Interoperability Specification,* www.imsproject.org/digitalrepositories/.

Jones, E. (2002) *The Exchange of Serials Subscription Information,* www.niso.org/Serials-WP.pdf.

Library of Congress (n.d.) *Bibliographic Control of Web Resources: a Library of Congress action plan*, http://lcweb.loc.gov/catdir/bibcontrol/actionplan.pdf.

National Library of Australia (1999) *Preservation Metadata for Digital Collections*, www.nla.gov.au/preserve/pmeta.html.

National Library of New Zealand (2002) *Metadata Standards Framework – Preservation Metadata*, www.natlib.govt.nz/files/4initiatives_metaschema.pdf.

NEDLIB (2000) *Metadata for Long Term Preservation*, www.kb.nl/coop/nedlib/results/preservationmetadata.pdf.

OCLC/RLG Working Group on Preservation Metadata (2001) *Preservation Metadata for Digital Objects: a review of the state of the art*, www.oclc.org/research/pmwg/presmeta_wp.pdf.

OCLC/RLG Working Group on Preservation Metadata (2002), *Preservation Metadata and the OAIS Information Model: a metadata framework to support the preservation of digital objects*, www.oclc.org/research/pmwg/pm_framework.pdf.

Rinehart, R. (2003) MOAC – A Report on Integrating Museum and Archive Access in the Online Archive of California, *D-Lib Magazine*, **9** (1), www.dlib.org/dlib/january03/rinehart/.

Sperberg-McQueen, C. M. and Burnard, L. (eds) (2002) *TEI P4: Guidelines for Electronic Text Encoding and Interchange*, Text Encoding Initiative Consortium, www. tei-c.org/P4X/.

Western States Digital Standards Group (2003) *Western States Dublin Core Metadata Best Practices, Version 1.2*, www.cdpheritage.org/resource/metadata/documents/WSDCMBP_v1-2_2003-01-20.pdf.

15

Metadata applications in developing countries: the example of China

Wei Liu

Introduction

According to the literature and statistics from digital library related projects, there has been a metadata movement in China since 2002. This paper reviews and highlights all the main efforts on the research and implementation of metadata standards, specifications and applications, by the institutions of national science and technology, education, and culture, and as well as the private sector.

The need for metadata arises from the ubiquity of digital resources and digital libraries. The term 'metadata' has become a buzzword in China in recent years, much like 'digital library', which inherited too much meaning and became almost meaningless. China is a large country with a great imbalance in the distribution of its population and resources, and therefore also in the development of the economy. Most of the industries as well as the universities and scientific research institutions are located around the coastal regions. This results in varying levels of librarianship and information literacy. The development of digital libraries and the research and implementation of metadata is usually based in Beijing – the capital city – and some other big cities that are located in the coastal areas.

The majority of funding for metadata projects comes from the central government, mostly from the national foundations for science and technology R&D, and the funds earmarked for construction of the national information infrastructure. A small part comes from provincial institutions and affiliated libraries. One new development is that digital library research institutes have been established by some big universities (Beijing University, Tsinghua University and Shanghai Jiaotong University), large public libraries (Shanghai Library) and corporations (Shanghai Changjiang Computer Group) to deal with the increasingly common requirements for the integration of digital resources and the digitization of traditional materials. The metadata research is no longer just a part of big digital library projects or other R&D projects to provide a method for resource organization. The standalone project 'the Building of Standards and Specifications for Digital Libraries in China' (*see* below) was approved by the State Science and Technology Ministry in October 2002. This brings the construction of national standards and specifications to the state level.

Brief history

Research into metadata in China began in 1997. Apart from some domain-specific research and development on Geographic and Educational Information Systems, the National Pilot Digital Library Project (www.library.sh.cn/libnet/sztsg/fulltext/reports/1998/metadata.html) was a milestone for metadata research in China. It was the first digital library project in China, and was initiated by the Ministry of Culture and the State Planning Commission. The research partners include the National Library of China and five other large public libraries. Before this project, there were few reports on metadata research, giving only a brief introduction to projects or standards from abroad.

In April 1998, the project task force proposed a draft metadata profile, which defines a core (minimum) set of metadata elements and provides refinement rules and markup guidelines. It suggested that the minimum metadata element set should adopt the Dublin Core Metadata

Element Set, provided HTML 4.0 and XML/RDF markup samples, and recommended a two-tier metadata application model in which the first tier is DCMES and the second is MARC, TEI Header or another rich metadata format. The first tier does not have to physically exist; it can be transformed dynamically by the mapping or bridge mechanism. The profile calls for the implementation of the two-tier model in the resource development phase of the pilot digital library project.

Although it was not taken up in its entirety by the project, the metadata profile had a big effect on subsequent metadata research, application, implementation and promotion. Since 1998 there have been many research and development digital library projects initiated by many universities under the Ministry of Education (formerly the State Education Commission of China) and the science and technology research institutes, which are led by the Ministry of Science and Technology (formerly the State Science and Technology Commission of China) and the Chinese Academy of Science. Chinese Vice Premier Li Lanqing commented that 'the library operation model in the future is the digital library' when he visited the National Library of China in October 1998. After that, many key programmes and projects were launched, and metadata research and application has become a hot topic in China.

Bibliographic analysis

A literature search was conducted on published papers collected from CNKI (www.cnki.net) and Chongqing VIP Database (http://202.119.47.6/). The China National Knowledge Infrastructure comprises seven databases: journals, newspapers, monographs, dissertations and conference proceedings, and two specializing in the medical and education fields. The Chongqing VIP Information Services company produces a periodicals database. The search returned hits for 43 professional periodicals in which the highest count was six papers related to metadata in 2002. According to this search there were only three papers related to metadata research before 1998. The total increased to around 10 in both 1999 and 2000 as shown in Table 15.1. The majority of the papers were about geographical information systems, data warehousing and other computer software topics. In 2002 there was a sudden explosion of 68 papers on metadata research, and most of these are related to digital libraries.

Table 15.1 *Yearly number of metadata-related research papers*

Year	1997	1998	1999	2000	2001	2002
Number	1	2	8	11	8	68

The increase in the number of papers related to metadata research in 2002 is extraordinary. Table 15.2 gives a content analysis (by sub-category) of the metadata-related papers of that year, with up to three sub-categories given for each paper.

Table 15.2 *Papers from 2002 by subject categories*

Subject	Entries
The application of metadata	21
The general introduction of metadata	17
Computer science related (data warehouses etc.)	14
DC related	10
GIS related	7
Educational information system related	5
Metadata model	5
MARC and cataloguing	3
XML/RDF	3
Archiving	3
Metadata format	3
Preservation	2
Interoperability	2
Metadata capturing	2
Multimedia metadata	1
Administrative metadata	1

There also have been three monographs on metadata published in Chinese. They are: *DC Metadata* by Dr Jianzhong Wu (the director of Shanghai Library), published in 2000 by Shanghai Scientific and Technological Literature Publishing House; *Introduction to Metadata* by

Liu Jia, published in 2001 by Beijing Huayi Publishing Company; and *The Research and Application of Metadata* by Zhang Xiaolin (the director of the Chinese Academy of Science library) published in 2002 by the National Library Publishing House.

There have been some practical achievements in metadata research in recent years, as well as the papers and books mentioned above. A number of metadata standards, specifications, guidelines, profiles and best practices which aim to diversify the use of resource description for a wide range of subjects have been issued by many kinds of institutions at different levels. Here below are some advanced schemes.

Metadata for Sustainable Development of China

Commissioned by the State Ministry of Science and Technology, the Metadata for Sustainable Development of China project (http:// nfgis.nsdi.gov.cn/sdinfo/login.asp?file=sdinfo_metadata_standard.pdf) is conducted by the National Fundamental Geographical Information Centre (http://ngcc.sbsm.gov.cn/). At the time of writing, the status of the standard is 'draft for approval' and it is recommended for use. It is based on ISO 19115 *Geographical Information – Metadata* (formerly ISO 15046-15), which is proposed by ISO/TC211 and refers to the Content Standard for Digital Geospatial Metadata v.2.0 (FGDC-STD-001-1998) approved by the Federal Geographic Data Committee (FGDC) of the USA in June 1998. (Please *see* the website of Chinese TC211 working group: http://nfgis.nsdi.gov.cn/isotc211/default.asp.)

The research into metadata standards is one of the outcomes delivered by the pilot project Information Sharing on China's Sustainable Development (97-925), which started in 1997. It is one of the National Key Projects for Science and Technology of the Ninth Five-Year Plan of China, to be followed by the System R&D of Sustainable Development of China project (www.sdinfo.net.cn/) in the Tenth Five-Year Plan. The primary goal is to build an information-sharing system in a distributed heterogeneous environment so as to share databases of natural resources, environmental protection and technology, biological diversity and comprehensive natural disaster information, all of which are closely related to the sustainable development of China. The information covers plant and crop species, natural disasters, the environment and its protection, geological and mineral resources, climate and weather, ocean resources, etc. Each of these domains has its corresponding descriptive metadata set to be built. For example, the Forestry Metadata Specification which is mapped out by the Resources and Information Institute of the China Academy of Forestry is one of the second-level metadata standards for specific domains in its framework (http://202.204.255.31/share/meta_standard.htm). The main task of the project is to set up a central GIS and database server array decentralized with domain servers to provide information sharing services.

Metadata specifications in the Metadata for Sustainable Development of China project are divided into two levels. The first level contains the core metadata entities and elements which can be considered as the minimum set that fulfil the basic requirements of description. There are about 70 entities and elements on the first level which can describe the digital object or collections in general or collectively. The second level contains all the entities and elements needed to describe an entire dataset file. There are seven sections and more than 100 entities and elements on this level. Except for the property of entity or element, every entity and element is conditional or optional. The detailed content of the seven sections on the second level should be declared in the metadata dictionary. The specifications regulate the range of value for the entity or element and the qualified code such as the codes for responsibility, dataset refinement classification, dataset status, data space type, reference frame, etc.

Learning Object Metadata Specification information model

The Learning Object Metadata (LOM) Specification of Chinese e-Learning Technology Standard (www.celtsc.edu.cn/DOCS/CD/CELTS-3.zip) was established by the Chinese e-Learning Technology Standardization Committee (CELTSC) of the Ministry of Education, which also acts as the Subcommittee for Educational Technology of the National Standard Committee for Information Technology (TC28). It is expected to be a national standard but the current status is 'CD (Committee Drafts)'.

Founded in 2000, the CELTSC (formerly the Modern Educational Technology Standardization Committee of the Ministry of Education) is in charge of the research, preparation and implementation of the distance learning technology standards (DLTS). The project changed its name to Chinese e-Learning Technology Standardization (CELTS) after the Committee changed its name. Lead by Zhu Zhiting, a professor at East China Normal University, the Committee members come from Tsinghua University, Beijing University and other major Chinese universities.

The CELTS includes 27 specifications, which are grouped in five categories: general, resources, audience, educational environment and service quality. It aims to establish the entire system of modern distance learning standards with Chinese characteristics by introducing, adopting and learning from related international standards and specifications, including the IMS (Instruction Management System) Learning Resource Metadata, the IEEE Learning Technology Standards Committee's Learning Object Metadata, OCLC's Dublin Core Metadata Set, etc. It will promote the sharing of educational resources, the interoperability of e-learning systems and guarantee the quality of distance learning services. The CELTS mainly follows IEEE 1484. The Learning Object Metadata Specification of CELTS is equivalent to IEEE 1484.12.

The Learning Object Metadata Specification can be used to describe any learning object (i.e. learning resource) normatively, provide technical assistance to the educator or learner on searching, evaluating, obtaining and making full use of learning resources, and guarantee the shareability, re-usability and exchangeability of the resources and the system. The specification contains nine categories of 47 metadata elements (sub-elements not included in the 47) for learning objects. The categories are: general, life cycle, meta metadata, technical, educational, rights, relation, annotation and classification. There can be at most nine properties of each element: name, name in English, definition, obligation, range, order, example, range or value, and data type.

The Establishment of Standards and Specifications for Digital Library Construction in China (ESSDLC) project

In September 2002, the 'Establishment of Standard and Specifications for Digital Library Construction in China project was proposed to the Ministry of Science and Technology by the National Science and Technology Library, National Library, China Academic Library and Information System (CALIS), Beijing University Library, Chinese Academy of Science Library, Institute of Scientific and Technological Information of China, and Shanghai Library, among others. This is a truly collaborative project whose members come from all the leading organizations related to digital resources. Most partners have led one sub-project; six sub-projects had been started by the end of 2002. Three more projects are to start very soon and there are still several sub-projects being proposed. The six current sub-projects are:

- the Overall Framework and Strategy of the Standards and Specifications for Digital Libraries in China
- the Opening Development Mechanism for the Establishment of Standards and Specifications for Digital Libraries in China
- the Standards and Guidelines for Digitization
- the Application of Unique Universal Identifiers for Digital Objects
- the Metadata Standard for Cross-Domain DO Description
- the Metadata Standard for Domain-Specific DO Description.

The three other sub-projects which are about to start are: the Metadata Standard for Digital Collection Description, the Standard for Searching, Retrieval and Accessing of Digital Resources, and the Open Registration System for Digital Library Standards and Specifications.

The goal of the ESSDLC is to generate a series of national standards and specifications regarding the construction of digital libraries in China. It is also a feasibility study to determine via the sub-projects the need for each of these standards and specifications.

Although the project is supported by the Ministry of Science and Technology and led by the National Science and Technology Library, the head of the project is Dr Zhang Xiaolin, who is the director of the

Chinese Academy of Science library. The members of the project are from the research side of digital libraries and related fields in China, and so far there has been wide participation. Before that, Dr Zhang led another project called Open Description of Information System in the Distributed Environment, approved by the Chinese Academy of Science, which is a pilot study for building a national digital library of science. It gives a framework for the standard system of a digital library, which is needed for resource description applications in the construction and services of digital libraries in the distributed open environment. The project is a practical application of the ESSDLC project.

The proposal says:

> As a digital resource and service providing system on the Internet, the digital library has to establish and follow a set of standards and specifications about digitization processing, resource description and organization, system interoperating and services. It should adopt all kinds of existing related standards and specifications of content encoding, data communication, intellectual property protection, system security, management, service and operation, so as to assure the usability, interoperability and sustainability of the resources and services of the digital library.
>
> Xiaolin, 2002

The ongoing project has already issued several reports in professional journals.

Chinese Metadata Standard

The National Library of China (NLC) has made great efforts towards standardization in developing digital libraries since 1996. In most of the digital library projects sponsored or initiated by the NLC, such as the early National Pilot Digital Library Project and the most significant and costly Digital Library Project (www.nlc.gov.cn/dloff/), the research and compiling of metadata standards and specifications have been very important. But the NLC realized that it would not achieve any success on a national standard without considerable openness and wide representation. Therefore it has done a lot in popularization and training on digital library technology and metadata applications. This has helped to reach a consensus on the importance of the standardization and has brought together many of the stakeholders to take part in the promotion.

The First Conference on Construction and Sharing of Chinese Documents, which was held in Beijing in June 2000, recommended a Chinese Metadata Standard to fulfil the need for Chinese information resources construction. There were 62 delegates from 42 institutions attending the meeting. The delegates came from mainland China, Taiwan Province, Hong Kong, Macao, Singapore, the USA and Holland, among others. They argued that the Chinese Metadata Standard is fundamental to building Chinese digital collections and should provide a basis for the steady development of Chinese online information. The conference urged the NLC to lead the work of drafting the standard. The Ministry of Culture approved the project proposed by the NLC. In June 2001, using foreign research and its own long-term experiences in this area, and integrating these with the characteristics of Chinese documents, the NLC finished the first draft version (www.cdi.cn/download/dmds.pdf).

The standard adopted an overall framework which followed the reference model presented by OAIS. The metadata element set is similar to those of the Library of Congress, the National Library of Australia, the Cedars project, the NEDLIB project and the Dublin Core Metadata Initiative. The core metadata set contains most of the Dublin Core Metadata Set, but adds many supplementary elements for the description of intellectual properties and abstract format of digital resources. The draft version of March 2002 consists of 25 core elements, their qualifiers and the encoding schema with DTD and RDFs. It has been considered to have suitable coverage for the characteristics of Chinese documents, with adequate descriptive ability, functionality, operability and simplicity. The elements are as follows:

1 Title
2 Subject
3 Edition
4 Abstract
5 Content Type

6 Language

7 Coverage

8 Creator

9 Contributor

10 Date of Creation

11 Publisher

12 Copyright Holder

13 Identifier

14 Related Objects

15 Digital Publisher Name

16 Digital Publisher Date

17 Digital Publisher Place

18 Rights Warning

19 Actors

20 Actions

21 Original Technical Environments

22 Ingest Process History

23 Administration History

24 Authentication Indicator

25 UAF-Description.

The Chinese Metadata Standard Framework and its Application (www.idl.pku.edu.cn/pdf/metadata_framework.pdf)

The Institute of Digital Libraries of Beijing University (IDLBU, www.idl.pku.edu.cn/index.html) was founded in 1999 by the Beijing University Library, Beijing University Centre for Information Science and CALIS. It is a combination of computer science specialists, librarians and professional administrators. It has focused on metadata research from the start. The Chinese Metadata Standard Framework and its Application was one of its achievements in 2001.

The need for a metadata standard comes directly from the collection digitization project of Beijing University Library, which has the most valuable, numerous and unique ancient documents of all the universities in the country, including rare books, rubbings and manuscripts. It is a great challenge to work out a unified metadata profile for the description of such a rich and varied collection. The researchers of IDLBU started to solve the problem by introducing a methodology framework. This became the outstanding feature of the study and promoted the progress of Chinese metadata research and development.

The Metadata Standard Framework of IDLBU analysed the description needs for different information resources in the various phases of their life cycle, examined the whole procedure of generating and utilizing metadata, and made restrictions for related entities according to their different roles. It provides a few principles for generating a practical metadata profile and outlines a three-tier metadata elements structure and its extension rules. It also discusses theory and gives some application and implementation approaches for the framework.

Other metadata research

Like the Digital Library Institute of Beijing University, Shanghai Library has formulated a scenario of metadata implementation for the application of resources digitization and integration. Some other institutions, such as the Tsinghua University Library and the Institutes of the Chinese Academy of Science, have done some work on metadata standardization and research but have not made their results public.

Many companies involved in digital library construction are heavily involved in metadata research. Some of them, such as Tsinghua Tongfang Corporation   (www.cnki.net/daobao/cnkidaobao5/cnkibzh02.htm), Wanfang Data Corporation (www.wanfangdata.com.cn/), Chongqing VIP Information Corporation (http://www1.tydata.com/productor/vipservice.htm), Beijing Superstar Corporation (www.ssreader.com.cn) and Beijing Shu Sheng Corporation (www.21dmedia.com), have developed simple metadata solutions.

Discussion and trends

In May 2002, a Forum on Standardization for the China Digital Library Project (www.nlc.gov.cn/dloff/standard4/st_2.htm) was hosted by the Office of the Joint Committee of the China Digital Library Project, and sponsored by the National Standardization Committee of IT and the Digital Library Subcommittee of the Chinese Library Association. Its main purpose was to guide the China Digital Library along the right track of standardization, as well as to sum up past research, bring together the experts to co-ordinate national standardization, and plan for the future on cross-domain co-operation.

Although Chinese metadata practitioners learn a lot from foreign pioneers, they are not very active in international forums, perhaps because of the language barrier. Inevitably they are repeating and debating many topics already discussed over and over again by their foreign colleagues, such as the contradiction between simplicity and functionality, and how to reach acceptable flexibility, extensibility and scalability, etc. After years arguing, they come to a consensus on the functionality of the metadata. But how to encode metadata in an information system and make it functional as promised is another story. That's why there are many metadata specifications and profiles but few metadata applications. The metadata myth still exists. Especially for librarians, who compare any other metadata format unfavourably with MARC. However, they realize it is time to change.

There are two directions of current metadata research and application in China. First, there is the introduction of reference models for setting up co-ordinates to investigate if the metadata profile has suitable extensibility and enough interoperability, for example, the Functional Requirements for Bibliographical Record (FRBR) model from IFLA and the Open Archival Information System (OAIS) model from CCSDS (www.ccsds.org/documents/pdf/CCSDS-650.0-R-2.pdf). The FRBR model is used for comprehensive systems that contain alternative objects with different formats in different phases of their life cycle. It provides a framework that is perfect for recording the intellectual properties of the different manifestations of the same object, while the OAIS model is good at describing the preservation systems needed urgently by many traditional libraries and archives. The two models provide a balanced methodology for choosing the appropriate approaches in all kinds of metadata applications.

Second, metadata standardization is becoming more systematic and hierarchical. There are general cross-domain as well as special domain-specific metadata standards or specifications. There are national and ministry-level standards as well as those just for intra-institution usage. There are draft national standards, recommended specifications, guidelines, best practices and examples. So it can be expected that the metadata movement in China will continue. And there will be many advanced metadata applications in the years to come.

Conclusion

As a developing country, China's experiences with metadata standardization and implementation are comparable to those of many other countries:

- The importance of information resources has become more and more evident after many countries have built up their basic information infrastructure. For the sake of long-term preservation of digital resources, and for the purpose of widespread sharing and re-usability in a distributed environment, standardization is very important.
- Keeping track of research on digital library standardization in developed countries is more important than research and development by developing countries. Many standards are not as simple as they look; they are supported by a large amount of investment in basic research. It is unnecessary to reinvent the wheel, as standards and specifications can be used directly. However, there is much work to do in localization and customization.
- The popularization and training of the standards and specifications is of the same importance as the establishment of them. The current metadata standards in China are mostly well designed with rich description but less flexibility and interoperability, and limited in some disciplines. There should be efforts made to distribute them in professional circles and improve the situation. Only by this means will it be possible to make amendments to the standards for practical applications.

Acknowledgements

The writing of this paper was encouraged greatly by Dr Jianzhong Wu, the director of Shanghai Library. Also I was fortunate to have the support of my colleague, Mr Leon Zhao, for occasional discussions, and I was helped with bibliographic data on the research in metadata and digital libraries in China by Cuijuan Xia and Xiangying Lou.

Reference

Zhang Xiaolin (2002) The Trends on Standardization for Digital Libraries, *The Journal of Chinese Librarianship*, **6**, 7, www.nlc.gov.cn/newpage/publish/xuebao/2002_6.htm.

Index

Page numbers in *italics* indicate references to figures.